Learning and Teaching

in Secondary Schools

Achieving
QTS

Learning and Teaching

in Secondary Schools

Third edition

Edited by Viv Ellis

LearningMatters

First published in 2002 by Learning Matters Ltd.
Reprinted in 2002.
Reprinted in 2003 (twice).
Second edition published in 2004.
Reprinted in 2004, 2005 (twice) and 2006.
Third edition published in 2007.
Reprinted in 2007 (twice).

British Library Cataloguing in Publication Data
A CIP record for this book is available from the British Library.

ISBN: 978 1 84445 096 1

The right of Rob Batho, Jane Briggs, Sue Brindley, Alan J. Child, John Clay, Viv Ellis, Patrick Fullick, Rosalyn George, Gary D. Kinchin, Kate Mackrell, Lynne Parsons, Miranda Peverett, Richard Pring, Geraldine A. Price, Sue Walters, Cathy Wickens and Charlotte Wright to be identified as authors of this work has been asserted by them in accordance with the Copyright, Designs and Patents Act 1988.

Cover design by Topics – The Creative Partnership
Project management by Deer Park Productions, Tavistock
Typeset by PDQ Typesetting, Newcastle under Lyme
Printed and bound by Bell & Bain Ltd, Glasgow

Learning Matters Ltd
33 Southernhay East
Exeter EX1 1NX
Tel: 01392 215560
info@learningmatters.co.uk
www.learningmatters.co.uk

Contents

Part 4: Professional knowledge: inclusion

Contributors

Rob Batho, Senior Adviser, Secondary National Strategy

Jane Briggs, Senior Lecturer in Education, University of Brighton

Sue Brindley, Senior Lecturer in Education, University of Cambridge

Alan J. Child, Regional Director (North West), The Personal Finance Education Group

John Clay, Senior Inspector for Ethnic Minority Achievement, London Borough of Greenwich

Viv Ellis, University Lecturer in Educational Studies, University of Oxford

Patrick Fullick, Lecturer in Education, University of Southampton

Rosalyn George, Reader in Education, Goldsmiths, University of London

Gary D. Kinchin, Senior Lecturer in Physical Education, University of Southampton

Kate Mackrell, Freelance Mathematics Consultant

Lynne Parsons, Regional Adviser, (Behaviour and Attendance), Secondary National Strategy

Miranda Peverett, Teacher of English, Bartholomew School, Eynsham, Oxfordshire

Geraldine A. Price, Lecturer in Specific Learning Difficulties, University of Southampton

Richard Pring, Lead Director of the Nuffield Review of 14–19 Education, England and Wales; University of Oxford

Sue Walters, Lecturer in Educational Studies, University of Edinburgh

Cathy Wickens, Senior Lecturer in ICT Education, University of Brighton

Charlotte Wright, Teacher of English, Hanson School, Bradford

Acknowledgements

The editor and contributors would like to thank the following people for their support and assistance in the development of this book:

Ros George and John Clay for their contribution to the Introduction; Dave Simpson for his contribution to an earlier version of Chapter 5; Julia Baxter and Matthew Beasley for inspiration; the PGCE secondary English group at the University of Brighton (2000–2001); Tony Burgess; Maggie Miller; Deb Davies; Kath, Kim and Nicole; Kate Spencer Ellis; Chris Childs; Graham Corney; Nathalie Manners; Julia Morris; Jennifer Clark; staff and students at Woodway Park School and Community College and Castle High School; all those who have reviewed the book or have provided feedback to the publisher.

This book is dedicated to CF, HDS and the FF

1
Introduction
Viv Ellis

This book was written for anyone undertaking a course of training leading to Qualified Teacher Status (QTS) for the secondary (11–18) phase. If this applies to you, then you may be registered at a university or college on an undergraduate degree programme with QTS, you may be taking a Post Graduate Certificate of Education (PGCE) course, or you may be following one of the employment-based routes to QTS such as the Graduate Teacher or Overseas Trained Teacher programmes. Whatever the particular route, you will be based in schools for most of your time and working with tutors and mentors towards the same goal: becoming an effective new teacher and achieving the Professional Standards for the Award of QTS. This book offers you useful guidance and support during your initial teacher education and shows how the information and guidance it provides relate to the QTS Standards.

The title of this book is *Learning and Teaching in Secondary Schools*. Our intention here is to emphasise the *learning* for two reasons: first, to acknowledge that this is what you – the trainee teacher – will be engaged in for a significant period and with some intensity. For this reason, the book addresses you directly, provides some classroom-based illustrations, and offers practical and reflective tasks and further reading to consolidate your understanding. The second reason is that fostering, developing, assessing, planning for and managing student learning is your primary role as a teacher. This may sound obvious but very often trainee teachers will initially focus on the performance aspects of teaching – how teachers look, behave and sound – rather than how and what their students are learning. We hope you will find it reassuring when we say that very good teachers do not need to be extrovert or overtly 'charismatic' performers; very good teachers listen to students carefully, think about what they see, hear and read analytically and treat students and colleagues with sensitivity.

Learning to teach

Becoming a teacher is a rewarding, stimulating and challenging process. Do not under-estimate the changes in your life and circumstances that may occur during this process! This is not to say that undertaking a course leading to QTS will inevitably lead to divorce, stress-related illness or the decision to keep a small-holding on Skye. It is fair to say, however, that the process of becoming a teacher involves personal, intellectual and profes-sional transformation and that, for many trainees, it requires them to consider what is important and meaningful to them for the first time. As a consequence, most trainees feel that – at the end of their initial training – not only have they learned a lot about teaching and learning but they have also learned a lot about themselves. For most, this acts as confirma-tion of their initial desire to teach and confirms that they have entered a profession that they will find rewarding. For some, however, whether early on or at the end of the course, it will confirm that teaching is not for them. This is an important decision that carries with it no sense of failure.

One of the most interesting writers about the process of becoming a teacher is the American psychologist Seymour Sarason, and his book *You Are Thinking of Teaching?* is recommended as further reading at the end of this introduction. Sarason's point is that any decision to enter the teaching profession must be an informed one: you must understand why you want to become a teacher *and* what it means to be a teacher (the responsibilities and the constraints):

> If you conclude that teaching is for you, it should be on the basis that you know who and what you are, the ways in which you will be challenged, and that you are prepared to be other than a silent, passive participant in the socially fateful and crucial effort to improve our schools; that is, the particular school or schools in which you work.
>
> (Sarason 1993, p. 4)

In addition to knowing why you want to become a teacher and that you understand its active and socially important role, Sarason also draws attention to the 'political' dimension of teaching, with which you might feel uncomfortable. Couched in the following terms, however, it is difficult to disagree with the view that teachers effect this kind of change:

> It is unfair and unrealistic to expect teachers to change the society. It is not unfair or unrealistic to expect teachers to change, in part if not wholly, the conditions in which they and their students experience personal and intellectual growth.
>
> (*ibid*., p. 5)

The new Professional Standards for the Award of QTS recognise that this kind of change is at the heart of the teacher's role.

The current context for teacher education and training

Teaching standards

To be awarded QTS, as beginning secondary school teachers, the new Standards that come into force in September 2007 require you to understand and uphold the professional code of the General Teaching Council for England (see Chapter 2). These are a set of values that have to be put into practice to demonstrate your understanding and commitment to working for equality, diversity and inclusion. There is a shift in emphasis in the new standards framework from previous guidelines that came into effect in 2002. It makes explicit the role of the teacher as a 'change agent' working as part of a multidisciplinary team leading learning and having a role in managing and leading support staff.

The framework of professional standards for teachers defines the characteristics of teachers at each career stage, from beginner teachers awarded QTS progressing through to experienced teachers at a senior level within the profession. Specifically, it provides standards for:

- the award of QTS (Q);
- teachers who have successfully completed their Induction (I);
- teachers on the Upper Pay Scale (Post Threshold Teachers) (P);
- excellent teachers (E);
- advanced Skills Teachers (A).

The framework of standards is arranged in three interrelated sections covering:

1. professional attributes;
2. professional knowledge and understanding;
3. professional skills.

All the standards are underpinned by a document called *Every Child Matters* (discussed later) and the six areas of the common core of skills and knowledge for the children's workforce. It is intended that the work of practising teachers be informed by an awareness, appropriate to their level of experience and responsibility, of legislation concerning the development and well-being of children and young people expressed in the Children Act 2004, the Disability Discrimination Acts 1995 and 2005 and associated guidance, the special educational needs provisions of the Education Act 1996 and the associated special educational needs code of practice (DfES 2001), the Race Relations Act 1976 as amended by the Race Relations (Amendment) Act 2000, and the guidance on safeguarding children in education (DfES 2004a). This body of legislation is referred to as appropriate in the chapters that follow; all of it emphasises the importance placed on achieving educational inclusion in practice.

All aspects of the education system in the UK have been subject to rapid and substantial change for at least 18 years. The pace of change can be bewildering and can leave some teachers feeling disoriented. As a new trainee, you will also be faced with new initiatives and further change but it is perhaps fair to say that some significant changes will have started to 'bed down' by the time you become a newly qualified teacher. Teachers and teacher educators have already struggled with the demands of Curriculum 2000, Standards-based teacher training and much of the secondary National Strategy. Of the new developments, you are most likely to experience significant change in two: some aspects of the Secondary National Strategy, the 14–19 curriculum and the *Every Child Matters* agenda.

Every Child Matters

The government in England announced its intention to take a new approach to the care, education and well-being of children and young people in 2003, following the tragic death in care of a young girl called Victoria Climbié. *Every Child Matters* was published (along with the Children Act) in 2004 and represents the national strategy for professionals working together on the well-being of children and young people from birth to age 19. The intention is that organisations such as hospitals, schools, social services departments, the police and voluntary groups team up in new ways, share information and work together so that young people have the support they need to:

1. be healthy;
2. stay safe;
3. enjoy and achieve;
4. make a positive contribution;
5. achieve economic well-being.

Together, these statements have become known as the five outcomes of the *Every Child Matters* agenda. Over the next few years, the potential for changes in the way that professionals (including teachers) work with young people and *work together* are quite significant. This is known as multi-agency working and is leading in some settings to an extended form of professionalism in work with young people. Further information is available from: **www.everychildmatters.gov.uk** and references are made to the implications of *Every Child Matters* in the chapters that follow.

Secondary National Strategy

There are six strands in the Strategy. These are:

1. English (including Literacy across the curriculum);
2. Mathematics (including Numeracy across the curriculum);
3. Science;
4. ICT (Information and Communications Technology);
5. Foundation subjects;
6. Behaviour and attendance.

The English and Mathematics strands of the Secondary National Strategy were introduced to all schools in England in 2001 with science, foundation subjects and ICT following in 2002 and behaviour and attendance in 2003. The aim of the Strategy is to raise standards by strengthening teaching and learning across the curriculum. Literacy is one of the cross-curricular elements of the Strategy.

All secondary trainees will need to be familiar with the cross-curricular elements of the Strategy as well as any strand that applies to their specialist subject. During your time in schools, you will undoubtedly be part of training that is related to the Strategy. Its main principles – derived from the Key Stage 3 strategy that came before it – are concerned with improving learning and teaching in the classroom and can be summarised as follows.

Set high expectations and give every learner confidence they can succeed
- Demonstrate a commitment to every learner's success, making them feel included, valued and secure.
- Raise learners' aspirations and the effort they put into learning and engage, where appropriate, the active support of parents or carers.

Establish what learners already know and build on it
- Set clear and appropriate learning goals, explain them, and make every learning experience count.
- Create secure foundations for subsequent learning.

Structure and pace the learning experience to make it challenging and enjoyable
- Use teaching methods that reflect the material to be learned, match the maturity of the learners and their learning preferences, and involve high levels of time on task.
- Make creative use of the range of learning opportunities available, within and beyond the classroom, including e-learning.

Inspire learning through passion for the subject
- Bring the subject alive.
- Make it relevant to learners' wider goals and concerns.

Make individuals active partners in their learning
- Build respectful teacher/learner relationships that take learners' views and experience fully into account as well as data on their performance.
- Use assessment for learning to help learners assess their work, reflect on how they learn, and inform subsequent planning and practice.

Develop learning skills and personal qualities
- Develop the ability of learners to think systematically, manage information, learn from others and help others learn.
- Promote learners' confidence, self-discipline and an understanding of the learning process.

The Secondary Strategy also emphasises the *personalisation* of learning, specifically:

- exciting whole-class teaching, which gets the best from every child;
- extra small group or one-to-one tuition for those who need it, not as a substitute for excellent whole-class teaching but as an integral part of the child's learning;
- innovative use of ICT, both in the classroom and linking the classroom and the home.

The Secondary Strategy differs from its predecessor the Key Stage 3 Strategy not just in its whole phase focus (11–16) but in its encouragement of innovation and its flexibility.

To be successful, the Strategy depends upon teachers – and trainee teachers like yourself – using and interpreting its principles, guidance and materials in ways that are focused on improving learning and teaching in the classroom. In order to be able to do this, the core of your initial teacher training will focus upon the fundamental principles underlying learning and teaching in your specialist subject. For up-to-date information on the Strategy, go to the Department for Education and Skills Standards website at **www.standards.dfes.gov.uk/ secondary/**. In addition, Chapters 8, 9 and 10 of this book address three key cross-curricular strands of the Secondary Strategy.

The 14–19 curriculum

At the time of preparing the third edition of this book, proposals were made to restructure the 14–19 curriculum, change the post-16 qualifications and increase choice and flexibility in what is currently GCSE provision and beyond. There is potential here for radical change that may have a profound impact upon the way we organise our schools and colleges. This is dealt with in more detail in Chapter 11 of this book, but for up-to-date information, go to the Qualifications and Curriculum Authority (QCA) website at **www.qca.org.uk/ca/14-19/** and the website for the Nuffield Review of 14-19 Education in England and Wales **www.nuffield14-19review.org.uk**.

How to use this book

The chapters in this book are presented in what we hope is a logical and progressive sequence. The reality, of course, is that none of you and none of your courses will necessarily progress through the same sequence.

Each chapter is prefaced by a short statement that references the content of the chapter to the Professional Standards for Teachers. You will notice that the Standards are divided into three sections:

1. Professional attributes;
2. Professional knowledge and understanding;
3. Professional skills.

Of the three sections, this book focuses on the first, Professional attributes, and the third, Professional skills. Some chapters – particularly those addressing the cross-curricular elements of the Secondary Strategy and special educational needs – do refer to the Professional Knowledge and Understanding section but the main focus in these Standards is on your specialist subject, how children make progress in this subject and your understanding of your subject's development in the primary phase. This subject-specific understanding is outside the remit of this book.

You will notice that a chapter may refer to all three Standards areas and that some Standards are referenced more than once. This is the nature of teaching and of learning to teach: they are not activities that can be atomised or isolated within the whole of what teachers really do in classrooms.

In the classroom

Some chapters also contain vignettes that illustrate aspects of the content of the chapter in a classroom context. These are introduced by the heading 'In the classroom'. In Chapter 4, for example, some of the principles of formative assessment are illustrated in a dialogue between teacher and student. The classroom stories are not meant to be exemplary templates or models to be imitated, however. They are examples of individual cases and fully enmeshed in a particular context. You will find them useful as cases when formulating your own ways into teaching.

Practical and reflective tasks

Each chapter includes a number of practical and/or reflective tasks. You can use these tasks in a number of ways.

- **To explore the relationship between the general principles outlined in the chapter and the policy of the schools in which you are training.**
- **To develop and consolidate your understanding of important skills or issues.**
- **To connect the principles informing your initial training and the practice of particular schools.**

You may find that the tasks would be a useful focus for some of the ongoing work with your mentor.

Moving on

Some chapters in this book have sections entitled 'Moving on'. These are intended to offer suggestions to those of you particularly interested in the topic or theme of the chapter as to what you might like to read or do. These sections are in addition to suggestions for further reading.

The structure and content of the book

This book arises out of the contributors' work in teacher education over many years and in many different contexts. Throughout, it is informed by recent and relevant research and scholarship, including evidence from inspections and surveys by the Office for Standards in Education (Ofsted). The principles discussed in each chapter have not emerged from the ether; they have grown out of a body of evidence built by teachers and researchers over many years. In learning to be a teacher, you should not see any division between theory and practice. This is a fallacy. Even the most apparently commonsense approaches to teaching are informed by a view of learning and teaching that is a theory. Effective teachers do not perform random acts; effective teachers do not simply apply the same 'solution' to every 'problem'. Underlying what effective teachers do are a set of principles that allow them to deal with very different learners in very different contexts. The development of such a set of principles in each trainee will be the aim of any course of initial training.

The 14 chapters in this third edition are arranged into three broad sections: professional attributes and learning; professional skills (planning and assessment); professional knowledge (across the curriculum); and professional knowledge (inclusion). The new edition adds a chapter on teaching students with English as an additional language, includes an entirely new chapter on the 14–19 curriculum, and every other chapter has been thoroughly revised to include new material.

Chapters 2 (Fullick) and 3 (Brindley) set the direction of the book by emphasising the shared values teachers hold and are expected to hold about young people, learning and achievement and by also emphasising the tentativeness and responsiveness of teaching suggested by the phrase 'teaching as professional inquiry'. The third chapter in this section (Chapter 4, Kinchin) opens out the subject of 'Learning' for consideration and proposes that teachers' efforts to understand their students' learning is at the heart of the enterprise.

In the second section – Professional skills: planning and assessing learning – Wright, Ellis and Peverett (Chapter 5) discuss the core professional skill of planning learning and consider approaches to planning over various time frames. This is complemented by Briggs and Ellis's chapter on assessment for learning (Chapter 6) and Child and Parsons' chapter on managing behaviour for learning (Chapter 7). All three chapters focus to some extent on creating the conditions for learning and understanding progress.

The third section on Professional knowledge: across the curriculum addresses three important strands of the Secondary National Strategy and the current reforms of education and training 14–19. Batho (literacy, Chapter 8), Mackrell (numeracy, Chapter 9) and Wickens (ICT, Chapter 10) offer proportionately more practical and reflective tasks than the other chapters and focus on teaching strategies and approaches. In Chapter 11, Pring offers an overview of the rapid and substantial change in the 14–19 phase and asks more fundamental questions about the aims and values of education and training.

In the final section of the book – Professional knowledge: inclusion – Price provides an overview of the frameworks and teaching approaches relevant to special educational needs (Chapter 12). Walters' chapter (Chapter 13) has a similar purpose with reference to teaching students with English as an additional language and Clay and George (Chapter 14) focus more particularly on issues of equality and diversity and the new teacher's responsibility to work for positive change in young people's lives.

Reading this book and engaging with the tasks alone will not enable you to become an effective teacher and to demonstrate achievement against the QTS Standards. This book can only support the intensive and interactive training you undertake as part of your course in schools and in higher education. The Professional Standards for the Award of QTS offer training providers – universities, colleges, local authorities and schools – the opportunity to design courses that regard teacher development holistically rather than as the 'ticking off' of separate technical competences that need to be 'evidenced' in wheel-barrows full of paper. Such courses acknowledge that values and dispositions (towards young people, to learning, to society, to teaching as a profession, etc.) accompanied by an understanding of how we learn and how we promote and assess learning, together with delight in a particular subject, and combined with skills of planning, organisation and communication are what effective teaching is all about. The contributors offer this book in support of such training programmes.

FURTHER READING FURTHER READING FURTHER READING FURTHER READING

Ellsmore, S. (2005) *Carry On, Teacher! Representation of the Teaching Profession in Screen Culture*. Stoke. Trentham Books. An entertaining and thought-provoking study of the charismatic, inner-city school teacher in film and what practising teachers have to say about this character.

Sarason, S.B. (1993) *You Are Thinking of Teaching? Opportunities, Problems, Realities*. San Francisco. Jossey-Bass. This is one of the best books available on the reasons why (or why not) to become a teacher. Sarason discusses the challenges that new teachers face in many aspects of their lives. He also explores issues of change in the lives of more experienced teachers. Although difficult to find in some libraries, this book is worth locating.

PART 1
PROFESSIONAL ATTRIBUTES AND LEARNING

2
Professional values and the teacher
Patrick Fullick

Professional Standards for QTS

Q1, Q2, Q3, Q4, Q5, Q6, Q7, Q8, Q9

To be awarded QTS you must have high expectations of children and young people including a commitment to ensuring that they can achieve their full educational potential and to establishing fair, respectful, trusting, supportive and constructive relationships with them. You should be able to demonstrate the positive values, attitudes and behaviour that you expect from children and young people.

You must be aware of the professional duties of teachers and the statutory framework within which they work, and of the policies and practices of the workplace and share in collective responsibility for their implementation.

You must be able to communicate effectively with children, young people, colleagues, parents and carers.

You must recognise and respect the contribution that colleagues, parents and carers can make to the development and well-being of children and young people and to raising their levels of attainment, and should have a commitment to collaboration and co-operative working.

You should be able to reflect on and improve your practice, and take responsibility for identifying and meeting your own developing professional needs, identifying priorities for your early professional development in the context of induction. You should have a creative and constructively critical approach towards innovation, and be prepared to adapt your practice where benefits and improvements are identified. You should act upon advice and feedback and be open to coaching and mentoring.

You may find it helpful to read through the appropriate section of the handbook that accompanies the Standards for the Award of QTS for clarification and support.

What do people think about teachers?

So you've decided that you want to teach. The contributors to this book are very pleased to hear it. But why teaching? It may seem rather strange to suggest to student teachers that they should begin their course by asking themselves this question, but as I hope you'll soon see, there are some very good reasons for doing so. Before we begin the process of reflecting on reasons for wanting to teach, let's look at what some people have said about teachers and teaching.

- **A man who knows a subject thoroughly, a man so soaked in it that he eats it, sleeps it, dreams it, this man can always teach it with success, no matter how little he knows of technical pedagogy. (H. L. Mencken)**
- **For every person wishing to teach, there are 30 not wishing to be taught. (W. C. Sellar)**
- **He who can, does. He who cannot, teaches. (George Bernard Shaw)**
- **It was God who made me beautiful. If I weren't, then I'd be a teacher. (Linda Evangelista)**
- **He was my favourite teacher in the school. If he hadn't been at the school, I don't think I would have been that clever. He's told me everything that I really want to know. (Training and Development Agency for schools publicity)**

PRACTICAL TASK PRACTICAL TASK PRACTICAL TASK PRACTICAL TASK PRACTICAL TASK

Think about each of the statements above. You may be able to add others about teaching that you have come across. Each statement carries a message about teachers and teaching.

- **Write down two or three sentences setting out what you think lies behind each statement.**
- **Now write two or three sentences setting out what these statements say to you about your choice of teaching as a career. A possible starting point for this is to think about what kind of reasoned response you would make to someone who made one of these statements to you.**

If you have the opportunity, discuss your reactions to these statements with other beginning teachers, and with experienced teachers too. To what extent do you think stereotypical views of teachers are inevitable? Are such stereotypes a bad thing?

Of course, I have been highly selective in the quotations I have chosen to use – whenever we teach we use quotations and examples that will support the ideas we are trying to convey! But these quotations illustrate a number of things that have been said to me, or to my colleagues and my students, in my years as a teacher educator. The overall gist of these is:

- to be a successful teacher, you've got to know your subject well;
- which will make teaching it pretty easy;
- although you'll still have to deal with a lot of kids who just don't want to know;
- so maybe teaching is something that you do if you haven't got anything better to do;
- although if you're successful, it can be quite a fulfilling job.

If you find these messages about teachers and teaching a bit confusing, then you find yourself in the same position as most seasoned teachers and educators. In my experience, it does not get less confusing when we look outside my (selective) quotations at the messages coming to us from the media, from friends and colleagues – most of these sources provide a great mixture of ideas about what teachers and teaching are all about. Just why this is the case could form the basis of a whole book in its own right. But for the moment I want to encourage you to think about the following points.

- Although adults are often unclear about what they expect of teachers, students are much less so.
- Teachers need to be clear about the expectations that other people have of them in order to behave appropriately.
- Teachers also need to be clear about the expectations they have of themselves as part of the process of deciding how to behave.
- Codes of behaviour and professional standards set out by government and by professional bodies are necessary starting points for deciding on one's own personal, professional standards of behaviour – but they are insufficient on their own.

In thinking about these points, you will not necessarily come to any quick and simple answers, but you will have begun an important process, involving a journey towards a set of personal professional values that are rooted in your own beliefs and values, as well as in what other people require of you.

Expectations – adults vs children

At first sight it seems surprising that there should be so much confusion about people's expectations of teachers. After all, teachers are a set of people of whom we all have experience at some point in our lives, and most people probably feel that they are pretty clear about just what it is that teachers do and how they should behave – their *professional ethics*. In a review article, Haydon (1996, p.301) points out that the term *professional ethics* is 'more likely to bring to mind issues about the practice and attitudes of lawyers or doctors than of teachers in schools', noting that there is 'a lack of certainty or clarity about the status of teaching as a profession'. In a lengthy discussion following these points, Haydon compares the activities of teachers with those of other professionals such as doctors and lawyers. What seems to give rise to the confusion about teaching is that, while most people can reasonably readily agree about the 'good ends' that professionals like doctors and lawyers pursue (in the case of doctors, health, and in the case of lawyers, justice), people are generally much less clear about the 'good end' pursued by teachers – education – even though it can be argued that health and justice are not, in themselves, necessarily straight-forward concepts.

Whatever the source of the confusion, at this point in deciding on your own professional values there is little that you can do other than to acknowledge it, and then move on. But while adults as a whole may be unclear about the kind of values they expect teachers to have, there is evidence to suggest that among students there is a fair degree of agreement about the values that teachers should have. In addition, teachers themselves are also in general agreement about these values, while the same evidence also provides some support for the idea that teachers and their students agree quite closely about values; and not only those values that should apply to teachers, but those that should apply to students too.

Research in the area of teachers' values is rather thin on the ground. In those empirical studies that do exist, one interesting strategy employed both with children and with student teachers is the use of drawing. Coming from the field of cultural studies, research methods involving drawing are based on the idea that 'writing paints pictures with words, while drawings speak with lines and colours' (Weber and Mitchell 1996, p.304). Such methods have been widely used by researchers exploring such diverse things as children's images of scientists (Tuckey 1992) and what it means to be healthy (Wetton and McWhirter 1998).

PRACTICAL TASK PRACTICAL TASK PRACTICAL TASK PRACTICAL TASK PRACTICAL TASK

Before reading on, take time to think about how you see yourself as a teacher. Now draw a picture to answer the question 'How do you see yourself as a teacher?' (Don't worry about how good your drawing is technically – the ideas it's conveying are the important thing!) If possible, carry out this task among a group of student teachers who are at the same stage of their professional development as you. Share your drawings with one another and discuss what they convey. What similar ideas do you have? What ideas are different?

How do your drawings compare to those in Figures 2.1 and 2.2?

Weber and Mitchell's research was carried out with student teachers on courses in the USA, producing a diversity of images with strong themes of 'nurturing' and 'controlling' running throughout. (See Figures 2.1 and 2.2.) As well as a research tool, Weber and Mitchell see drawing as a means of helping student teachers reflect on and explore their conceptualisation of their developing ideas about how they see themselves as a teacher during their course.

Figure 2.1. A traditional portrayal of a teacher (from Weber and Mitchell 1996, p.306).

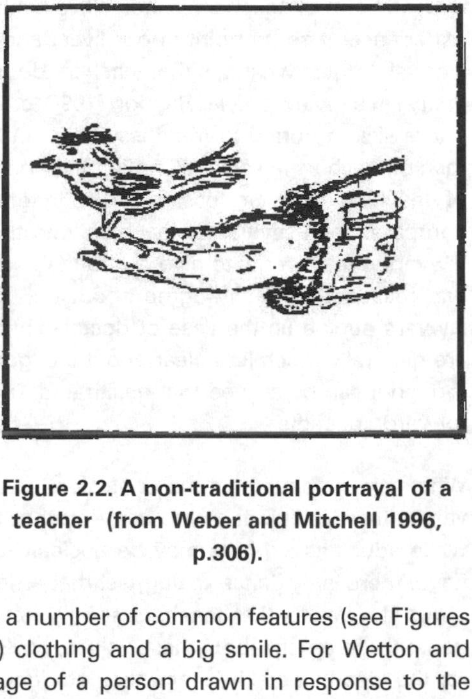

Figure 2.2. A non-traditional portrayal of a teacher (from Weber and Mitchell 1996, p.306).

Children's drawings of teachers like these share a number of common features (see Figures 2.3 and 2.4), most notably their bright (smart?) clothing and a big smile. For Wetton and McWhirter, the presence of a smile in an image of a person drawn in response to the instruction 'Draw a healthy person' indicates the need for mental health as part of overall healthiness. However, researchers exploring images of teachers are less certain about the meaning of a smile in a drawing of a teacher's face:

**Figure 2.3. Mrs Richards by Sophie D, 4R
(from Porth Junior School, 2000).**

**Figure 2.4. Mr Morris by Carys B, 4R
(from Porth Junior School, 2000).**

> What does a smile signify? Surely the female teachers' smiles are intended to indicate good will, a lack of threatening intent. But a smile, as it is often unconsciously practiced [sic] by females, also signifies a lack of threat that may be interpreted as a submissive attitude, a desire to please. Why do the male teachers not need to smile so continuously? Does this reflect male and female socialization, and if so, what does it mean for the role of female teachers both in the classroom and in the larger contexts of school and society?
>
> (Trousdale 1994 quoted in Weber and Mitchell 1996, p.311)

While draw-a-teacher research provides some insight into teachers' values, text-based research provides insights into the extent to which students and teachers share ideals. Researchers in Finland (Verkasalo et al. 1996) administered a questionnaire to 428 15-year-old students and 134 of their teachers. Analysis of the responses showed that both teachers and pupils were in close agreement as to the values that an ideal teacher should display – especially highly rated were:

- **benevolence (incorporating such ideals as loyalty, honesty, helpfulness, responsibility and forgiveness);**
- **and universalism (broad-mindedness, social justice, equality, world at peace, unity with nature).**

There was less agreement about the values held by students. Students were asked to rate the values that they regarded as most important for *themselves* and for *an ideal student*. Answers to these questions showed that students felt that values which they regarded as the most important for themselves (true friendship, freedom, meaning in life and sense of belonging) were not the same as the most important values that an ideal student should hold. However, teachers also saw the students' personal values as very important in an ideal student. This means that we have the interesting situation that, while teachers and students are broadly in agreement about the values held by ideal teachers, students do not see their own values as being those of an ideal student, although teachers do ascribe these values to ideal students!

Although this research has not been replicated in the UK, another study with teachers only (Walker and Newman 1995) shows that teachers hold a large number of values in common when asked to rate agreement or disagreement with statements about teaching.

Expectations – what are yours?

We began thinking about developing a set of values to guide you through the early part of your teaching career by posing the question 'What do people think about teachers?'. Having given this some thought, and looked at the kinds of expectations placed on teachers by others (adults and children) and by themselves, as part of the process of clarifying your own values I should now like to invite you to consider your reasons for wanting to teach.

Why teach?

Whatever your answer to this question, I suggest that it is possible to classify it into one of six different 'teacher portraits', as follows (I am grateful to my colleague Mike Smith for these portraits, and for their descriptions):

- 'it pays the rent/mortgage';
- the missionary;
- the imitator;
- the child;
- the bully;
- the radical.

Let's look at each of these in turn.

It pays the rent

While no-one denies a teacher's right to be fairly remunerated, the idea that the job of a teacher can be viewed purely as an economic transaction (labour in exchange for money) is one that is difficult to sustain. Being a professional carries responsibilities, and the role of a teacher is not one that is susceptible to the simple equation x hours of labour = y amount of money. A professional approach to the job is therefore something that must be at the heart of every teacher's set of values.

The missionary

At an early stage in their career, many teachers want to act as a shining example to others, both as a person and as a professional. Yet in the messy world of schools and teaching many compromises are necessary, which can lead to disillusionment. While initial missionary zeal may not necessarily turn to cynicism in every case, every teacher needs to be able to temper their ideals in the short term in order to achieve what they set out to do in the longer term.

The imitator

As we set out to become teachers nearly all of us will have someone in mind who inspired us in the past. It is all too easy to remember that great teacher who taught us as students and to seek to become 'just like them' – the problem is, you're not them. For one thing, you are working at a different time to them, and almost certainly in a different setting. You have a different set of skills and characteristics to them (no matter how much training you do), and you have a completely different set of experiences.

The child

If we're lucky we have many happy memories of our own childhoods. In order to work with young people effectively we need to move on from childhood and leave childish things behind. The teacher who seeks to relate to children as a friend is on dangerous ground – in more ways than one. Leaving the legal aspects of teacher-student relationships aside, students need a teacher who is able to guide, to offer explanations and to encourage. To do this teachers need to develop a professional relationship with students that is based on respect, but which is not simply a meeting of equals. Never confuse being friendly (good) with being a friend (bad).

The bully

While it is not appropriate here to explore what makes someone a bully, there is a fine line between being assertive and being a bully. There will be many occasions when you will need all your powers of persuasion to convince a class that what you are asking them to do is reasonable – be it to discuss a Shakespearean sonnet on a wet Friday afternoon, or to solve a maths problem for homework. While we may feel that we need to 'bully' children into doing things, we should never do this on the basis of abusing the power that we have as teachers, either as an authority figure or as a person who is older and/or bigger than our students. Any coercion has to be based on our own enthusiasm, to persuade students that they can and should achieve something, and that to do so is both good and desirable, even if it does not seem to be so in the short term.

The radical

While many of us may come into teaching wishing to change the world, there is a world of difference between encouraging discussion and debate among our pupils and fomenting revolution. While all teachers should feel that they have the duty (and not just the right) to encourage debate of controversial issues in their classrooms, to lead that debate by encouraging students to formulate a particular view is something that lies outside the remit of the teacher. Learn to make it clear to students when you are expressing a personal view about something – and to make it clear to them that other people may hold different views. Better still, ensure that they are able to hear more than one side of any argument that may excite particularly strong feelings.

Your reasons for teaching

As you think about these portraits, many of you may find yourselves thinking 'but my reasons for teaching are like that...' or something similar. I certainly do not want to argue here that none of these reasons for wanting to teach is valid, or that any of them alone accurately represents a viewpoint that aspiring teachers necessarily hold. However, I do believe that any of these portraits, taken on its own, represents a seriously deficient model for a teacher to have, and encourage you to think more widely. In particular, you should be very clear about your motivation for teaching, whether you see it rooted within your subject, or within a desire to work with young people. Hopefully by this point you are beginning to think in terms of visualising the teacher as someone whose desire to teach comes from both of these sources – you will certainly need a good understanding of your subject to teach it at secondary level, and it will be a difficult job to do if you don't like your students.

Take time to think about your reasons for wanting to teach. No doubt you wrote about this on the form when you applied for your course, and it was certainly explored at interview with your tutors. At some point in your career someone is bound to ask 'what do you teach?' when they find out that you are a secondary teacher. If you reply 'maths' (or whatever your subject is) they might say 'but what about children – don't you care about them?'. On the other hand, if you say 'children' they might say 'but what about your subject – isn't that important to you?'. What will you say?

Professional frameworks

For anyone seeking to be awarded the status of a qualified teacher in England, it is necessary to be able to demonstrate the ability to meet the requirements of the government's Standards for the Award of QTS – and in this chapter we are concerned with the statements relating to Professional Attributes in the document. As I hope you will already have gathered, my point to you as a beginning teacher is that you should see the values contained in these standards as a statement of what you have to do in order to achieve QTS rather than a set of values *in their own right*. I have tried to set out the reason for this in what has gone before in this chapter – that every teacher needs to understand the basis of their own professional values and those of their colleagues, and to have some idea about from where they are derived. This is not to question the values in the Standards document – but we do need to be clear about these values in order to make them our own. It is also important that we do this to ensure that we abide with values in the Standards not just in the detail of what they say but also in the spirit of their meaning.

Other professions have had codes of behaviour for a very long time – most people will be familiar with the Hippocratic Oath of the medical profession, for example. Derived from this oath, the General Medical Council has produced a document called 'The Duties of a Doctor', which is reproduced below. Effectively this is the equivalent of the attributes in the QTS Standards.

Good Medical Practice (2006)

The duties of a doctor registered with the General Medical Council

Patients must be able to trust doctors with their lives and health. To justify that trust you must show respect for human life and you must:

- Make the care of your patient your first concern
- Protect and promote the health of patients and the public
- Provide a good standard of practice and care
  - Keep your professional knowledge and skills up to date
  - Recognise and work within the limits of your competence
  - Work with colleagues in the ways that best serve patients' interests
- Treat patients as individuals and respect their dignity
  - Treat patients politely and considerately
  - Respect patients' rights to confidentiality
- Work in partnership with patients
  - Listen to patients and respond to their concerns and preferences
  - Give patients the information they want or need in a way they can understand
  - Respect patients' right to reach decisions with you about their treatment and care

---

– Support patients in caring for themselves to improve and maintain their health
• Be honest and open and act with integrity
  – Act without delay if you have good reason to believe that you or a colleague may be putting patients at risk
  – Never discriminate unfairly against patients or colleagues
  – Never abuse your patients' trust in you or the public's trust in the profession.

You are personally accountable for your professional practice and must always be prepared to justify your decisions and actions.

www.gmc-uk/org/guidance/good_medical_practice/duties_of_a_doctor.asp

---

PRACTICAL TASK PRACTICAL TASK PRACTICAL TASK PRACTICAL TASK PRACTICAL TASK

Compare the values in the QTS Standards with those in 'The Duties of a Doctor'.

1. Doctors' 'clients' are their patients – who is the 'client' in the case of teachers?
2. Doctors have to respect patients' confidential information – what duties do teachers have in the case of information about students?
3. Patients have rights to be involved in decisions about their care – what rights attach to decisions about students?
4. What other values are present in the QTS Standards, and what are their equivalents for doctors?

While the professional standards for teachers are demanding, I have every confidence that hard work and diligence during your course will mean that you will have no problems in meeting the standards, and in setting a fine example, both professionally and personally. As you reflect on and evaluate your practice during the course, return to the Standards and to the ideas about your own values that you have thought about as you have read this chapter. Ask yourself 'Is this how I would wish others (students, parents, colleagues) to see me, and to think of me?' If the answer is 'yes' – well done! If not – why not – and what will you do about it?

A SUMMARY OF **KEY POINTS**

> Being clear about expectations forms an important part of determining codes of behaviour for professionals.

> Expectations of teachers expressed by teachers, students and others may be at variance – in clarifying expectations it is therefore important to know to whom an expectation belongs.

> Expectations of teachers form the basis for setting professional values for teachers.

> Text and drawings form the basis of two important classes of research tools for clarifying values.

> Beginning teachers must understand their own expectations of what it means to be a teacher in order to begin to build their own value set.

> Meeting the requirements for QTS means that a beginning teacher must be able to demonstrate behaviour consistent with the Professional Attributes outlined in the Standards.

> Beginning teachers must build a value set which is consistent with the Standards and which is based on a thorough understanding of the role and expectations of a teacher as expressed by all of the stakeholders in education.

Moving on

Obtain a copy of the relevant part of each of the professional codes of conduct for teachers, lawyers and doctors. (For example, the part of each code that relates to confidentiality.) Compare the three codes – what do the codes have in common, and where do they differ? What does this comparison tell us about 'profession' as a concept?

FURTHER READING FURTHER READING **FURTHER READING** FURTHER READING

General Medical Council guidance on Good Medical Practice (available from **www.gmc-uk.org/guidance/good_medical_practiceindex.asp)** *and The Guide to the Professional Conduct of Solicitors* (available from **www.guide-on-line.lawsociety.org.uk/**). These two professional codes for doctors and lawyers provide an interesting comparison with the GTCE code.

GTCE Professional Code for Teachers (available from **www.gtce.org.uk/standards/disc/ StatementOfProfValues).** The Standards make reference to this Professional Code – it is obviously in the interests of all beginning teachers to have read this document and ensured that they have understood it.

Koehn, D. (1994) *The Ground of Professional Ethics*. London. Routledge. For anyone wishing to consider professional ethics in more depth, this book provides a good starting point – although it is not for the faint-hearted! Teachers reading this book will find much of interest, although (as Haydon 1996 notes) they will find it necessary to infer what Koehn's arguments mean for teachers, since she refers to teaching only briefly, when discussing practices that might be considered as a profession.

For further information on professional values and the teacher, visit **www.learning matters.-co.uk/education/learnteach/chapt2.html**

3
Teaching as professional inquiry: the importance of research and evidence
Sue Brindley

Introduction

By meeting the Standards you are reading about in this book, you'll certainly qualify to be a teacher. But is there anyone reading this who wouldn't claim to want to be not just a teacher, but a *good* teacher? That is, someone who actively thinks about teaching and learning; who wants to keep up to date with their subject; who wants to keep their enthusiasm for teaching and education. The Standards quoted above are short statements, easy to overlook – or underestimate in importance. These standards, however, will be the hallmark of the good teacher, the critical thinker, rather than the technician, encapsulated in Donald Schön's term, 'the reflective practitioner' (Schön 1983). It's the quality which the best mentor you have worked with displayed – the ability to articulate good practice, to explain beyond the anecdotal level why strategies work in the classroom – in short, to construct a conceptual framework that allows you to transfer the knowledge from one teaching situation to another, and to know why you are choosing to do so. It is absolutely clear from the positioning of this Standard in Professional Attributes, and the alignment with the General Teaching Council's Professional Code, that research and evidence go hand in hand with teaching as a professional activity.

PRACTICAL TASK PRACTICAL TASK PRACTICAL TASK PRACTICAL TASK PRACTICAL TASK PRACTICAL TASK

As part of this chapter, you will be encouraged to keep a research diary. You can choose to do this either electronically, or using pen and paper. The purpose of this research diary is twofold: to allow you to record your own progress as a researcher over time, and to keep a record of those articles and sources you find useful in supporting your own professional development.

Research diaries are also a useful methodological tool (see, for example, Robson 1993, pp.254–255) for any research you decide to undertake. Robson refers to diaries as 'a kind of self administered questionnaire' and it may be helpful to use this description as a starting point.

> • **Design a research diary. Ensure you have a section to record your own story of becoming a researcher, and one which will allow you to record sources of evidence you discover during your own research. Using research you have already undertaken for an assignment, record your first diary entry.**

Evidence

What do the Standards mean by evidence? In terms of teaching in 2007 and beyond, it encapsulates a thrust of thinking that challenges teaching to become 'an evidence based profession'. Teachers are exhorted to use educational research to inform practice, with the associated agenda of 'raising standards' ever present. But this apparently straightforward link carries with it a constellation of issues.

The debates

The area, and indeed the legitimisation of educational research, is fiercely contested and debated. A brief, recent history may serve to give you the flavour of this.

It was perhaps Stenhouse who first gave the notion of teacher as researcher real currency. In 1975, in his book *An Introduction to Curriculum Research and Development*, he argued that 'a research tradition which is accessible to teachers and which feeds teaching must be created if education is to be significantly improved'. The role of the teacher was that of active researcher.

> The idea of teachers exploring their own practice then became enshrined in Schön's 'reflective practitioner' where the good teacher was the teacher who evaluated their teaching either through 'knowledge in action' or 'reflection in action' (Schön 1983).

Where teachers (and schools) took up these ideas in practice it was often through action research – an approach first described by Kurt Lewin (1946) and which has as its methodology a cycle of planning, acting, observing and reflecting. Action research has become a significant way for teachers to incorporate research into their teaching, with a focus on improvement:

> ... firstly, the improvement of a practice of some kind; secondly, the improvement of the situation in which practice takes place those involved in the practice being considered are to be involved in the action research process in all its aspects.
>
> (Carr and Kemmis 1986, p. 165)

Other views

Things were livened up by David Hargreaves, then Professor of Education at the University of Cambridge, and subsequently Chief Executive of QCA, in his address to the Teacher Training Agency (1996). Hargreaves was addressing primarily the 'professional researchers' and claimed that educational research lacked rigour, and was neither read nor seen as useful by the 'client group' of teachers. He compared teaching with the medical profession which, he pointed out, used evidence to develop practice in ways which teaching had not. (It is also worth reading Hargreaves' later address to BERA 2001 to see how his thinking developed on this theme.) Hargreaves' call to revitalise – indeed re-invent – educational research was taken up with enthusiasm by Chris Woodhead, then HMCI of Ofsted and not noted for his support of academics (or teachers, it may be said). Woodhead commissioned (ironically) research into Hargreaves' claim, appointing James Tooley, now Professor of Education Policy at the University of Newcastle Upon Tyne and then director of the training and education unit at the Institute of Economic Affairs, a right-wing think tank, to lead this. Tooley's report, some would say unsurprisingly in the light of his perceived political positioning, was highly critical of educational research (see Tooley and Darby 1998). In an incestuous move, Tooley's position was then criticised by a number of academics, not least for claimed flaws in his research methodology (see for example Goldstein 1998, Armstrong 1999).

In 1998, the DfEE commissioned the Institute for Employment Studies at the University of Sussex to produce a review of educational research. Their report (Hillage et al. 1998) called for 'more partnerships' in research and the need for 'evidence based policy'. As part of their findings, the report called for a central research body which would advise educational researchers on the needs of the education community, the 'users' of research. The proposal was that this committee would include teachers who would give the practitioners' perspective. This was an interesting development. Seemingly a pragmatic response to the identified problem of irrelevance, it nevertheless drew a warning response from Harvey Goldstein, arguing strongly on the basis of intellectual freedom in research, stating that '... if the recommendations of this report were to be implemented I would have very grave concerns for the future of educational research in this country' (1998). In fact, a National Educational Research Forum was set up in 1999, to advise on key areas to research in education.

A range of perspectives

The theme of pragmatics in educational research – or centralisation and control of knowledge, depending on the ideological frame you bring to this – was developed in some sectors with enthusiasm and rapidity. The Teacher Training Agency (TTA – now the Training and Development Agency for Schools, TDA), for example, took the theme of 'classroom focused' as their central tenet to define 'good' educational research, and used the criterion of 'raising standards' as the purpose for undertaking educational research. I want to discuss later the routes that their thinking has taken, but I think it's important to note that the research commissioned by agencies such as the TDA is just one representation of educational research. As trainee teachers, you will want to engage with a range of perspectives, not least so that you are able to distinguish and select from a range of research positions, and to understand the principles that underpin that research and thus to become 'research critically literate' – able to explore the production of knowledge and test its claims to authenticity.

REFLECTIVE TASK
REFLECTIVE TASK

In your research diary, record your own views and experiences, if any, on the purposes and potential of research in education. You might like to consider:

- **the place of research in your own subject area;**
- **the place of research in your own professional development;**
- **the views of those already involved in the debate (as outlined above, and others you may want to call upon).**

Add a record of any other readings you have discovered on the place of research in education, and in your own subject area.

Research – when?

The temptation with pressures of time, both now in your training period and in your equally busy career as a teacher, is that you will be seduced by the 'what works *now* in my class-room' approach to research. I do not want to deny the place of such explorations. But I want to extend this, and to do so in an appeal to the notion of professionalism. In a longitudinal project currently being undertaken in my own institution, led by Professor Donald McIntyre and looking at the developing expertise of beginning teachers (DEBT Project), two major reasons given by trainee teachers for coming into teaching are:

- **a desire to continue to be engaged with the subject;**
- **and an interest in how children learn.**

In interviews we conducted later in their careers, it became clear that these interests were still present – in fact were stronger. But there is also evidence that the teachers often cannot pursue these central concerns. Instead they have become marooned on an island of 'busy-ness' where time to develop their own thinking has become low priority in the onslaught of 'things to do'. My own research on 'Becoming an English Teacher', undertaken with my colleague Jackie Manuel at the University of Western Sydney, echoes these findings where teachers we have interviewed in both the UK and Australia say the same thing – we want to do this, but where's the time? It's a legitimate cry. But we also know that a parallel statement from teachers is that they're being asked to do more and more – and somehow, they do. They 'make' the time to administer more, or mark more, or teach more. So it's not simply about time (though nobody in their right mind would claim teachers have enough) – it's about *legitimising time to research,* that is, seeing research as something which is important enough to prioritise in the welter of day to day tasks. And to see it in this way because:

> At a time when teachers' work has intensified, when there are more bureaucratic pressures, you might expect teacher research to be pushed aside. But instead it is flourishing. It flourishes, I think because research leads teachers back to the things that lie at the heart of their professionalism, *pupils, teaching, and learning.*
>
> (Ruddock 2001)

Well, why – and how?

Recently I interviewed a series of teachers who had chosen to become involved in school-based, small-scale research projects. I wanted to know why they had chosen to spend (or legitimise) time exploring areas of teaching in this way. I had expected replies to refer to promotions or school development plans. Whatever their original motivation, the teachers I interviewed virtually all expressed surprise at their own findings about this; that the greatest pleasure – indeed the almost addictive pleasure to be found in research – was the return to being a learner:

> Emma: I've been in teaching four years – this is coming up to my fifth, and I'd forgotten what a buzz I get from being a learner. It's funny, isn't it, that my job's about learning – I'm constantly telling the kids, students, to concentrate on their learning or to think about their learning or whatever, but it's taken this [her research project] to remind me that I really enjoy learning. I used to go home and perhaps moan about this or that to my partner – but now he can't stop me talking about this work. I love it, I just love finding me again.

Paul: When I took this on, mainly because you made me, I really didn't think there'd be any value in it at all. Couldn't see the point of wasting valuable time reading all that stuff about what others knew about teaching. I've been teaching for years – what were they going to say that was new? But to my own surprise, well, shock, in fact, I've become caught by the research. As I'm teaching, I catch myself thinking differently about the reactions of the students, and classifying them, for God's sake! I feel like I'm learning about teaching in ways I'd forgotten I could. I feel energised by it.

I want to use this evidence about teachers as learners in relation to both using and undertaking research.

A staging frame

The 'How' question takes us a bit further in thinking about the significance of the demands of the standards. If, for the purposes of this chapter, we use a broad definition of research as concerned with the creation and development of knowledge, involving a systematic collection of evidence framed around a question and mapped against existing knowledge, we can see that it is a demanding activity.

What I should like to suggest here is a 'staging framework' for describing ways of responding to the Standard Q7 as a trainee teacher.

The first stage we might term 'exploration', reflecting the distinction made between using and doing research.

Exploration

As trainee teachers, it is likely that you will 'use' research findings – to support your own assignment writing, to develop ideas of your own in your teaching area, or perhaps in another construction of research – curriculum development – to research materials for your own lesson plans.

In the 'exploration' stage you will be examining the findings and ways in which others in the field have mapped this area. In practical terms, you are likely to have found this information in education journals, either in the library or online. You may well have undertaken a search around a particular area using methods, although probably not sources, familiar to you from your degree course. Part of the work you will be doing here is to establish which sources are going to be of particular use to you: some deal with diverse issues related to education, some specialise in particular areas. It is through reading and building knowledge of these sources that you will begin to build a concept map of key issues, key thinkers and key developments. It will also begin to reveal where the tensions and gaps are in knowledge and where you, as a developing professional, might be able to contribute to the knowledge base in your field.

Reading and sourcing research: practical advice

If you are as yet inexperienced in using research, you might find it helpful to have the following guidelines:

Reading

In a sense, this is almost a skimming and scanning activity, though of a particular type. In the first instance, you will be building a range of resources to read and you will need to undertake rapid first evaluations of how useful a text may be. Rather than attempting to speed-read the whole article, read the abstract (if there is one) and the conclusion. Note keywords if there are any printed at the beginning of the article, a convention with some journals; look at the bibliography and note any names that recur over a number of articles – you will begin to build a picture of those who are the central participants in that debate. If an article looks useful, read the first (topic) sentence of each paragraph. If it's well written, this will allow you to see the key ideas that are explored in depth within the article. After filtering out a number of articles this way, you will be able to spend time sensibly on reading in-depth articles directly useful to you. It's likely by now that you will have developed your own note taking style – but if you haven't, try simply writing a sentence on each key paragraph, noting down the central idea. Most importantly, when you do use a text, record author, title, date and publisher, or web source. 'Endnote' is a useful piece of software to record sources and quotations if you have access to that, or simply use library index cards. Spending hours on trying to find that useful quote from a pile of papers is frustrating and hugely time consuming.

Sourcing

Two major sources for written texts are libraries and online references. It is likely that you will have the facility in your library to consult research databases – collections of articles, papers, books that have been published and which the library can usually source for you through inter-library loans if they are not available on the library shelves. Two commonly used databases are BEI (British Education Index) and ERIC (Educational Resources Information Centre). Although straightforward to use, you will almost certainly need a password, so the library is the first stop here. For simple online searches, you could simply use a search engine such as Google at **www.google.com** and enter key words to take you to articles. However, two caveats should be borne in mind.

- **The keyword selection is critical. You need to be as specific as possible, and be prepared to narrow down your search if you find you have entered a word such as 'numeracy' which will source literally thousands of articles. Think carefully and precisely about the exact aspect you want to read about (numeracy+ICT). Similarly, it is all too easy to follow interesting but fundamentally unproductive (for your current purposes) lines of enquiry as you proceed through the articles that the search engine has identified. This is electronic displacement activity – don't let it lull you into thinking it is useful!**
- **The second caveat refers to provenance of text: there is no control over publication on the Internet – and so no guarantee that what you find there is valid or worth your while reading. Unless you know the source, it's probably best to avoid quoting from such articles as if they were seminal texts.**

Perhaps a more secure route is to access education journals, including those from your own professional organisations, online. Again, you can use a search engine with the name of a journal and keywords for your research. You will find that increasing numbers of publishers have online versions of their journals that you can access. There are still some who require subscription either from you as an individual or from your library, so it is worth checking with your library about that aspect.

Indeed, librarians themselves are invaluable when it comes to sourcing information. They will know not only the larger sources of information such as those mentioned here, but also the more local resources you can use. It is always wise to use the librarians themselves as a resource.

As a final note, just as you should consider the provenance of text on the Internet, you need to consider the provenance of research when you read reports. It is worth establishing whose needs are served by the published work and who funded that work. It can – although it shouldn't in the spirit of 'pure' research – impact on what is reported and what, often more significantly, is left unsaid.

Government sources

Government publications and websites offer a significant range of evidence that you should use to inform your own research. Many of the major government agencies now address the concept of research and evidence directly. In this section, I want to direct your attention to five main sources of research and evidence.

Department for Education and Skills (DfES)
The DfES commissions and publishes its own research across a wide range of areas. Details of the DfES research programme can be found at: **www.dfes.gov.uk/research/ programmes/research/.index.cfm?type=0.**

Teachernet
The website **www.teachernet. gov.uk** has an outline of research currently being undertaken in the UK and information on research opportunities in education. At the time of writing, the website outlines its intentions thus:

> You can find out why research can help you in your teaching and how to become involved in research, find out about research networks, access publications and articles and get hold of the latest statistics as well as discover sources of useful information on education systems in other countries.

Potentially, this is a useful site for research and evidence and one worth noting.

Office for Standards in Education (Ofsted)
The third government resource for research and evidence is Ofsted. The database of information on schools held by Ofsted is extensive. Although they do not have a dedicated research area on the website, there are publications that form a research database. Part of using research in a professional capacity in teaching is accessing and interpreting external statistical information and Ofsted's national statistical base is probably not equalled elsewhere in the UK.

Qualifications and Curriculum Authority (QCA)
QCA styles its research centre as 'research and statistical information'. They define their approach as 'research and statistical analysis, [with] evaluation activities support [ing QCA's] efforts to develop effective policies to raise achievement and improve learning'. A range of publications available through the website at **www.qca.gov.uk** extend the evidence base available.

British Educational Communications and Technology Agency (Becta)

Becta focuses on ICT in education. Its research and evidence aim is to 'engage in a range of evidence-gathering activities regarding the use and impact of information and communications technology (ICT) in education' and it does this through a series of projects. A useful source is the ICT Research Network which 'seeks to encourage the exchange of information between all those with an interest in research on ICT in education, in order to inform the national agenda and professional practice'. This site also welcomes contributions from teachers on ICT and research.

National Foundation for Educational Research (NFER)

Whilst not government funded, an additional UK and international source which you should be aware of is the National Foundation for Educational Research. NFER undertakes research for government but also for a wide range of other users. The website (**www.nfer.ac.uk**) offers a comprehensive overview of current and completed research both UK and internationally based. They define their work as:

> Improving education and training nationally and internationally by undertaking research, development and dissemination activities and by providing information services by being the leading independent educational research institution in the UK, with a diversified portfolio of research, information and development activities that spans all sectors of education and training.

Of particular use is the comprehensive book list to be found on current topics of research. You can access this at **www.nfer.ac.uk/infoservices/hot_topics.asp** NFER can also be contacted directly via the website.

There are of course an almost infinite number and range of resources to support this stage of exploration. Those discussed here are a beginning point for your own research activity. The next section asks you to consider how.

How? A research 'thinking frame'

Perhaps one of the most striking discoveries identified by the trainees and teachers with whom I work is the mindframe of enthusiasm for exploring education that researching activity generates. After all, it's likely that you came into teaching precisely because you enjoyed thinking about your subject area. That intellectual curiosity is a key part of professionalism. Stale teaching often reflects stale thinking and as a professional, it's a part of your job to draw students in by demonstrating your own ongoing interest in the field. It links to the quality that has emerged time and again in the DEBT project in response to the question 'what makes a good teacher' – the answer given is enthusiasm. This powerful characteristic is a way of thinking. It is about excitement in exploring knowledge and about wanting to share that excitement. So the activity of engaging with research is valuable in itself – the intellectual energy created through discovery and the rigour of organising the knowledge gained into relevant frameworks. The teachers quoted earlier, Emma and Paul, draw us back into the idea of teachers as learners – and the strengths to be found in this positioning.

Generating and networking research

> ... access to ideas that enable people to conceptualise alternatives are crucial to learning.
>
> (Young and Lucas 1999)

This section is really a glimpse into the future. You are indeed a rarity if as a trainee teacher you have the opportunity to engage with research beyond the exploration stage or small-scale assignment level work, so I am going to extend the 'increasing' part of the reference in the Standard 1.7 'tak(ing) increasing responsibility for their own professional development' into your career post initial training. This bridging move makes sense too in terms of the Career Entry Profile, a document designed to ensure continuity between your training and your year as a newly qualified teacher (NQT), and the implicit assumption that the PGCE year isn't the end of your training. Perhaps it's where teacher education begins instead.

Generating and Networking Research is the stage where exploration begins to shade from 'using' into an active approach to research. It is also arguably where you begin to make the links between 'theory' and 'practice' through the application of ideas to classroom practice. Generating research is really about developing your own identity as a researcher. It may be that during your training year you have found yourself intrigued or excited by an area of teaching and learning that you have not had the time to pursue but which now could form the basis of a profitable area for action research. It may be the type of research which the current Best Practice Research Scholarships support: small scale, classroom focused, extending over a year. It may well form the focus for you as a professional to contribute to what Calderhead (1987) refers to as 'a body of specialised knowledge acquired through training and experience'.

A research example

The type of research I am thinking of here is exemplified through the work of Rachel, who, like Paul and Emma, is also a teacher researcher. Rachel is in charge of Key Stage 2/3 transition and, following some preparatory reading, was interested to see whether the experience of English by Year 6 pupils was the same as that of Year 7 pupils. The research is still in progress, but she chose to record, over a short period of time, parallel classroom activities in English in a partner primary school and in her own secondary school, and then to interview teachers and pupils about what they thought constituted 'English'. It seems to be emerging that English in the primary school she is working with has ceased to exist and 'literacy' has taken its place. When pupils come into the secondary school, they encounter a subject whose name is familiar, but where the content is largely text based. Unfinished as it is, it is still possible to predict that Rachel's research will supply an interesting insight into pupil transfer, progression and achievement for her department to use to inform planning.

REFLECTIVE TASK

In your research diary, note areas emerging from your PGCE work which would be of interest to you to begin to research in your early years of teaching. Ensure that you transfer these to your CEP for discussion with your induction tutor.

Plan to develop your identity as a researcher, and to make it an integral part of your own professional development. Use the research you plan to discuss with your induction tutor as the beginning of this process. Share your findings with colleagues either informally through departmental meetings, or more formally through CPD days, or in due course, by contributing to conferences and by publication.

Continue to use the diary over this time. At the end of each term, review how your views and experiences of research have changed. You will discover that the diary will form a valuable record of your own professional development.

Networking

Associated with the generating stage is that of 'networking' knowledge, that is, the linking together of generated research projects to contribute to that notion of a 'community of practice' (Lave and Wenger 1996). Briefly, this theory states that 'real life' learning takes place in a necessary context: 'situated learning'. They go on to propose, however, that 'legitimate peripheral participation' means that people learn by participating in 'communities of practice': that not just the individual learns through engaging in specific activities, but the whole community learns. Networking research records and establishes that learning. Building understanding in teaching is about being active in bringing about a community of learners and expanding the community of practice that is part of being a profession. This is the area which should feature in the next stage of your own professional development, not as a further 'task' but as part of the pleasure of being a teacher.

I am going to let Emma have the last word:

> I don't think I could have anticipated the impact this research has had on me. I don't think about just teaching any more – I think about education. I belong to this community still (department and school) but to a wider community too – the research community. I just feel like I'm learning so much and it's good. It really is good.

Moving on

There are a number of subject teaching associations in England which organise professional development and research opportunities for teachers and local, regional and national conferences. Ask your mentor or tutor for details of associations in your subject area and look at their websites to decide if membership would be beneficial for you.

FURTHER READING FURTHER READING **FURTHER READING** FURTHER READING

Guides to undertaking educational research

Hart, C. (1998) *Doing a Literature Review*. London. Sage. A useful, practical guide to producing a formal account and analysis of existing literature in the field. Examples at the end of each chapter. Sample contents list includes classifying and reading research, argumentation analysis, organising and expressing ideas, mapping and analysing ideas.

Hitchcock, G. and Hughes, D. (1995) *Research and the Teacher*. London. Routledge. Written for practising teachers, focusing on qualitative research. Helpful section on designs and approaches.

Hopkins, D. (2002) *A Teacher's Guide to Classroom Research*. Buckingham. Open University Press. A good overview with a strongly practical approach to researching in the classroom.

Robson, R. (1993) *Real World Research*. Oxford. Blackwell. A comprehensive, and comprehensible, guide to research methodology.

Useful journals

There are a range of subject specific and general educational journals. For particular reference to research issues, you might try:

AERA (American Educational Research Association): publishes a number of journals which focus on education and research (see **www.aera.net**). A very good source for accessing research beyond the UK perspective.

British Educational Research Journal (BERJ): Carfax (see also **www.bera.ac.uk** for details of conferences). Well known and well respected journal which focuses largely, but not exclusively, on educational research in the UK. This is the journal of the British Educational Research Association (BERA) which holds annual conferences, usually in September.

Educational Research Abstracts: Taylor and Francis (online). Useful overview via abstracts of current research in education.

Educational Action Research: *Triangle Journal* which focuses on both the methodology of action research and articles exemplifying this approach.

For further information on teaching as professional inquiry, visit **www.learning matters. co.uk/education/learnteach/chapt3.html.**

4
Understanding learning
Gary D. Kinchin

Professional Standards for QTS:

Q10, Q16, Q19a, Q23

As a teacher you will know the content of the subject you are trained to teach. You will be able to assess the learning needs of those you teach and set challenging learning objectives. You will know how to adapt your teaching, learning and behaviour management strategies to personalise learning to enable all learners to achieve their potential. You will support and guide learners to reflect upon the progress they have made. You will teach lessons that employ interactive teaching and group works approaches and encourage active and independent learning where students take greater ownership of their learning.

You may find it helpful to read through the appropriate section of the handbook that accompanies the Standards for the Award of QTS for clarification and support.

Introduction

Learning is clearly central to achieving the aims of education and thus to making a difference in the classroom. As a soon-to-be-qualified teacher or new member of the profession you are also central to raising standards further within the education system as set out within some most recent White Papers (e.g. DfES 2004, 2005) and pivotal to some of the key educational reforms including *Every Child Matters* (DfES, 2003).

The authors of this book hope you will agree that all teachers have a responsibility to know their subject and teach in ways which enable their students to learn (Bleach 2000). As Pritchard (2005) states: 'A basic understanding of processes of learning is essential for those who intend to develop activities that will have the potential to lead to more effective learning in classrooms, that is teachers' (p.2). *A student learning what was intended* has been identified by some as the basis for describing effective teaching (Capel *et al*. 1995, Kyriacou 1997).

While student learning should be your first consideration in planning and teaching, it is well documented that trainees and early career teachers possess only the beginnings of a knowledge base to achieve this objective and at the same time are more concerned with:

- how they are going to cope with their workload and survive in the teaching environment;
- their classroom management and being regarded as a 'real teacher';
- being liked;
- developing a professional image that is accepted by students (Behets 1990, Fuller 1969, Kyriacou and Stephens 1999, Monk 2001).

These may be anxieties that you have felt yourself.

Whereas the above concerns may not foreground learning or make direct reference to the different ways in which students learn, the promotion of learning will always remain one of the things that a teacher is concerned about across their careers. You will find teaching most enjoyable and satisfying when your students are enthusiastically engaged in their learning and you feel you have got them to the *point* of the lesson.

Assuming that you are at the initial stages of beginning to understand the nature of learning, learning theories, and how students might prefer to learn, the purpose of this chapter is fourfold.

1. To get you thinking about learning, what it is, and how you might consider it in one classroom and promote it in yours.
2. To provide a description and critique of some of the learning styles which might exist within classrooms.
3. To consider the implications for learning in light of some key reforms in education and in particular the growing interest in personalised learning.
4. To consider some implications of the new Standards for the Award of Qualified Teacher Status (QTS) for enabling student learning.

What is learning?

This is indeed a difficult question to answer. Theorists do not all agree what learning is and how it occurs. Learning is a broad concept and perspectives on how learning takes place have been put forward by psychologists, linguists, neurophysiologists and philosophers. There is clear agreement that learning is important. Gredler (2001) has provided some pertinent reasons why the ability to learn is so crucial.

- **Learning is important to the individual.**
- **Learning develops competencies in a variety of school subjects in both childhood and adolescence.**
- **Learning aids the acquisition of a variety of perspectives, values, and ways to interact with one another.**
- **Learning enables an individual to carry out a diverse lifestyle.**
- **Learning develops the capacity for lifelong learning.**
- **Learning helps to preserve cultural values and traditions.**
- **Learning aids new discoveries and inventions.**

The word 'learning' would seem to imply 'change'. Although learning can occur in both formal and informal settings, Stevenson and Palmer (1994) argue that learning might occur implicitly (without the individual being aware of it) or explicitly (where there is conscious and deliberate effort). Most definitions suggest that learning is an enduring change in an individual as a consequence of an experience in a particular situation (Driscoll 1994). This definition, however, would seem to exclude changes which might occur due to maturation/growth and development (Long 2000).

As you begin your career in teaching, Kyriacou (1997) offers one of the most helpful definitions of learning, stating 'Student learning can be defined as changes in a student's behaviours which take place as a result of being engaged in an educational experience' (p.22). The changes implied here can span the some of the many outcomes possible within a secondary school curriculum, as the following illustrate: greater knowledge of dates in history; having different attitudes towards certain issues or ideas in contexts of personal, social and health education; the improved ability to play a musical instrument; demonstrating an understanding of photosynthesis in science through a group presentation; knowing all major cities in France; or the application of a particular defensive strategy in an invasion game in physical education. Learning here therefore suggests the capacity to do something different to what could be done earlier (Schunk 1996).

Understanding learning: one view from inside the classroom

In an effort to understand learning it is important also to understand the dynamics of classroom life. You and your students will spend considerable time in one another's presence. Creating teaching environments that are both orderly (which we know you are concerned about) and which meet the needs of individual students will be difficult professional work. Your role as a teacher is to enable learning, which could suggest the direction of influence in class is solely from you to the student in terms of influencing their learning gains. In the dynamics of classroom life this is not always the case, and you may have experienced this. Students can sometimes exert great influence. For example, there may have been times when what is completed and hopefully learned by students feels almost 'negotiated' between you and them, and that they are exploring the boundaries.

Given the current educational climate (explored a little later in this chapter) it is highly likely you will be faced with varying student needs and learning styles and with the expectation that you will begin to personalise learning and teaching, focusing as you will on each child's learning in order to enhance their progress, achievement and participation. Your students are also likely to have varying levels of motivation to be in class and to learn. Being with their friends and fulfilling their own agenda for social interaction (which you might regard as disruptive) may already have competed with your efforts to engage students with the lesson content. Such a situation can impact on learning in the classroom, as an explanation to the following 'model' indicates.

Doyle (1979, 1981) viewed the classroom as 'ecology'. A brief insight into his model will provide one way of understanding the daily realities of classroom life and the challenges this poses for thinking about and enabling teaching and learning for individual students. Doyle viewed the class in a way that saw the management, instructional, and student social systems interacting and developing around a series of tasks to be completed by students. If the ecological balance between these systems was right in the eyes of students then the instructional element is normally foregrounded and learning tasks and gains become priority. If not, then students may tend to fix the balance in their own way to make the tasks or work they are doing something they can achieve and enjoy, or they may go off-task and do something else which requires you re-establish order and control.

Of relevance to some of the content of this chapter (in particular sections where you are asked to consider some learning theories) Siedentop and Tannehill (2000) indicate that good teachers tend to be able to promote learning gains by blending the student social system into the instructional system by:

- **offering an exciting and relevant curriculum;**
- **employing strategies such as group-work which demand student interaction;**
- **promoting peer teaching and cooperative learning.**

It therefore seems important that we are able to develop students' positive attitudes towards learning, and the use of the above suggestions while acknowledging how Doyle views the classroom may in one way help you see and appreciate the complexities of classroom life.

Theories of learning

As a beginning teacher or new entrant into the profession, do you have your own personal theory or theories of how learning best takes place? Most teachers do, so it is very possible that you do too. You are a learner yourself and have spent many hours observing teachers teaching you in their efforts to enable your learning.

REFLECTIVE TASK

As you ponder over your own personal theory of learning, take a few minutes to consider some of the following questions. What did you learn in and out of school? How did you learn these things? Under what circumstances did you learn best? What circumstances or arrangements tended to impede your learning? How might you use your own experiences as a learner to inform your efforts to enable learning in the classroom?

Your responses to the above task might suggest your learning occurred differently for different tasks (some that were simple, some that were more complex). There may have been things that you learned either in the absence of a teacher (e.g. being with your class-mates) or you felt could only have been learned with a teacher present. You might have recalled examples when class discussions and group-work with others helped your learning or when you were required to recite facts successfully from memory alone.

Every intentional teaching/learning experience is built on assumptions about how learning happens, whether this is implicit or explicit (Rink 2001). When these assumptions about learning are formalised or abstracted to a more general level, we call them learning theories. According to Driscoll (1994) a learning theory represents 'a set of constructs linking observed changes in performance with what is thought to bring about those changes' (p.9). In essence, learning theories have attempted to understand how individuals relate to their environment in ways that enhance their ability to use themselves and their environments more efficiently and more effectively.

As you may be aware, writers have put forward a vast number of theories in an effort to explain or describe how learning occurs. Not all theories, however, are applicable to those who work in education but there are some that appear more dominant and have received greater attention in the literature. Child (1986) reminds us that 'no one theory has provided all the answers to the kinds of questions of concern to teachers . . . no one single theory has yet been formulated which satisfactorily accounts for all the facts' (p.82).

The following section will set out the main premise of some of the positions/theories of learning. It is not intended that these theoretical perspectives be seen as polarised but that they are available for teachers as fit. The difference between the perspectives involves different ways of focusing on learning but both provide important insights into the processes of effective performance and learning. As Phillips and Soltis (1998) state: 'We must be content to deal with a number of theories of learning, each useful perhaps in a different context' (p.5). Roblyer (1996) also reminds us, and the following section will attest, that there are opposing views as to whether learning should be structured and directed by teachers or that students should take charge of constructing their own knowledge, in essence having more ownership of that learning, but again the situation will dictate. In summary, an aware-ness of learning theories can be helpful to you in the following ways.

- They can inform your planning and teaching.
- They can help you to evaluate your practice.

- **They can assist in the diagnosis of in-class problems.**

Some theories of learning

All twentieth-century learning theories can be classified into two broad families: firstly, conditioning theories (behaviourist family), and secondly, interactionist theories (cognitive family). There are differences across these two families, particularly centring upon the behaviourist position that humans are passive beings and therefore react to stimuli while cognitive theorists support the position that learners are interactive. However, no learning theory can ignore the critical nature of the level of student engagement or that motivation is a key factor influencing whether learning does or does not take place. High achievement in learning is more likely when the student is highly motivated as motivation represents a key factor influencing the extent to which students can achieve desirable learning outcomes.

We shall examine perspectives on learning promulgated by theorists within the behaviourist and cognitive families, which some claim to have had the most significant impact upon learning and teaching within schools (Child 1986).

Behaviourist family

If as a teacher on placement you have used immediate praise and positive feedback to students as examples of positive reinforcement or have applied consequences for inappropriate behaviour such as detentions, or you have taught and re-taught with feedback how you want your students to enter and exit the classroom, then you have already incorporated aspects of Skinnerian theory in your teaching. If you are looking to use Skinner's ideas further then as a teacher you will be predominantly concerned with finding ways to get your learners to respond and then reinforce that response. The resultant behaviour should subsequently be reinforced for it is more likely to occur again under similar circumstances.

Skinner

B.F. Skinner (1968), as the founder of operant conditioning, is considered by some to be the most influential to have impacted on education and learning. Advocates of behaviourism viewed learning as a permanent transformation in behaviour with an emphasis upon measurable changes or outcomes. Learning is seen as a conditioning process concerned with a response to a stimulus. The stimulus is deemed the cause of learning which acts upon the individual, evoking the response or increasing the chances of a response. In the absence of this reinforcement the behaviour is less likely to occur. Learning is therefore interpreted in terms of the strength of the stimulus–response connection. Behaviourists suggest teachers should therefore:

- **create environments that enable students to respond properly to stimuli;**
- **be specific about what are appropriate responses;**
- **model good behaviour;**
- **shape appropriate behaviour by rewarding positive responses.**

Cognitive family

If during your teaching to date you have:

- **provided opportunities for your students to learn in problem-solving settings;**
- **included content that students are passionate about – that is, you see the importance of making the learning experiences relevant and meaningful for your students with an awareness of the students' current knowledge;**
- **used teaching which concentrated on the unknown using the known as a basis;**

then not only may you see on a practical level elements of Doyle's thinking, but you have already begun to incorporate aspects of cognitive learning theory in your teaching, as the following will explain.

Cognitive theorists have attended to more holistic perspectives on learning with specific interest in the ways learners solve problems. Vygotsky (1962) and Bruner (1966) are considered some of the most influential theorists within this family. According to Bruner (1966) the acquisition of knowledge is an active process. Individuals construct knowledge by connecting the incoming facts to previously acquired knowledge. It is here that the individuals make meaning.

Cognitive theorists typically place action and problem-solving at the centre of learning. Learning is viewed as a process of gaining or changing insights, views or outlooks as individuals make meaning of previously learned facts. Learning is inferred from what people say or do. Thus, the learning process is primarily social and learning occurs through socialisation carried out in a variety of contexts such as the school, the family or peer group. (You will recall within Doyle's model there was a very heavy emphasis upon the social task system and how teachers might develop this to achieve instructional objectives.) The assumption here is that students will learn when placed in these groups – or other interactive settings, as much of what is learned is learned from others (Vygotsky 1962).

Constructivism
According to Marlowe and Page (1998):

> passively accumulating disconnected knowledge is not learning…To learn a student has to be mentally and often physically active. A student learns when she discovers her own answers, solutions, concepts and relationships and creates her own interpretations (p.12).

The above statement offers one rationale for constructivism as a school of thought on learning. Of late, constructivism and situated learning have become quite popular orientations to teaching and learning as a part of the cognitive family (Rink 2001). The constructivist approach has had a significant impact upon instruction and learning (Capel *et al.* 1997, Kyriacou 1997), and is viewed by some as a component within the cognitive sciences (Terwel 1999) and as a theory about how we learn (Marlowe and Page 1998). Constructivist approaches support the position that learners are not passive recipients of transmitted knowledge. Constructivism emphasises the active role students play in acquiring knowledge personally and socially through engagement with meaningful tasks situated within their immediate environment. Rather than being given specific information on how the task is to be performed, constructivist approaches encourage learners to find their own way through the tasks, developing and creating their own knowledge. Learner autonomy and initiative are accepted and encouraged and knowledge is created by doing, researching and experiencing real-life situations (Roelofs and Terwel 1999). In effect, as the term suggests, learners attempt to 'construct' individual meanings based upon what they currently understand and know. Constructivism assumes that all learners have had different experiences, therefore individual understanding cannot be the same between people.

Constructivist approaches foreground the knowledge structures students currently possess, termed 'conceptions' within the educational literature. Research that originates in cognitive psychology provides considerable support for the presence of students' prior knowledge: that is, students come to every new learning experience with some knowledge about the topic already established (Dodds *et al.* 2001). For learning to take place the student must understand the new material in terms of their existing prior knowledge (Taber 2001). There is a growing literature across a number of the subjects – including science, maths, PE, health, geography, and history – on students' conceptions, that is, what they know and believe about a topic (see Barratt and Hacking 2000, Galili and Bar 1997, Griffin *et al.* 2001, Myhill 2000, Pendry *et al*. 1997, Placek *et al*. 2001). These conceptions have been labelled preconceptions, misconceptions, alternative conceptions, or alternative frameworks. An understanding of alternative conceptions is critical if genuine learning is to occur (Palmer 2001), as it is quite common for learners to enter classrooms with ideas related to topics which are at odds with expert opinion or viewpoints (Taber 2001).

PRACTICAL TASK PRACTICAL TASK PRACTICAL TASK PRACTICAL TASK PRACTICAL TASK

You are planning to teach a lesson in your subject area. During the closure of the preceding lesson introduce the next topic(s).

- **Ask the students to write down what they currently know or believe regarding the topic and what they consider to be some of the sources of their present knowledge.**

Collect the written task before you read the responses.

- **Predict and write down what you expect your students to possess some prior knowledge of in relation to the topic(s).**
- **List what might be some possible sources of this knowledge.**

Read the responses and attempt to collate them.

- **Compare and contrast your predictions with the present knowledge and sources of knowledge among the students. What emerged?**
- **How did the nature of their knowledge compare with your conceptions of the topic that you are about to teach?**
- **What are the implications of these findings for enabling learning in your subject?**

Marlowe and Page (1998) offer some implications for work in classrooms if teachers wish to move to adopting the constructivist perspective:

- **Teachers should emphasise the promotion of learning via questioning and problem-solving.**
- **Teachers should de-emphasise the 'transmission' of knowledge.**
- **Work in the classroom should retain the importance of the content to be unearthed and reflected upon.**
- **Individuals' conceptions of the content are foregrounded to help learners decide between the relevant/meaningful and the irrelevant.**

In summary:

- **learners construct knowledge actively and socially;**
- **learners already possess ideas about the learning situation;**
- **learners take greater responsibility for and ownership of their learning.**

If you take account of what you currently do in your teaching and consider some of your most recent experiences with your classes, it may be quite possible that you have used some activities/tasks which illustrate the above positions on learning. If you can associate yourself with some of the activities below then you could well have incorporated some elements of them in your classrooms already. Have you:

- **asked your students in their groups to predict the outcome of a science experiment before they begin?**

- used punishment to discourage certain types of activities?
- developed an interactive multimedia presentation to make a topic more interesting in geography?
- asked students to count to 50 in French and then praised them for this?
- allowed your students in your class to set their own personal targets in physical education when fulfilling a role of their choice (e.g. team leader)?
- structured an environment in a citizenship session where your students engaged in critical thinking?
- used a reward to encourage your students to complete a task in history?
- played background music to encourage a mood or stimulate a group routine within dance?
- provided your students with the materials to create their own presentations in IT?

At the surface you may not realise that the fundamental underpinnings across these tasks are quite different, but part of becoming an effective teacher will be your ability to quite skilfully blend these different approaches and positions on learning for different classroom-based situations.

Learning styles

There is a large body of research on learning styles or preferences for learning new information and then connecting this information to something that is already known. Specifically, research and writing on learning styles have attended to efforts to define learning styles and have documented elaborate attempts to understand and categorise elements that make up different learning styles. While writers have put forward multiple definitions (Cano-Garcia and Hughes 2001), throughout educational research the idea of 'learning style' typically refers to how people prefer to learn (Heffler 2001, Kolb 1984, Sternberg 1997) and thus access and process ideas and new information.

You may have been informed as part of your training or induction that one reason why learning may not take place is a possible mismatch between a student's preferred learning style and the learning opportunities and tasks they face. Indeed this is often true. As Fleming and Baume (2006) state: 'Teaching often reflects the teacher's preferred style, rather than the student's preferred learning styles' (p.5).

There is general agreement that individuals do indeed differ in their preferences for gathering and processing information. Like adults, children and students learn in different ways. Felder and Silverman (1988) and Barbe and Malone (1981) claim students and young people could be considered hear-learners, see-learners or do-learners. Individuals will rely upon a consistent set of behaviours or approaches to learning and seeking meaning (Van Zwanenberg *et al*. 2000) which are determined by a combination of hereditary and environmental factors, and the demands of the present environment.

Research on teaching to different learning styles is not conclusive with reference to the impact upon students' academic achievement (Muijs and Reynolds 2001) and as will be seen later, there are some who have questioned the use of learning styles, Regardless, a number of writers have attempted to 'catalogue' a range of learning styles that appear to exist across individuals or have produced inventories to enable learners to self-report their preferences. An extensive review of the learning style literature is not appropriate here. The reader is encouraged to consult Riding and Raynor (1998) and Honey and Mumford (1982). For the purposes of this chapter the work of Kolb (1976, 1984, 1985), and Honey and Mumford (1982) in the area of learning styles will be discussed followed by some attention to Gardner's Theory of Multiple Intelligences.

Kolb: Learning Styles Inventory (LSI)

One of the most noted writers in the area of learning styles is Kolb. Kolb's LSI is arguably the most widely documented instrument for measuring and analysing learning styles (Kolb 1984). Kolb (1976) identified four adaptive learning modes, which are summarised in Table 4.1.

Table 4.1: Summary of Kolb's Learning Modes and Associated Characteristics

Learning mode	Unique characteristics
Concrete experience	Responds to kinaesthetic elements of the experience
Reflective observation	Learns by introspection and reflection
Abstract concept	Comprehends information conceptually
Active experimentation	Learns by environmental manipulation

The construct of learning style as identified by Kolb included two dimensions. Firstly, perceiving, which describes the concrete and abstract thinker, and secondly, processing, which describes the active or reflective processing ability. When these dimensions were integrated by Kolb some alternative ways of relating to the world were expressed as four types of learning styles.

1. Divergers: who learn by personal experience gathered from feelings.
2. Assimilators: experience is grasped through abstract comprehension.
3. Convergers: use abstract reflection.
4. Accommodators: process information concretely and actively.

Kolb (1984) offered a conceptualisation of learning through the 'experiential learning cycle'. This model described learning as a continuous cyclical process of experience, reflection, theory and preparation. The ability to learn, according to Kolb, can commence at any point in the cycle. The individual elements of the sequence are described as follows:

- **Experience: represents an active experience where new information is fed in.**
- **Reflection: process of learning change, the individual now passively thinks about what has just happened.**
- **Theory: the individual thinks about the new information and now contrasts this with other ideas and theories.**
- **Preparation: this is where the learner considers what to do next.**

Honey and Mumford

Honey and Mumford (1982) applied Kolb's experiential cycle to produce a learning styles model that consisted of four descriptions of individuals who prefer to learn at the respective stages of the Kolb cycle. Their 20-item questionnaire enables the individual to locate their preferred learning style. Cotton (1995) offers a useful summary of the characteristics of each learning style, which has been outlined in Table 4.2.

Table 4.2: Summary of Honey and Mumford's Learning Styles with Associated Characteristics

Style	Stage of Kolb's Experiential Learning Cycle	Characteristics
Active learners	Experience	Welcome new experiences, rush into new experiences, take centre stage, easily bored, happy to combine with others, and like opportunities for problem solving. **Activists** are individuals who learn by doing, enjoy novel experiences, and generally dislike structured situations
Reflective learners	Reflection	Are cautious, tend to take a back seat, are calm, prefer to take their time, generally have a low profile and are more disposed to observational experiences. **Reflectors** are individuals who learn through feelings and experience, enjoy asking questions and try to predict outcomes
Theorists	Theory	Learn by investigation, carry out tasks in logical steps, and think through application of general rules. **Theorists** are individuals who learn through observation and investigation and tend to focus upon logic and systematic planning
Pragmatists	Preparation	Tend to try out ideas in practice, want to get on with things, and thrive on direct work experience. **Pragmatists** are individuals who learn by thinking and engaging in problem-solving and role playing

Multiple intelligences

Gardner

As we have seen, many learning styles can be found within one classroom. The intellectual strengths and weaknesses each student possesses will determine how easy or difficult it is for this individual to learn the subject matter presented in a particular way by the teacher. As an attempt to recognise the different abilities and talents of students, Howard Gardner (1983) proposed a new concept of intelligence and formulated a list of seven intelligences:

1. Logical-mathematical intelligence: logical thinking, deductive reasoning (mathematical and scientific thinking).
2. Linguistic intelligence: mastery of language to remember information.
3. Spatial intelligence: development of mental images to solve problems.
4. Musical intelligence: recognition of musical tones, pitches and rhythms.
5. Bodily-kinaesthetic intelligence: mental ability is used to co-ordinate bodily movement.
6/7. Personal intelligences: include interpersonal feelings of others, and intrapersonal intelligence, which is the ability to understand one's own feelings and motives.

Gardner claimed the intelligences are needed for productive functioning in our society, that they rarely operate alone, but are used concurrently when facing problems or acquiring skills.

Gardner suggests some implications for teachers:

- **think of all the intelligences as equally important;**
- **present material which attends to most if not all the intelligences;**
- **use knowledge of the intelligences to reinforce the subject matter in multiple ways;**
- **implement different assessment techniques to enable learners to show what they know, understand and can do (journals, portfolios, creative tasks);**

Guidance on the teaching with multiple intelligences is available, such as Jasmine (1996).

> **PRACTICAL TASK** PRACTICAL TASK PRACTICAL TASK PRACTICAL TASK PRACTICAL TASK
>
> Select a topic/concept. Using your understanding of Gardner's Multiple Intelligences plan and teach a lesson where you aim to address most if not all of these intelligences. What different ways will the material be presented which attends to these intelligences? What alternative evaluation practices might you use? What do you notice about the level of participation within the class and the work the students produce?

As a beginning teacher do you sense that some of your students might prefer structure, or some might prefer learning on their own, or with others in groups? Are there some students who seem to prefer situations when the room is silent or there is noise? Do you recognise these seven intelligences within the classes you teach?

Learning styles: a critique

At was intimated earlier within this chapter, the notion of learning styles has been challenged by some. Fleming and Baume (2006) offer the following possible reason: 'This is probably because it is very difficult to measure learning (in) part because it is difficult to define learning in useful way(s), especially if one wants to know when learning happened or to what it can be ascribed' (p.7). Other scholars are of the view that most learning style models have limited efficacy and that more work must be undertaken to validate these theories through research, as there seems to be some variability in the evidence (Demos 2005). Readers are encouraged to consult the following sources for a useful critique of learning styles and a discussion of the theoretical base upon which they rest: Coffield *et al.* (2004); Franklin (2006); Demos (2005).

A trend towards personalisation of learning

Some writers have deemed the use of learning styles as 'superficial quick fixes, and do not lead to sustainable personalisation of learning' (Aspect, 2006). As has been mentioned in this chapter, the present educational climate, in part, speaks to a long-term, learner-focused provision designed to meet the needs of students and which teaches learners how to learn. The development of the personalisation agenda within public policy is concerned with meeting the individual needs of children and young people in an effort to maximise their individual achievements and standards. It also sets the agenda for learners to have far greater involvement in the ways in which they are taught. Specifically, the current Gilbert review includes within its main points that: 'every secondary student has a learning guide who will meet with them at least once every half-term, monitor their progress and act as their advocate in the school' (*Times Educational Supplement* 2007, p.1).

In 2004 a speech by David Miliband (former Minister of State for School Standards) first identified five components to the government's conception of personalised learning (Milliband 2004). These were: 1) Assessment for learning, 2) Effective teaching and learning, 3) Curriculum entitlement and choice, 4) Organising the school, 5) Supported by effective teaching and learning strategies. Personalised learning requires teachers, in conjunction with a range of other adults, to develop knowledge of a student's strengths and weaknesses using feedback that is provided to and obtained from students to inform their planning. The teacher's role is to develop the confidence and competence of each student using appropriate teaching strategies that aim to build upon individual needs, including information and communications technology (ICT) and being aware of the various student intelligences.

Catering for such an array of individual needs will be a challenging task for trainees and newly qualified teachers when interacting with large groups of learners. There are a number of references to personalisation and the need to know the strengths and weaknesses of individual students within the present Standards. In order to progress towards meeting the Standards for the Award of Qualified Teacher Status (QTS) it is important that beginning teachers are aware of the different learning styles that might exist in their classes and what might be some characteristics of individual learning preferences. Such information will inform how you organise the curriculum, select appropriate teaching strategies and their accompanying learning experiences or tasks to enable access to the content for all students.

The QTS Standards: implications for student learning

What might be some implications for trainees in enabling student learning in light of the language and intent of the new Professional Standards? In this section, attention is drawn to some aspects of the Standards that appear most relevant for enabling learning.

It must be stated that the Standards can be viewed as a progression from qualified teacher to excellent teacher status. These Standards also reflect the enhanced professionalism that accompanies the *Every Child Matters*, Extended Schools, and the workforce remodelling agendas.

Mention was made earlier in the chapter of the typical concerns/fears which are apparent in most inexperienced teachers during the very early stages of their development and training, which could limit the range of teaching approaches which are adopted. New in-service teachers will also experience a range of stressors during a period which Katz (1972) referred to as 'survival' and which is a time when the teacher is coping on a daily basis, and may be questioning their ability to teach. Acknowledging Fuller's three-stage model of teacher development (Fuller 1969), moving from (1) concerns about self, to (2) concerns about tasks, to (3) concerns about students and the impact of teaching, seems pertinent here and leads us to ask whether trainee teachers are capable of achieving such a focus upon outcome rather than on self so early in their development as teachers.

The new Standards also emphasise the need to support and guide students to reflect upon the progress they have made as part of an ongoing dialogue and collaboration with them. The ability of students to talk about their experiences and make adults aware of their views is a key issue in personalisation. Consulting students about teaching and learning, as one aspect of 'student voice', has received considerable attention within the literature (Cullingford 2006, McIntyre *et al.* 2005, Thomson and Gunter 2006). Engaging in dialogue with students will, in part, help you as teacher become better informed about how and when they learn.

It has been documented that inexperienced teachers tend to adopt more direct forms of instruction that both lead to less developed independent learning skills among students (Gipps and McGilchrist 1999) and do not 'connect material' (Muijs and Reynolds 2001, p.15). Indeed, in some subject areas Ofsted (1995) have highlighted that experienced teachers have tended to use more command styles of instruction. Attention to some of the personalisation literature foregrounds groupwork as one instructional approach considered significant in the shift towards personalisation (TLRP 2004). Many have advocated the benefits of groupwork (e.g. Cohen 1994) and the educationally worthwhile outcomes that groupwork can promote including enhanced student motivation, developing social communication, and better relationships with students. If indeed there are commonly used pedagogies that fit within the more teacher-directed mode, then this trend would seem to be a little counterproductive to enabling a more learner-focused provision. Student teachers will be expected, within the context of the current reforms in education, to have good subject knowledge and to be able to contribute to the workforce via contact with a range of support staff, other professionals and parents. Beyond this, can we indeed expect trainees to have sufficient pedagogical knowledge to provide, monitor, and manage learner-centred environments (couched within cognitive/constructivist schools of thought) when they are typically 'getting to grips' with subject and curricular knowledge? If we aim to develop the very best teachers then the answer to the above question has to be yes. However, all of us involved in initial teacher education realise the difficulty and complexity inherent in this process and one of the primary functions of any teacher education programme has to be the provision of support in the achievement of this goal. It is perhaps timely to heed Kyriacou and Stephens' (1999) remark in their study of Postgraduate Certificate of Education students;

> If student teachers believe that students should be occupied principally to keep bad behaviour at bay, future generations of teachers are going to be more pre-occupied with the management of 'order' than the cultivation of learning (p.28).

A SUMMARY OF **KEY POINTS**

This chapter has offered a very brief insight into the nature of learning and learning styles. The key points of this chapter are as follows:

> **Student learning should be the first consideration in teaching a lesson.**

> **Learning theories typically fall within one of two umbrellas (behaviourist and cognitive), should be applied as the situation demands, and critically examined within the dynamics of classroom life.**

> **Learning styles refer to how individuals prefer to learn. Several learning styles and their associated characteristics have been identified by researchers (Kolb, Honey and Mumford) and that children possess different abilities (see Gardner).**

> **Individuals with different learning styles possess some unique characteristics.**

> **Constructivism represents a dominant school of thought on learning. An understanding of students' prior conceptions is critical to helping them connect new learning with established knowledge structures.**

> **The concept of personalised learning puts forth a system where the child is at the centre and where teachers engage in dialogue with children so their voices are heard.**

FURTHER READING FURTHER READING **FURTHER READING** FURTHER READING

Aspect (2006) *Personalised Learning: From Blueprint to Practice*. Wakefield. Aspect.

Bleach, K. (2000) *The Newly Qualified Secondary Teacher's Handbook*. London. David Fulton Publishers.

Coffield, D., Mosely, D., Hall, K., and Ecclestone, E. (2004) *Should We Be Using Learning Styles: What research has to say on practice*. London. Learning and Skills Research Centre.

Cohen, E. (1994) *Designing Groupwork: Strategies for the Heterogeneous Classroom*. New York. Teachers College Press.

Cullingford, C. (2006) Children's own vision of schooling. *Education 3–13*, 34(3), 211–221.

Demos (2005) About Learning: Report from the Learning Working Group. London. Demos.

DFES (2003) *Every Child Matters*. London. DfES.

DFES (2004) *Five Year Strategy for Children and Learners*. London. DfES.

DFES (2005) *Higher Standards: Better Schools for All*. London. DfES.

Fleming, N., and Baume, D. (2006) *Learning styles again: VARKing up the right tree.* Educational Developments, SEDA Ltd 7(4), 4–7

Franklin, S. (2006) VAKing out learning styles why the notion of learning styles is unhelpful to teachers. *Education 3-13,* 34(1), 81–87.

Kyriacou, C. (1997) *Effective Teaching in Schools: Theory and Practice (2nd ed.).* Cheltenham. Nelson Thornes Ltd.

Milliband, D. (2004) Personalised learning: building a new relationship with schools. Speech made to the North of England Education Conference, 8 January 2004, Belfast.

McIntyre, D., Pedder, D. and Rudduck, J. (2005) Student Voice: Comfortable and uncomfortable learnings for teachers. *Research Papers in Education.* 20 (2):149–168.

Pritchard, A. (2005) *Ways of Learning: Learning Theories and Learning Styles in the Classroom.* London. David Fulton Publishers.

Thomson, P., and Gunter, H. (2006) From consulting students to students as researchers. *British Educational Research Journal,* 32(6), 830–856.

Times Educational Supplement (2007, January 5) Students' personal advisers, p1.

Tirosh, D. (2000) Enhancing prospective teachers' knowledge of childrens' conceptions: The case of divisions of fractions. *Journal of Research in Mathematics Education*, 31(1), 5–25.

TLRP (Teaching and Research Programme) (2004) Personalised learning: A commentary by the teaching and learning research programme. ESRC.

PART 2
PROFESSIONAL SKILLS: PLANNING AND ASSESSING LEARNING

5
Planning for learning
Charlotte Wright, Viv Ellis and Miranda Peverett

Professional Standards for QTS

Q3, Q7, Q22, Q23, Q24

As a teacher, you will, of course, need to demonstrate high expectations of your students. You will carefully evaluate your own work so that your contribution to raising students' educational achievements is as effective as possible. You will be aware of the general teaching requirements of the National Curriculum and be able to plan lessons and sequences of lessons in your specialist subject that are related to particular students' abilities and interests and the expected standards for their age. Your planning may involve the deployment of additional adults to support students' learning as part of your differentiation of work for students of different abilities. Your students will understand what it is you want them to learn and why and your skills of time and resource management will support the learning process.

You may find it helpful to read through the appropriate section of the Handbook that accompanies the Standards for the Award of QTS for clarification and support.

Introduction

This chapter addresses the key issues of teacher preparation and planning for learning. It follows on from the themes of Chapter 4, with its overview of theories of learning and learning styles, and anticipates those of Chapter 6, a chapter concerned with the vitally important and inseparable issue of assessment of – and *for* – learning. Underlying this chapter as a whole is the assumption that the processes of teaching and learning are inextricably bound up with domains of knowledge, that teachers and students are dealing with what is often referred to as 'content' and that – in the UK context - this is often specified by the National Curriculum, National Strategies or examination syllabuses. But Herbert Kohl (1986) reminds us to give equal attention to the interpersonal dimension of teaching as an activity - interacting with students and contributing positively to the development of learners' identities:

Teaching . . . involves helping students acquire understanding, knowledge, and skills they didn't previously have. To do this, it is essential to enable students to feel good about themselves as learners and to create an atmosphere that enables them to focus energy on learning.   (Kohl 1986, p. 90).

Curriculum and learning

The word 'curriculum' means a course of study or a set of ideas (to be taught and developed). In England and Wales, the first ever National Curriculum was implemented in 1989 (Scotland and Northern Ireland have never had a National Curriculum). This was the first time that a range of subject knowledge, understanding and skills had been specified across the 5 to 16 age range. The National Curriculum became a statutory instrument and its implementation has been monitored ever since through the inspection system. These new arrangements supplemented the syllabuses for 16+ and 18+ national examinations with which secondary teachers have worked for a very long time. Since September 2001, secondary schools have also been asked to work with the Key Stage 3 Strategy (subsequently, the Secondary National Strategy). This non-statutory but recommended initiative has been designed to address the difficulties many students experience on transition from the primary phase in accessing the secondary curriculum and also the problem of student regression (in terms of attainment) between Key Stage 2 and the early years of Key Stage 3.

> **REFLECTIVE TASK**
>
> In your school (and preferably in your own subject department), find a teacher who was teaching prior to the introduction of the National Curriculum in 1989. How did this teacher design a course of study – a curriculum – for students then? What are the differences now? What are the benefits and drawbacks (for individual students, teachers and society) of a National Curriculum?

The activity of teacher planning, then, has become more complex over the last 16 years as more detailed curriculum prescription in terms of 'content' – combined with a more recent emphasis on recommended teaching methods and strategies – means that individual teachers (through their work in subject departments) have had to 'map' their curriculum against national frameworks as well as examination syllabuses. This complexity arises from the obvious requirement to consider the children to be taught first (their needs, interests and ways of learning), the available resources (physical, including the classroom, sports equipment, textbooks, musical instruments, computers, library stock, etc.; and human, including classroom assistants and teacher expertise) and the students' entitlement to the National Curriculum, Key Stage 3 National Strategy and what is generally referred to as the ideal of a 'broad and balanced curriculum'. Complex planning at this level is discussed later in this chapter but, as a trainee, you will need to develop an awareness of how your work – and that of your department – relates to the rest of a student's experience of the secondary curriculum.

Different traditions in planning for learning

One of the most influential models of teacher planning and preparation was that of Tyler (1949). Tyler's original theories of instructional design were based on rational, behaviourist approaches to learning. The psychologist Jerome Bruner (1966) later expounded theories of teaching and learning that were focused on the processes of mental growth and the teacher's role in facilitating this. Glaser (1976, 1984) critiqued what he saw as 'process-based' approaches to instruction but proposed a 'knowledge-based' or 'competency' model that to some extent reflected Bruner's notion of 'optimal structures' of knowledge:

> . . . a theory of instruction must specify the ways in which a body of knowledge should be structured so that it can be most readily grasped by the learner. 'Optimal structure' refers to a set of propositions from which a larger body of knowledge can be generated . . . since the merit of a structure depends upon its power for *simplifying information*, for *generating new propositions*, and for *increasing the manipulability of a body of knowledge*, structure must always be related to the status and gifts of the learner. Viewed in this way, the optimal structure of a body of knowledge is not absolute but relative.
>
> (Bruner 1966, p. 41; emphasis in original)

Recent inspection evidence from Ofsted (2002) suggests that effective departments in secondary schools do not necessarily have more detailed or thorough schemes of work but that what exists clearly specifies what knowledge, skills and understanding should be developed with a class and how students can make progress.

For many beginning teachers, this is one of the most difficult aspects of planning. How do you represent ideas or model skills that you have developed at the graduate level to, say, a bottom set Year 9 last thing on a Friday afternoon during a force eight gale? The Standards for the Award of QTS – and this book – assume that much of your training will concern the principles of developing 'optimal structures' in your own specialist subject and providing you with opportunities to practise this development in classrooms.

The question of teacher knowledge

The Standards for the Award of QTS specify that you should understand the subject knowledge requirements of your own specialist subject. The *transformation* of your subject knowledge in the context of the secondary classroom will be an important part of your training.

When discussing teaching strategies, Kohl drew our attention to the importance of the teacher's knowledge of the subject:

> There are many other modes of explanation, such as drawing diagrams, providing examples, or even improvising a dramatic presentation of an idea. All these techniques require a mastery of the content you are teaching so that you are free to play with it.
>
> (Kohl 1986, p. 102)

In other words, in order to teach effectively, matching 'content' and method to the particular children's needs – and to analyse what the children have learned – teachers need to be able to be able to reshape ideas, to represent knowledge in different ways. This is only possible if teachers have confidence in their own knowledge, and thus the process of training will continue throughout each teacher's career. Good teaching is born out of a recurring process: successful teachers continually update their own understanding, reflect upon the process of learning that they themselves are constantly undertaking, and then use that subject and pedagogic knowledge into their planning for students' learning.

Planning for learning over time

Teaching is sometimes described as a cycle of planning, transaction and evaluation.

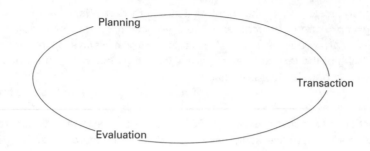

Simply put, planning goes on before teaching; transaction is what happens in the classroom with students; and evaluation occurs after teaching. However, the reality is much more complex.

The *planning stage* includes a consideration of aims, justifications, concepts, strategies, assessment and resources. It is ongoing and plans are adjusted based on assessment information.

The *transaction stage* is the execution of the plans made earlier (although in practice the transaction may involve changes of plan in response to the emerging and unforeseeable responses of the learners). Simultaneous evaluation of the transaction can lead to changes in planning. Transaction – implying, as it does, interaction and interplay – is a term that is used in preference to 'delivery'. Deliveries can be made while the intended recipients are 'out'.

The *evaluation stage* includes a comparison of the learners' achievements in the lesson with the teacher's plans; and an evaluation of the effectiveness of the teaching strategies and resources used. The evaluation is the start of the planning stage for the next and subsequent teaching activities/lessons.

But why bother writing lesson plans?

It is worth stating explicitly here that your initial training's emphasis upon careful and thorough planning, and reflective, critical evaluation, is to ensure high standards of teaching and learning (the 'transaction') through which your students will make progress. Planning and evaluation are not simply administrative requirements. There are at least two main reasons why trainees are asked to plan carefully and thoroughly.

1. For new teachers without substantial classroom experience, the planning process is often difficult. In trying to plan teaching that is successful for you and your students and draws upon your own strengths (rather than simply trying to copy successful lessons you have observed), you will need to spend time thinking about what you want the students to learn and how you will help them to achieve this. The very process of trying to write a plan – including the inevitable re-drafting and revisions – will help you to develop planning skills. There is a body of research that views writing as a mode of learning (see, for example, Emig 1977) and so writing lesson plans can be seen as being

useful to you, the trainee.

2. As a trainee, you will need to demonstrate – consistently and over a period of time – certain skills and attributes, including those contained within the QTS Standards. You will need to evidence your achievement of these Standards to a variety of people to whom you are accountable: your mentor and tutor, an external examiner and, perhaps, an inspector during an inspection of your training course or school. The evidential requirements for trainee teachers are sometimes seen as greater than for fully qualified teachers. This shouldn't be surprising. That said, qualified teachers seeking threshold payments or applying for Advanced Skills status (or indeed going through Ofsted inspection or post-Ofsted special measures) all have to produce detailed plans and records as part of portfolios of evidence.

Nevertheless, you will be aware that experienced teachers do not appear to 'need to plan' as much as you do. This doesn't mean that experienced teachers' plans aren't as detailed as yours; rather that 'experienced teachers more often rely on their extensive experience to form a mental framework of how they want the lesson to proceed' and that their plans and their ability to adjust them to the specific needs of each class 'have become internalised through repetition' (Kyriacou 1991, p. 17).

Long-term planning: schemes of work or key stage plans

A scheme of work is a description of the work planned for pupils over a specific period. Sometimes, they are known as key stage plans if they relate to the groupings of National Curriculum years. The planning of these is the responsibility of the whole subject department in a secondary school, co-ordinated by the head of department with all members of staff contributing to the planning process. It is at this level that the links between planning and teacher development become clear: different teachers with differing strengths contribute to the design of a curriculum for students in which teacher expertise is shared.

Long-term plans usually give an overview of the year or key stage. At departmental level, a scheme of work is made up from a series of units of work which describe:

- **how a school's curriculum policy is to be translated into effective teaching;**
- **how the curriculum will be implemented;**
- **how human and material resources will be used efficiently.**

To develop a scheme of work, departments will need to decide on an overall programme with regard to the range and depth of experiences/topics/activities they teach and ensure progression and continuity of student learning. The National Curriculum and the relevant national strategies and examination syllabuses will inform this process, which is sometimes called 'curriculum mapping'.

PRACTICAL TASK PRACTICAL TASK PRACTICAL TASK PRACTICAL TASK PRACTICAL TASK

Talk to your mentor about your subject department's approach to longer-term planning. How does the department go about planning at this level and reviewing their plans? What kinds of long-term planning records are kept?

The cover sheet to one department's key stage plan is reproduced on the next page. It is not intended to be exemplary and we would need to see the detailed (medium-term) planning that followed it. It does, however, give us the opportunity to see how one secondary department (in this case, English) represents its Key Stage 3 programme on one side of A4.

Medium-term planning: units of work/sequences of lessons

These are the plans for the teaching of one of the components of the scheme of work, i.e. a topic, text or activity, which will involve a series of lessons, perhaps over a five- or six-week period (one-half of an average term). The planning of these is sometimes the responsibility of individual teachers, although departments often collaborate in this process. In some cases, the unit of work is detailed to the level of content of individual lessons. As a beginning trainee, you will not normally be asked to design an entire unit of work straight away but, instead, you are likely to be given specific content and asked to plan an individual lesson. As you progress, however, you will be given increasing responsibility for designing your own units of work.

An effective medium-term plan shows how lessons fit together, indicates the progress expected and is a way of identifying targets for progression that apply to groups rather than individual students. An effective medium-term plan should:

- **identify what pupils will learn over a half-term/term;**
- **be based on assessments of what students already know, understand and can do;**
- **show evidence of progression, in line with the department's scheme of work or key stage plan; this may be in the form of differentiated expectations (see below);**
- **give recommendations for teaching and learning approaches;**
- **identify opportunities for assessment.**

An example of a medium-term plan (unit of work) proforma used by one training provider is given in Figure 5.1. It is not presented as an example of good practice. As a guiding principle, we should recognise that different secondary specialist subjects will have different planning requirements and that any generic proforma is meant to be adapted or used in the development of personalised planning formats.

Medium-term planning will ideally start at the *bottom* of the proforma, with the expectations and differentiated outcomes. This should then inform the *sequencing* of tasks/activities so that cumulative and directional learning can take place.

You will notice that a good deal of information is required on this plan and that some of it will require considerable thought. Remember that some departments' units of work may not be as detailed but, in the context of your training, a proforma like this gives you the opportunity to demonstrate your understanding (briefly and meaningfully) of a number of key areas related to planning such as the cross-curricular learning specified at the beginning of each National Curriculum document and in the Secondary National Strategy.

Learning across the curriculum

All teachers have responsibility to develop their students' capacities in a number of areas. The National Curriculum specifies a number of general teaching requirements (including the

Key Stage 3 Plan for English		
Induction unit: making a student prospectus; – writing non-fiction	writing/telling autobiography – differences between speech and writing	class novel study *Holes by Louis Sachar* – language awareness – social variation
extended simulation activity – *Escape from Kraznir* – – drama (role-play, writing in role, etc)	expressive arts project – based on the *Beowulf* story – – ICT focus (multimedia)	diaries – integrated project – *Diary of a Survivor* – pre 1914 non-fiction
Individual poetry anthology – writing poetry – using quotation	the language of advertising (media focus) – media languages – audiences	drama text for class study – *Frankenstein* – (inc. comparison with Mary Shelley's novel)
class novel study – choice of Anne Fine texts	individual/group extended narrative – – narrative POV	Introduction to media studies – media technologies
presenting a written argument – response to non literary texts – – persuasion	forms of poetry – ballads and sonnets –	class novel study – theme: different generations – choice of Robert Westall or Aiden Chambers texts
drama text as class study – Shakespeare –	control of narrative – twist in the tale –	newspapers – their production and impact – ICT focus

(Row groups labelled **7**, **8**, **9** in the left margin)

– independent reading programme
– literacy skills programme level)
– ICT available – limited but systems in place for use
– information skills (Year 7)
– storytelling (Year 8)

KS3 starter activity units – word and sentence

} cross curricular projects

Figure 5.1: Key Stage 3 plan

use of language, ICT and citizenship across the curriculum) and seven aspects of cross-curricular learning:

1. key skills;
2. spiritual, moral, social and cultural development;
3. thinking skills;
4. work-related learning;
5. education for sustainable development;
6. enterprise and entrepreneurial skills;
7. financial capability.

As an individual trainee, you shouldn't feel obliged to take full responsibility for all aspects of students' learning across the curriculum. This responsibility can only be assumed by the school and planned for collaboratively across departments and pastoral areas. You should, however, be interested in whether your specialist subject can make a contribution and be aware of how your own teaching might contribute. The sections on the unit of work proforma concerned with key skills and spiritual, moral, social and cultural development/ other learning across the curriculum would only be completed if there were obvious ways in which the unit contributed to the development of students' capacities in these areas. For examples of how secondary subjects can contribute to these areas of cross-curricular learning, go to: **www.nc.uk.net/** and follow the link for 'Learning across the curriculum'.

The Secondary National Strategy supports the development of cross-curricular literacy, numeracy and the use of ICT. For further details, see Chapters 8, 9 and 10.

General teaching requirements: health and safety

One of the general teaching requirements specified by the National Curriculum is that of ensuring the health and safety of students. This requirement applies particularly to teachers of design technology, art and design, physical education, science and ICT. Training in these specialist subjects will include attention to this important aspect of planning and teaching. On a medium-term plan, it is useful to draw attention to particular health and safety issues associated with the topic or activities so that a more detailed risk assessment can be made. On the generic proforma, health and safety issues can be identified underneath a list of any particular resources needed for the unit.

Differentiated expectations

In this section of the proforma, you would briefly indicate the level of attainment (expressed as a National Curriculum level or examination grade) you expect of the different groups within your class. In this way, you are setting targets for groups of students based upon your knowledge of class. The (three) groups are broken down in the following terms:

1. 'After completing the unit, **most** students will have ...': this is what you expect of the majority of the class; the core, the key concepts and basic skills related to an appropriate level of attainment.
2. 'After completing the unit, **some students will not have made as much progress** and will ...': this is where you indicate the level at which you expect the lowest attaining in the class to achieve; this may arise out of a different task for these students.
3. 'After completing the unit, **some students will have progressed further** and will ...': this is where you indicate what you expect the highest attaining students to achieve; this may arise out of a different task or extension work with additional content.

| Secondary QTS **Unit of work** | Year Group: | Date developed: |
| | | Date revised: |

Unit title:	The rationale for this unit:
Focus:	
Aims:	Potential outcomes for summative assessment purposes:
Particular resources:	Opportunities to develop cross-curricular dimensions:
	Links to previous work:
Health and safety issues:	Language for learning/KS3 Literacy objectives:
	KS3 Numeracy:
	KS3 ICT:

Learning across the curriculum: Key Skills:

Communication
Application of Number
ICT
Improving own learning and performance
Working with others
Problem solving

Other learning across the curriculum:
Contribution to Students' Spiritual, Moral, Social and Cultural development/ Thinking skills/Work-related learning/ Education for sustainable development/Enterprise and entrepreneurial skills/Financial capability

| Tasks/Activities | NC Programmes of Study/KS3 Strategy Objectives/A-Level AOs | Teaching approaches (including use of ICT) |

Differentiated expectations:	AT and NC Level or exam criterion and grade, etc.:
1. After completing the unit, **most** students will have:	
2. After completing the unit, **some** students will **not have made as much progress** and will:	
3. After completing the unit, **some** students will **have progressed further** and will:	

Figure 5.2: Unit of work proforma

This model of setting differentiated expectations in medium-term plans was developed by the Qualifications and Curriculum Authority (QCA) in their exemplar units of work for Key Stage 3. To look at examples in National Curriculum subjects go to: **www.standards.dfee. gov.uk/schemes/**

Teaching approaches

This column on the unit of work proforma provides some information about teaching strategies that have proved or will prove to be effective. For example, in relation to a particular activity or task, it may be that teacher modelling of a particular skill will be most effective; or perhaps the use of ICT would effectively consolidate children's understanding. The teaching strategies necessary to include all members of the teaching group should also be mentioned here.

PRACTICAL TASK PRACTICAL TASK PRACTICAL TASK PRACTICAL TASK PRACTICAL TASK

Use this medium-term planning proforma in the development of a unit of work you are going to teach. What are the strengths and weaknesses of this format and of using proformas in general?

Short-term planning: lessons

You will probably begin to develop lesson plans fairly early in your training. Two definitions are useful here.

* **A lesson is a 'period for teaching something; an experience from which to learn'.**
* **A plan is an 'arrangement for carrying out future activity; an arrangement of parts in a system'.**

We have already made the obvious point that you – the teacher – are going to teach something that the students will learn. In this context, 'experience' refers to the methods or strategies that you use to connect what you want the students to learn to your assessment of that learning. The word 'arrangement' draws attention to the need to think carefully about the parts of a lesson: in what order do you put the experiences? How does the order influence the students' learning? In turn, that starts to take you back to the medium-term plan (unit of work) because a lesson plan comes from within this overview plan. A lesson plan is part of a sequence.

Although each lesson plan must be related to what has gone before and show how it is related to what is to come, it can appear to stand by itself. But it is a plan, not a script: it is something you work **from** and not **to**. There is the danger of planning too much and too little: too much detail can lead to you telling rather than teaching; too little can lead to a lack of focus in the teaching and to under-developing what it is you want the students to learn.

An effective short-term (lesson) plan should:

* **identify in detail what pupils should learn (the objectives or learning intentions);**
* **identify how you will know that progress has been made (the outcomes);**
* **identify opportunities and strategies for assessing the learning outcomes;**
* **show how lessons will start, end and continue;**
* **outline activities which show what pupils will do, how they will be grouped and what resources will be used;**
* **identify key teaching points and key questions;**

- show how students' learning can be supported or extended (differentiation);
- note how any support staff will be deployed.

Once again, this probably sounds like a daunting and unrealistically detailed list. In the example of lesson planning that comes at the end of this chapter, you will see how these requirements can be met manageably and meaningfully. At the moment, please remember that a lesson plan isn't a script nor is it an essay. It must be useful to you and allow an outside observer or examiner understand what – and how – you have been teaching.

PRACTICAL TASK PRACTICAL TASK **PRACTICAL TASK** PRACTICAL TASK **PRACTICAL TASK**

Referring to the checklist above, use ICT to prepare a lesson plan format that you would find useful in your specialist subject.

Differentiation

This aspect of planning involves matching your tasks or activities and your teaching approaches to the needs and preferred learning styles of the children in your classroom. For a more detailed discussion of differentiation and inclusion, please see Chapter 12. At this point, however, it will be useful to note some principles of differentiation as they would impact upon a lesson plan.

In planning lessons as in planning units, it is useful to think about a core of learning that you will plan for all students in a class. This would consist of the key concepts and basic skills. Based upon your assessment of all students' likely progress against this 'core', you may also plan for two eventualities:

1. A 'support loop' that could involve a different task or activity, a different teaching approach or the support of another adult for those who may have difficulties; it is essential that any other adults are aware of your plans before the lesson and what you see as their role in supporting an individual or small group.
2. Extension activities for those who will be able to progress further, which may involve additional content of greater challenge, more independent research or the development of higher order skills such as synthesis, evaluation or application to different situations.

On lesson plans, these strategies can be related to individual students by name. If a student has been assessed at Stage 2 or above of the Code of Practice for Special Educational Needs, you will need to refer to their Individual Education Plan (IEP) when planning differentiated work (see Chapter 12 for more information on planning for students with special educational needs).

Assessment

You will need to give some details of the assessment opportunities (what and who?) and the assessment strategies (how?) employed during the lesson. Assessment strategies could take the form of monitoring a few individuals and discussing their contributions to a whole-class discussion, observing a specific student at work, a question and answer session with a small group, reading any written work produced during the lesson or marking homework or classwork after the class. You will also need to be aware of the record-keeping requirements of your department and how your ongoing assessment of students' progress will need to be recorded. The next chapter in this book deals with assessment of – and for – learning in some detail but for the moment, the key questions to address in lesson planning are:

- who will your assessment activities focus on?
- what aspect of their work will you be assessing?
- how do you intend to achieve this?

Managing the lesson

An important aspect of planning a lesson involves thinking about the various stages or elements in the lesson's structure and the transitions between them. This will include the organisation of students (how they are grouped) and resources. The most common structure to lessons in secondary schools (especially at Key Stage 3) has three parts.

In the **introduction** (which may include a **starter** activity), the teacher:

- provides a clear, brisk start to the lesson;
- makes the purpose of the lesson and your expectations clear (very often, especially at Key Stage 3, this will involve sharing the objectives with the class explicitly);
- recaps on previous work;
- has strategies for ensuring all students take part;
- introduces key ideas through exposition, modelling, example, etc.;
- makes a smooth transition to the main part of the lesson.

During the **development/main activity**, the teacher:

- ensures students know what they are to learn;
- gives students a deadline for completion of work;
- ensures students know where to obtain resources, get help or receive further work;
- maintains pace by motivating students and keeping them on task;
- concludes the main activity smoothly and moves to the conclusion/plenary.

In the **conclusion** or plenary, the teacher:

- summarises important facts or key ideas;
- identifies what needs to be remembered for the next lesson.

A **plenary** may also involve the teacher managing:

- students presenting and explaining their work;
- students generalising a rule from a number of examples;
- students reflecting on and evaluating how they have been working;
- the setting of homework.

Managing behaviour

The justifiable assumption of this book is that if the teacher matches tasks or activities and teaching approaches to the needs and preferred learning styles of his or her students, then the potential for off-task or disruptive behaviour can be minimised. This applies to both 'ends' of the ability scale and the bored and unchallenged 'able' children pose just as great a disruptive threat as the confused and frustrated 'less able'. Further guidance on managing challenging behaviour in the classroom is the focus of Chapter 7 of this book.

Evaluation

Evaluations of learners' progress and your own effectiveness as a teacher will form the basis of written evaluations of your lessons. 'Good' lesson evaluations are honest and constructive and draw upon the student assessment information you have gathered during the lesson. The two most important evaluative questions that should be answered at the end of every lesson are:

1. To what extent were the learning objectives achieved?
2. Based on your assessment, what needs to be planned/taught next and why?

Your answers to these questions will have a direct influence on your planning for the next lesson and, indeed, for the remaining lessons in the series. This link between assessment and planning is discussed in detail in Chapter 6. The process of reflection and adjustment in response to your findings is crucial, and will need to be ongoing: analysis of the *actual* outcomes of the lesson in comparison with the *planned* outcomes will help you to consider what the students are trying to tell you about their own learning.

Sometimes, trainees are asked to complete a more detailed evaluation of their teaching on a weekly basis that will be used in meetings with their mentor or tutor to set targets. An example of such an extended evaluation form from one training provider is reproduced Figure 5.3 on page 58.

PRACTICAL TASK PRACTICAL TASK PRACTICAL TASK PRACTICAL TASK PRACTICAL TASK PRACTICAL TASK

Complete the evaluation proforma in Figure 5.3 yourself at the end of a week's teaching. Use your evaluation as the basis of a meeting with your mentor. What aspects of teaching and learning will you focus on next week (e.g. structure, timing and pace, or assessment opportunities)?

IN THE CLASSROOM: THE LESSON-PLANNING PROCESS

The following account of the lesson planning process was given by a PGCE English trainee (Miranda) near the end of her first block school experience.

Lesson commentary

Context:

This was a lesson given towards the end of my first school experience placement at an 11–18 technology college. The class was a Year 9 mixed-ability class of 22 students with attainment levels ranging from two to six. Eleven students were on the SEN register. One student was on a part-time timetable. In this lesson, there would be one teaching assistant.

I had been teaching this class throughout my placement, and by this stage, I felt I knew them well. The class had spent the past four weeks studying *Macbeth* in preparation for the Shakespeare section of the End of Key Stage 3 tests. This was the final lesson of a four-lesson scheme of work that I had developed independently to prepare the class for questions on dramatic interpretation of the play. In the previous three lessons, we had compared some versions of the play, and I had introduced the notion of dramatic interpretation while watching sections of a modernised film version (*Macbeth on the Estate*). The class were becoming more familiar with how actors and directors had

Secondary QTS Weekly Evaluation

Trainee's name:	Classes taught:

1. Planning and preparation

Did my lesson planning adequately cater for the activities and content of the lessons? How effective was my preparation?

2. Planned learning objectives and outcomes

How realistic were they? To what extent were they achieved?

3. Teaching and learning methods

How effective were my teaching methods in bringing about student learning?

4. Structure, timing and pacing

How effective were these?

5. Management and resources

How effective was my classroom management and the use of resources?

6. Students' tasks

Did I introduce points clearly? To what extent did students understand them? Did I provide opportunities for students to contribute to discussion?

7. Behaviour management

How effective was it? To what extent was I able to motivate the students?

8. Use of Information and Communication Technology

Did I exploit the available oportunities to enhance students' learning through the appropriate use of ICT? Did I exploit the potential of ICT to help me in planning, preparation, recording and presenting information?

9. Assessment opportunities

Did I share the criteria for assessment with the students? How did I provide feedback to students on the quality of work? Did I encourage student self-evaluation?

10. Individual students/students

Comment as appropriate on the progress of individual students

11. Future planning

What implications does this evaluation have for my future planning? What will be my focus for the next set of lessons?

Figure 5.3. Evaluation proforma

achieved different effects on stage or screen; now I wanted to use this final lesson to encourage students to complete creative work on their own interpretations.

Planning the lesson
My first step in planning the lesson was to develop the learning objectives and outcomes. I made the objectives student-friendly by turning them into 'key questions' to be written into student planners at the start of the lesson. I then considered the assessment opportunities I would have in the lesson.

In planning the activities, I considered the class's degree of prior knowledge about the topic. In preparation for the main activity, I had set a homework in the previous lesson where students were required to write down some ideas about where, when and how they would set the play if they were a director. I needed a contingency plan in case there were students who had been away, or had not done the homework, so I planned a starter activity to help students to revisit their own ideas and opinions about different versions of *Macbeth*, and to remind them of the previous work we had done on the film version. A simple matching activity would hopefully build confidence.

The range of abilities in the class made differentiation essential. I spent time considering how to explain the main task, and prepared an example of how to tackle it for weaker students. We were to watch the end of the film, but this still needed a focus for learning, so I planned questions to help students remember this scene clearly when designing their own staging of it. For more able students there would be an extension activity to allow them to develop their ideas about staging independently. I also needed to take into account those students with special educational needs. One student was not taking the same end of key stage test, and so was undertaking an individual project on *Macbeth* while the rest of the class did the more focused work for the tests. I therefore needed to plan one part of the lesson to allow him to participate, and one part when he would continue with his project.

I then considered how the teaching assistant could help with each activity, which students she would work with, what information she would need. Finally, I prepared my lesson resources.

As I made progress in my PGCE course, I found that time spent developing clear and detailed learning objectives and outcomes made planning the details of the teaching much easier. Having learning objectives clearly shared with students as 'key questions' also helped me to reinforce learning and assess progress during the plenary. I have experimented with a number of different planning formats to help me remember all the pieces of the jigsaw, but it has really been active experience that has caused all the elements to start to fall into place for me.

Evaluation of learning achieved
Most of the learning outcomes were met. However, we spent longer than anticipated on the first two activities, so there was less time for the main activity. The students showed secure knowledge of the events in the scene, and were able to make creative choices about the staging. Most could articulate why they had made these decisions by writing on the sheet, but some had more difficulty with this. I realised that all students would have benefited from more time to develop their ideas. Only a few students had time to move on to a more detailed set or costume design, and many

needed more help to enable them to articulate and write down why they had made their staging decisions with reference to the play.

Class: **9**	Date: **Thurs P2**	Scheme of work: **SATS, Macbeth, Dramatic interpretation**	Lesson 4

Learning objectives	Learning outcomes
Kn/U: Understand that the words of a play can be interpreted in different ways. Know the variety of aspects to be considered when staging a scene. See the events of *Macbeth* scene 5.5 as open to different staging possibilities. **Skills**: Explain decisions about staging with reference to the play. Visualisation of written text. **Values**: Appreciate their *own* ability to affect meaning through staging decisions – existing directors do not hold a monopoly!	*All* will make decisions about staging the scene that are appropriate and can be justified with reference to the play. *All* will consolidate their knowledge of the events in scene 5.5. *Most* will show creativity and originality in their choices about how to stage the scene. *Some* will be able to articulate the impact of staging choices on the audience. *Some* will extend their ideas through costume or stage designs.

Key questions: How would you direct scene 5.5 of *Macbeth*? What should a director consider to make their interpretation convincing?	Resources: Starter sheet x15, A3 direct the scene sheets x27, video of *Macbeth on the Estate*. Coloured pens, blu-tac.

Activities	Teacher	Students
Starter: Pictures of different film versions of *Macbeth*. 5 min	Explain L.O. and sheet. Explain purpose is to recognise the possible variety of interpretations.	Write L.O. – Emphasise that students may be asked to write an exam response as if 'directing' a scene in the SATS. Match a picture on the starter sheet to direction descriptions. Which one sounds the most interesting to you?

Main activity
Watch *Macbeth on the Estate*, and fill in chart of what is different to the Polanski film version.
20 min
	Prompt at key moments to make notes.
	Check understanding and last boxes on sheet filled in.
		Follow film, and fill in chart to show how the film is different to the play.
		Focus on how Macbeth reacts after Lady Macbeth dies.
		After watching, consider: What do you think will happen to Malcolm, now that he is leader?
		   Daniel: watch and follow the sheet.
		   (Differentiated version)

Annotate a picture to show how you would direct the scene. (5.5)
20 min
	Remind of the scene.
	Explain task.
	Model an example.
	Emphasise need to explain *why* as well as *what*.
		Remember what happens in Act 5 Scene 5.
		Answer questions in the box first – about setting and the feeling of Macbeth.
		Then draw Macbeth as you want him to look.
		Annotate with details about position on stage, gestures, costumes etc.
		Explain *why* you chose to do each thing.
		   Extension: begin costume or stage designs on the back.
		   Daniel: continue with Macbeth summary picture book.

Plenary Look at different 'Macbeths' on show.	How can the effect of a particular line be changed by the way it is staged?	Students to write their names on sheet and blu-tac to the board. Students to nominate a poster to be read out. Share good practice.
Assessment Notes on picture/chart. Q&A, talking with groups and individuals.	Homework: none set in this lesson.	Key words Interpretation, direction, scene, stage, lighting, costumes, gestures, expression, voice position.

Figure 5.4 Macbeth lesson plan

I do think the lesson was successful and caught the imagination of the class. In future planning, I would extend this scheme of work to allow another lesson for students to complete their designs and do a related practice question. I would also plan more time to teach students how to explain and justify their decisions, and to allow them to practise this.

Commentary on the lesson planning

This is a very detailed lesson plan that uses a format developed to meet the needs of a secondary English trainee. The evaluation at the end of the plan begins to address the two key, evaluative questions discussed earlier. The trainee's mentor or tutor would want to gather the following additional information when making any judgement about achieving the QTS Standards.

- **When will the trainee take the assessment opportunities mentioned (at what point in the lesson) and who (which students) will be her focus?**
- **The evaluation indicates that the starter overran. Were students given enough time to develop their own responses before the plenary?**
- **The evaluation also indicates that some students had difficulty with the worksheet. What adjustments would allow for more successful completion of this section of the lesson?**
- **The lesson was described as the final lesson in a sequence. How might the knowledge, understanding and skills fostered here be kept visible and current during further study of the play, and how might they be consolidated in terms of the department's longer-term plan for Year 9?**

This information would be gathered through lesson observation, discussions with the trainee and students, and an examination of both the resources designed by the trainee and samples of work actually completed in the lesson. Judgements about the effectiveness of resources and planning should not be reached without examination of actual outcomes.

Overall, it is clear that this trainee was beginning to consider the myriad aspects of planning for learning and beginning to integrate these in her lesson plans without undue anxiety or the production of over-detailed scripts.

PRACTICAL TASK PRACTICAL TASK PRACTICAL TASK PRACTICAL TASK PRACTICAL TASK

Work with your mentor as she or he plans a lesson in the format you devised earlier for your own lesson planning. Ask your mentor questions about the decisions they are making. This will help them to complete an activity that they will find fairly difficult (having already internalised a planning structure) and will help you to understand the planning process.

Then, observe the lesson being taught and notice how your mentor *adapts the plan* during the transaction of the lesson. Make notes about the adaptations and changes and speculate on the reasons for them. After the lesson, discuss your notes with your mentor.

A SUMMARY OF **KEY POINTS**

> **Effective planning builds on high expectations of students informed by a knowledge of their past and current achievements.**
> **Effective planning clearly identifies what is to be learned and the teaching strategies by which this will be achieved.**
> **Effective planning identifies the means by which learning will be assessed.**
> **Trainees need a good knowledge of their specialist subject so that they can plan over the long, medium and short term, ensuring student progression.**
> **Trainees need to be able to demonstrate the ability to plan for the development of students' learning across the curriculum and promote active and independent learning.**

Moving on

As your experience of planning progresses, consider how you might foster a greater degree of independence in your students. Don't neglect the importance of pursuing the students' perspectives. What can the (apparently) least motivated student in the class tell you in response to the question: 'What would you like me to do to help you learn more effectively?'

FURTHER READING FURTHER READING FURTHER READING FURTHER READING

Kyriacou, C. (1998) *Essential Teaching Skills (2nd ed.)*. The second edition of this popular book covers a wide range of topics, including planning and managing lessons; classroom climate and discipline; streaming and setting; assessment, and continuing professional development.

Ofsted (2002) *Good Teaching, Effective Departments*. This report presents the findings from a HMI survey of subject teaching in secondary schools during 2000–2001. There are many practical implications for trainees and mentors arising out of this report, including comments on planning for learning and managing teaching time.

6
Assessment for learning
Jane Briggs and Viv Ellis

Professional Standards for QTS

Q1, Q11, Q19, Q21, Q22, Q23, Q24

To be awarded QTS you need to be able to use a range of strategies to assess students' learning. You will use your assessment knowledge to plan appropriately for the range of learning needs in your classes. You will be able to identify how you assess, both during the course of teaching and after teaching. Your subject knowledge will be crucial, as it will enable you to analyse the students' learning and make decisions about what is to be taught next, and how it should be taught. You will focus sharply on how you take the students' learning forward. You will be aware of the importance of the quality of interaction between you and your students and of the need for explicit oral and written feedback. Your record keeping should help you reflect on students' progress and attainment and should also enable you to report to parents, carers and other parties involved in the students' education. You will need to use your knowledge and understanding of comparative data to help you make informed decisions about how such data relates to your own teaching. In order to teach effectively, you will recognise how central assessment is to teaching and learning.

You may find it helpful to read through the appropriate section of the handbook that accompanies the standards for the Award of QTS for clarification and support.

What do we mean by assessment?

Assessment is the process by which teachers analyse students' learning. It is central to the activity of teaching. In 1988, a group of experts given the task of devising an assessment framework for what was to become the first National Curriculum, put it this way:

> The assessment process itself should not determine what is to be taught and learned. It should be the servant, not the master, of the curriculum. Yet it should not simply be a bolt-on addition at the end. Rather, it should be an integral part of the education process, continually providing both 'feedback' and 'feedforward'. It therefore needs to be incorporated systematically into teaching strategies and practices at all levels. Since the results of assessment can serve a number of different purposes, these purposes have to be kept in mind when the arrangements for assessment are designed.
>
> (TGAT 1988, p. 4)

You will see this quotation in a good deal of writing about assessment. To an extent, it has become a definitive statement. Often, however, its meaning and its importance are not immediately grasped by trainee teachers. Assessment has come to mean all sorts of things. Perhaps, most commonly, the term is used to describe the practices of awarding marks or grades to students' work and recording these. Assessment in its full sense, however, is so much more. The purpose of this chapter is to familiarise you with the various aspects of educational assessment and to demonstrate the relationship between assessment and the processes of teaching and learning.

The various aspects of assessment

What follows is a brief overview of the various aspects of assessment that have come to be included in this umbrella term. There are suggestions for further reading about key aspects of assessment at the end of this chapter.

Teacher assessment

In its general sense, this is the ongoing analysis of students' learning that is the day-to-day life-blood of good teaching. By observing, reading, questioning and interpreting students' comments and actions, teachers learn whether students are learning what they had intended them to learn. This process is constantly influencing an effective teacher's interventions in the classroom with students and this is how a teacher's lesson plans are adapted as those lessons are being taught.

Teacher assessment is a term that is also used to refer to the judgements teachers make about students' attainment in National Curriculum levels at the end of Key Stage 3 and is contrasted with and reported separately from the levels students are awarded through the externally marked national tests.

Student self-assessment

This term refers to students' involvement in the assessment process. It begins with students understanding the learning intentions or objectives for the particular lesson and the success criteria for the specific task or activity. It develops into students' awareness of their own strengths and weaknesses in a particular subject (and as a learner in general) and the ability to identify their own 'next steps' or targets. It may include a formal review of the students' work over a period of time – perhaps using a target-setting or progress review document – at which teacher and student identify progress, negotiate future targets and then report these to parents or carers.

Formal tests

There is no shortage of formal tests or examinations in the secondary phase. Some – like the optional national tests for Year 7 designed by QCA – are fairly new. Others – like GCSE – have been around for a comparatively long time. Here is a list of some of the formal tests you may encounter in schools:

- **standardised tests such as CATS (Cognitive Abilities Tests) or tests of reading and spelling ability;**
- **school (internal) examinations such as end-of-unit tests or annual end-of-year examinations;**
- **optional 'Progress' tests for Year 7 in Literacy and Numeracy that are designed and published by QCA but marked by schools;**
- **End of Key Stage 3 National Tests (often referred to as 'SATS') in the core National Curriculum Subjects of English, maths and science that are marked externally;**
- **GCSE and other 'intermediate' national examinations taken at the end of Key Stage 4 that lead to certification;**
- **the multiplicity of post-16 examinations.**

For further information on the examination system from 14–19, see Chapter 11.

Record-keeping

Teachers are required to keep records of students' progress and attainment in school subjects. At the very least, this will probably take the form of recording whether a significant activity or task has been undertaken and the level of attainment. Some schools may issue teachers with customised documents or portable electronic devices in which to keep assessment records and marks; teachers in other schools may rely on their own mark books or 'teacher's planner'. You will need to find out about the expectations and requirements of your school. Assessment records should also provide teachers with information that can be used in their own forward-planning or in planning that takes place in departments across year groups.

Target-setting

There are several different layers to target-setting, all of which are designed to make the action required to raise standards explicit, to designate who is responsible for the action and the date by which progress will be reviewed.

- **LEA targets** are determined by local education officers as a means of monitoring and raising standards of achievement across groups of schools and may be expressed as the number of students expected to achieve a particular level in an end of key stage test by a particular date.
- **School targets** are negotiated between the LEA and the school's management team and, once again, may be expressed in terms of the percentage of a year group achieving five or more GCSEs at grade C or above.
- **Curriculum targets** are negotiated between a school's management team and a head of department or curriculum manager and would take into account past performance, student ability and the school's own targets.
- **Student targets** are negotiated between teacher and child following a review of the child's work; the student should be able to monitor their own progress and identify areas for future development; this is an aspect of student self-assessment mentioned earlier.

Reporting

You can probably remember your own school reports and may be surprised at how much they have changed over the last few years. Annual reports to parents and carers (including, for example, the End of Key Stage 3 test and Teacher Assessment results) now also detail strengths and areas for improvement in addition to the standards achieved.

Use of comparative data

Data means information and includes national and local End of Key Stage test results (KS2 and KS3) and GCSE results so that comparisons can be made between LEAs and between schools. Within school, the data can be used to identify trends with a view to setting curriculum and teaching targets; this will be increasingly important as you develop your career in schools.

At the moment, however, your first priority as a trainee is to develop the ability to analyse students' learning and to use the information you gather to inform your planning and teaching. By regarding assessment as an integral part of teaching you will be able to provide the continuous 'feedback' and 'feedforward' that are essential for effective student learning.

Why and how do teachers assess?

To take learning forward

> There is a firm body of evidence that formative assessment is an essential feature
> of classroom work and that development of it can raise standards.
>
> (Black and Wiliam 1998, p. 19)

As an integral part of the process of teaching and learning, assessment that is used to take students' learning forward can be described as 'formative assessment'. Teachers assess students' learning on a daily basis in order to be able to respond appropriately to their learning needs. Formative assessment is concerned with analysing students' comments and their answers to questions. It is concerned with listening to what students have to say and the way in which they go about a task. It is concerned with really looking at tangible end-products to find out what students know, understand and can do. It involves responding to information gained about students' learning during the course of teaching and afterwards to inform future teaching. Formative assessment means analysing, reflecting and acting in ways which will take students' learning forward. Formative assessment is an integral part of the interaction between teacher and students, informs future planning and teaching and provides information which enables the quality of teaching and learning to be evaluated.

We can, therefore, consider formative assessment as being:

- **the analysis of students' learning and appropriate response during the course of teaching;**
- **the analysis of students' learning and appropriate response after the teaching episode.**

The analysis of students' learning and appropriate response during the course of teaching

During teaching, you will be assessing students' learning continuously. Shipman describes this as:

> the thinking-on-the-feet that is one of the main skills of teaching.
>
> (Shipman 1983, p. 12)

While teaching, you will be interpreting what the students say and do in order to make judgements about their achievements. The ability to analyse the students' learning is vital if you are to make appropriate teaching points which help the students develop their knowledge and/or competence. You will be using your subject knowledge to help you identify what to look for and where to take the student next. You will need to listen, observe and question in ways which will enable you to give appropriate feedback or further instruction. It is crucial that feedback to students is explicit and indicates to them what they have achieved and how they can progress further. It is also crucial that you are able to interact with students in ways which enable them to take risks: you will discover much from students' errors and misconceptions. The ability to respond immediately, providing appropriate feedback and further teaching, can be much more meaningful for that child than waiting to the next day when the moment has passed. This is sometimes referred to as monitoring and the Professional Standards for the Award of QTS refer to 'Monitoring and Assessment'.

Black and Wiliam (1998) highlight the importance of assessment being used to enhance teaching and therefore to raise standards. They argue that the real way to raise standards is to improve the quality of teaching by enhancing teachers' ability to use formative assessment in the classroom. The Assessment Reform Group explores these issues further in *Assessment for Learning: Beyond the Black Box* (1999), including discussions about the involvement of students within the assessment process and the impact this can have on their motivation and self-esteem. They also stress the importance of teachers asking the right questions in order to analyse effectively. The work of the Assessment Reform Group (King's College) underpins approaches to assessment for learning within the Secondary National Strategy. Details can be found on the standards site **www.standards.dfes.gov.uk**

IN THE CLASSROOM

In a Year 7 maths lesson, the teacher was revising area and perimeter. The students were asked to find the measurement in centimetres of one side of a rectangle. They were shown a diagram of the rectangle on which the area had been written in (10cm squared) and the height (2cm). The students were asked to write their answers on their individual whiteboards and hold them up for the teacher to see. One child had written '3cm'. The teacher asked: 'Explain to me how you got that answer. How did you work it out?' The child explained: 'I added 2cm and 2cm to get 4cm. Then I took 4cm away from 10cm which left 6cm. Then I divided 6cm by 2 which gave me 3.' From this the teacher clearly realised that the child was confusing perimeter and area.

She then explained to the child what she thought he had done – that he had thought the perimeter was 10cm and used that information to work out the length of the rectangle. She repeatedly asked questions such as : 'Is that what you were thinking?' and 'Is that right?'. She then explained that 10cm squared was the area, drawing the cm squares onto the diagram to illustrate her teaching point. She demonstrated how to work out the length of the rectangle by counting the cm squares. Next, she asked the child: 'Can you explain to me the difference between perimeter and area?' He was able to explain that one was 'the total distance around the outside edge of the shape' and the other was 'the surface of the shape', pointing at the diagram appropriately as he spoke.

The teacher then demonstrated how to work out the area of the shape by multiplying the length by the height, writing on the board : '5cm x 2cm = 10cm^2'. She then reminded the student of the inverse operation : 10 divided by 2 = 5 and explained how to use the information about the area of an rectangle to find out details of the length of the sides. She carried out two more similar examples with the whole class, checking that everyone, and particularly that one boy, had the correct answer.

This example demonstrates how teachers need to ask the right questions in order to analyse students' misconceptions and errors. By using the whiteboard the teacher could see the child's error and respond immediately to rectify the misunderstanding rather than the child completing several examples incorrectly during the lesson and not learning of the mistake until the work had been marked and returned at a later stage. The teacher was able to make appropriate teaching points based on her analysis of the student's response to the task. In this, her questioning was vital.

The analysis of students' learning and appropriate response after the teaching episode

In order to evaluate your teaching and to make decisions about what to teach next and how, you will need to reflect upon the students' learning and make judgements about their attainment. Analysis after teaching will include looking at samples of the students' work, reflecting on their comments and actions and may also involve discussions with colleagues. It may be that you need to amend your plans to clarify misconceptions or to raise the level of challenge. It may be that you need to develop your own subject knowledge further in order to enhance the quality of experience offered to the students. You will need to think about the feedback which you will give to the students and how this can motivate them to further their own achievements. Assessment knowledge will, therefore, be used to inform future teaching and if used effectively should *enhance* future learning.

Formative assessment, then, can be defined as the process by which teachers make judgements about students' attainment and use this information to inform teaching and learning and planning in order to take students' learning forward. Involving students is a key element of formative assessment. Explicit feedback enables students to recognise what is required of them and how they can progress. They need to have ownership of their own learning and need to be able to identify their successes and areas for development. Students need to engage in meaningful dialogue with their teachers to reflect upon their learning and to work together effectively.

IN THE CLASSROOM

During a Year 7 unit of work on poetry, an English trainee had been working on the production of individual poetry anthologies with the class. He used the marking of these anthologies to inform his teaching in the remainder of the unit and to give positive and constructive feedback to the students that could inform the extended piece of writing they would prepare towards the end of the unit. His marking appears below:

Jane, your work was perfectly presented. I like the way you chose appropriate colours for each poem, eg, seaweed green near the lines about the stomach!

In your comments on the poems, your ideas are first-rate. I particularly liked your comparison of the sea to a 'plaything' for a child and where you examined how this brought to mind ideas of 'harmlessness' – why not think a little more about this idea by considering the question mark that comes after it? What effect does the poet achieve by placing the question mark here?

Although I thought you'd completed the difficult part of this task well, I don't think you were as successful with the easier part. When you are expressing your opinions about poetry, a good way of justifying these to a reader is by using quotations from the poem (as we discussed). So, although you say the writer compares the sea to beautiful things, you don't say that the phrase 'it runs in beads on their jackets' made you think this. We will work on this in readiness for the final piece of writing in the unit.

The trainee's marking is specific and focused on the student's work. It identifies positive achievements and demonstrates to the student that he has read and engaged with her work. The trainee has also identified an important skill that the student will need to develop and how this relates to what he plans to teach next.

In his marking of the completed individual poetry anthology, the trainee is beginning to engage in a dialogue with his students. This dialogue was developed during part of a lesson when the trainee worked with groups of students to review their marked work while the remainder of the class worked on an independent activity. Over a period of three lessons, the trainee had seen all the students about their work and used the marking as the basis for a dialogue about improvement.

From a lesson or lessons you have taught, identify examples of:

a. your analysis of students' learning and your appropriate response during teaching; consider your use of questioning, explaining, demonstration, etc.;

b. your analysis of students' learning and appropriate response after teaching; consider how assessment influenced your future teaching and was reflected in your plans.

In both cases, how did your assessment enhance your teaching and what impact did it have on the students' learning?

To make judgements about standards

Summative assessment is more commonly associated with testing or making judgements about students' overall achievement at the end of a period of time. It requires students to demonstrate their knowledge, skill or understanding as a means of what Harlen, Gipps, Broadfoot and Nuttall (1994) describe as 'summing up and checking up'. They describe the former as:

> a picture of current achievements derived from information gathered over a period of time in order to set future targets.
>
> (Harlen, et al. 1994, p. 223)

This picture of student achievement can be used to inform students of progress and to set future targets. It can also be used by teachers to reflect upon the quality of teaching and to inform future planning. Since the introduction of the National Curriculum and its assessment, teachers have increasingly been required to make judgements about standards of attainment within a criterion-referenced system. Barrs (1990) highlights the impact this can have when teachers' assessment practice becomes that of measuring attainment of previously identified criteria rather than considered analysis of students' learning.

With the current emphasis on national test results forming a key part of political agendas, the judgement of standards is more commonly linked to the evaluation of teaching performance. National test results are used as an indicator of school effectiveness and teacher performance. LEA and school targets influence the expectation of student attainment.

Information about standards of attainment can be considered from two key perspectives:

- **measuring progress and attainment;**
- **evaluating the effectiveness of schools.**

Measuring progress and attainment

Your judgements about students' attainment over a period of time will enable you to consider whether progress has been made and to identify future learning targets. You will need to look closely at students' work to identify what improvements there have been: this will require you to draw on your subject knowledge. You will also need to develop your ability to identify the National Curriculum levels at which the students are operating. Your record-keeping should enable you to consider what progress students have made and should help you identify ways forward for individuals. It is important that your record-keeping system is manageable and that you can use it to further your understanding of students' progress and attainment.

REFLECTIVE TASK
REFLECTIVE TASK

Examine examples of teachers' record-keeping in your department. Consider the following.

- **How 'learning-specific' are they? What do they tell you about the students' knowledge, skills and/or understanding?**
- **How would these records enable you to take the students' learning forward? What information do they contain that could inform future teaching and planning?**
- **How would these records support reporting to parents/carers (in writing and orally)?**

The use of comparative data can help you identify trends and patterns in student attainment but you will need to consider the data carefully as it can be limited. Teachers are now expected to be aware of students' attainment in national tests and to use comparative data across key stages to monitor progress. Clearly, only that which has been tested can be considered and teachers need to be aware of the limitations of testing and the reliability and validity of the data provided.

Evaluating the effectiveness of schools

Teachers are accountable to their students, their parents and carers, the school, the LEA and the wider community. Scrutiny of the standards of student attainment and their performance in national tests and examinations are key features of Ofsted inspections. This leads into an evaluation of the effectiveness of the school. Making simplistic comparisons between the examination results of different schools serving very different communities and with very different resources does not allow us to make valid judgements about the effectiveness of the teaching in those schools. For example, comparing the GCSE results of a selective grammar school in an affluent suburb with the results of a comprehensive school in a city where many students enter late in Key Stage 3 without fluency in English will not tell us much about the work that goes on in classrooms. To try to quantify the 'difference' made by teachers in schools, the notion of 'value-added' was developed whereby the effectiveness of teaching in a school is judged partly by the progress made by its students from a baseline assessment on entry to the school. Increasingly, school examination result league tables – and Ofsted and LEA reviews – are building in elements of 'value-added' assessment.

So what do trainee teachers need?

The Standards for the Award of QTS are a set of outcome statements that you must demonstrate. It is important to note that the Standards for Monitoring and Assessment come within Section 3 of the Standards that relates to Teaching: assessment takes its place between Planning and Teaching. The Assessment Standards make repeated connections with the ability to understand how students learn and how to plan lessons. It is in this spirit, therefore, that we offer the following list of skills and attributes that you will develop as an effective, beginning teacher:

- **the ability to interpret students' learning using a variety of strategies appropriate to your subject;**
- **a confident knowledge of your specialist subject in which you take delight and pleasure so that**

you can re-formulate lesson ideas, answer questions and represent concepts in a way that is appropriate to the needs of the learners in your classroom;

- the ability to make assessment a continuous and integral part of your teaching so that the information gathered has an immediate effect upon your interventions in students' learning as well as informing future planning;
- the ability to ask the 'right' questions that check understanding rather than simple recall and probe misconceptions;
- the ability to implement a record-keeping system that is manageable and meaningful to yourself, other members of your department and school and that is open to parents and carers;
- an awareness of the implications of formal, national tests for curriculum planning and your own professional development;
- an awareness of the use of comparative data in setting targets and understanding how your students' performance compares with those in other classes and other schools.

A SUMMARY OF **KEY POINTS**

> Assessment is an integral part of teaching and learning.

> It is a process by which we make judgements about students' learning.

> Effective formative assessment (including student self-assessment) is a key part of raising standards of attainment.

> Summative assessment is used to measure students' progress and attainment, but also school effectiveness.

> Trainee teachers need to be able to use their analysis of students' learning in a dialogue with parents, carers and others involved in the education of students.

Moving on

The Assessment for Reform Group define assessment for learning as:

> The process of seeking and interpreting evidence for use by learners and their teachers to decide where the learners are in their learning, where they need to go next and how best to get there.

> (Assessment Reform Group 2002)

Visit the DfES Standards website and search 'assessment for learning'. Read the digest 'How do pupils respond to assessment for learning?' Review the 'What are the implications?' section and consider how you might adopt some of the strategies/approaches described to enhance your own assessment practices.

FURTHER READING FURTHER READING **FURTHER READING** FURTHER READING

Black, P. and Wiliam, D. (1998) *Inside the Black Box: Raising Standards Through Classroom Assessment*. London. King's College. This short pamphlet offers a review of research into the ways in which formative assessment can have an impact on the quality of teaching and learning in classrooms. The authors put forward an argument for the improvement of formative assessment in order to raise standards.

Gipps, C. and Stobart, G. (1997) *Assessment: A Teacher's Guide to the Issues*. London. Hodder and Stoughton. This well-respected guide is available in most education libraries and is written in a lively and accessible way. It covers a wide range of assessment issues, including fairness and validity in assessments, baseline and value-added measures, and the National Curriculum.

For further information on assessment for learning, visit **www.learning matters.co.uk/ education/learnteach/chapt6.html**

7
Managing behaviour for learning
Alan J. Child with Lynne Parsons

Professional Standards for QTS

Q1, Q2, Q3, Q4, Q5, Q6, Q19, Q21

To be awarded QTS you must have high expectations of your students in terms of their work and behaviour. You must model high standards of respect and demonstrate positive values related to learning. You should know a range of strategies for managing student behaviour for learning in a safe and secure environment. You should recognise that some students' behaviour is influenced by complex factors outside the school and seek to manage these so that other students' learning is not adversely affected. You should be able to establish clear frameworks and manage students' behaviour constructively.

You may find it helpful to read through the appropriate section of the handbook that accompanies the Standards for the Award of QTS for clarification and support.

Introduction

This chapter title is an important emphasis in its own right because it is a natural instinct for a trainee teacher to seek to manage students' behaviour and then to focus on their learning. The key message is that the appropriate use of the knowledge and skills discussed in Chapters 4, 5 and 6 will enable the teacher to create a classroom climate in which the students' right to learn is matched by the teacher's right to teach.

Hardly a day passes without some horror story appearing in the press about the unacceptable behaviour of students in secondary schools. These headlines do not, of course, capture the reality in the vast majority of schools where students engage in learning and a culture of mutual respect exists. David Bell, former Her Majesty's Chief Inspector of Schools, said recently:

> Behaviour was found to be at least satisfactory in the majority of schools. The proportion where behaviour was good or better was greater than in the schools inspected in 2003/04, and the proportion where it was unsatisfactory was a little lower. However, generally across Key Stages 3 and 4, small numbers of pupils fail to respond appropriately when admonished and low level disruption interrupts teaching and learning. Even a small number of pupils of this kind have a disproportionate detrimental effect on learning; this can become a major problem.
> (HMCI Annual Report 2004/05)

In surveys conducted by the Training and Development Agency for Schools (TDA) amongst newly qualified teachers (NQTs), 50 per cent of respondents maintain that the training they received in behaviour management was inadequate to meet their needs in the first year of teaching. Some 45 per cent of teachers who decide to leave the profession cite student indiscipline and lack of respect for the teacher as major reasons for their decision to pursue an alternative career. So, quite clearly, if you have early concerns about how you will manage students' behaviour for learning, you are certainly not alone in experiencing some genuine uncertainty and perhaps a little trepidation at the prospect of working with a lively group of Year 11 students on a Friday afternoon.

All the analysis and research into effective teaching emphasises that unacceptable behaviour is likely to be minimised when the teacher:

- **aims to personalise the learning for each student and identifies the most appropriate learning style;**
- **supports and challenges students as well as planning activities and content which are interesting;**
- **monitors and recognises progress based on well developed assessment strategies.**

In addition to these pedagogical principles, effective teachers employ a range of techniques to encourage students who are disengaging from the learning to re-engage and be 'on task'; the very best classroom practitioners anticipate students' 'off task' behaviour and take pre-emptive action. If you have observed an experienced and effective teacher at work with a demanding class you might have had a mixed reaction: sheer admiration as you watched this paragon manage the learning of 30 Year 9 students with good humour, effortless transitions from activity to activity and real pace and momentum; some despair as you reflect that such multi-skilled, multi-tasked teaching is beyond you – an impossible dream.

In 2005 the report of the Practitioners' Group on School Behaviour and Discipline was published (Steer Report). The group focused on identifying practical solutions to a range of behavioural issues that most schools are dealing with on a day to day basis. The report is based on six core beliefs.

1. The quality of learning, teaching and behaviour in schools are inseparable issues and the responsibility of all staff.
2. Poor behaviour cannot be tolerated as it is the denial of the right of pupils to learn and teachers to teach. To enable learning to take place preventative action is most effective, but where this fails, schools must have clear, firm and intelligent strategies in place to help pupils manage their behaviour.
3. There is no single solution to the problem of poor behaviour, but all schools have the potential to raise standards if they are consistent in implementing good practice in learning, teaching and behaviour management.
4. Respect has to be given in order to be received. Parents and carers, pupils and teachers all need to operate in a culture of mutual respect.
5. The support of parents is essential for the maintenance of good behaviour. Parents and schools each need to have a clear understanding of their rights and responsibilities; and
6. School leaders have a critical role in establishing high standards of learning, teaching and behaviour.

(DfES 2005)

As you continue to read this chapter it is important that you reflect on how the strategies and techniques that are described are aligned to the core beliefs of the Steer Report.

REFLECTIVE TASK

In a school where you are working keep a diary to see if any of these core beliefs inform everyday practice. Where they are well established, how does this impact on student behaviour? What happens when positive beliefs do not inform practice sufficiently well? Share your reflections with your school mentor or your college tutor. If you know of other trainees who are undertaking a similar task, share your reflections with one another. Remember to respect the school in which you are working. Try not to present your findings as a negative list. Emphasis the positive and offer ideas to improve the situation. This may well include good ideas picked up from trainee colleagues.

Every teacher, at some point in their career, experiences challenging student behaviours. Often, factors are at play which relate to the student's home circumstances or with social groupings and influences outside the school environment. Although teachers so readily accept responsibility and endure intense reflection wondering how this awful moment could have been avoided, you will also no doubt meet some cynical staffroom commentary which alludes to the past ('things were better then'), falling standards ('we used to have a discipline policy here'), and the decline in family and society values ('what do you expect when programmes like *Footballers' Wives* are on TV?'). You might also be tempted by the quick fix ostensibly offered by some of the burgeoning catalogue of classroom management textbooks. The idea of tips for teachers needs to be dispelled as, at best, they are a short term strategy. You can gain from reading around the subject of behaviour management but success in the classroom is not predicated simply on the deployment of techniques.

Praise

There is ample evidence to support the effectiveness of teacher praise in creating a positive classroom environment and in motivating students into behaviour for learning. This is not to say that the teacher who uses praise in a cosmetic, artificial way will be successful. Praise used in the appropriate way is indeed a powerful force; praise used insincerely will undermine relationships and learning.

There are three important aspects to consider:

Personal: praise should be given to the individual or group so that it resonates personally. The most obvious thing to do is to name the students and to ensure that they receive the praise in a direct way with, for example, positive non-verbal signals like a smile.

Specific: praise should be firmly grounded in a particular achievement or attainment which is clearly referred to. For example, if a student has finished a task which has previously caused difficulty, the teacher's compliment should specify that the praise is for finishing the task and for the effort to overcome the particular problem.

Genuine: praise must always be given to students who have really achieved something. The careless, repetitive use of praise will undermine the value of other praise you want to give. Imagine how you have felt when in the presence of someone who overuses the words 'thank you': in a short time they no longer ring true and can, indeed, become irritating!

Praise which is offered in close proximity to the achievement or attainment is usually the most well received and the most powerful in motivating students.

You might need to consider some less public ways to praise senior students. Year 10 and 11 students may not welcome the embarrassment of public acclaim in front of their classmates.

Rules and routines

It is increasingly common in a school to find that not only has it a behaviour management policy but also some clearly specified classroom rules prominently displayed on noticeboards. Additionally you may come across other documentation (probably in the staff handbook) which advises on anti-bullying, anti-racism, attendance, school uniform regulations and even a code of conduct or key principles. This material can be quite daunting and far from easy to absorb. It is important, however, to do some research and reading about the school's key policies and practice as you are working in a context and need to be in tune with its key concepts and the practicalities. For example, a school might have a sophisticated system to manage challenging student behaviours like an on-call scheme involving the support of senior staff; or it might have access to a facility like a Learning Support Unit (LSU); or it might employ a school counsellor.

It can be a very reassuring and supportive environment if you undertake some of your training in a school which has very clearly expressed values, rules and routines. It can be very helpful if you work in a school where the staff have good relationships with students and can offer you insights into the effective management of learning for behaviour. You might, however, feel that the environment is so supportive that you are not actually developing your own skills but simply adopting the good practice of others. At the other end of the spectrum where you are left largely to your own devices, the challenge may be far too great and you may feel daunted and confused as you try to establish your classroom rules and routines.

Students do need the freedom to work within constraints. Classroom rules are an effective way to establish and develop the climate for learning. The general wisdom pertaining to classroom rules is that they should be:

- **developed and owned by the students and the teacher;**
- **few in number;**
- **expressed in positive language;**
- **about improving learning;**
- **reinforced and reviewed regularly.**

A classroom behaviour plan

You might find it useful to think about an overall approach for your classroom under several headings:

1. Movement.
2. Learning.
3. Communication.
4. Mutual respect.
5. Safety.
6. Problem-solving.

If you do this you will think about how students enter and leave your classroom, how they will work in groups, noise levels, common courtesies, using equipment and how to deal with challenges.

> **PRACTICAL TASK** PRACTICAL TASK **PRACTICAL TASK** PRACTICAL TASK **PRACTICAL TASK**
>
> Working with another trainee, develop five 'golden rules' for the classroom. Remember to phrase them positively and to produce rules which encourage behaviour for learning. Why not share these with other members of your group?
>
> You might like to compare your proposals with those you have seen published in your placement schools.

Consequences

In most schools, unacceptable student behaviour incurs a consequence. Commonly, schools operate reward strategies and a hierarchical set of sanctions. As a trainee it can be rather disconcerting to find yourself working in a school without a full appreciation of the systems. If you act idiosyncratically, the students will undoubtedly react, or possibly over-react, to your sanctions. Therefore, it is essential to know and follow the school's protocols. This can be a source of some tension if you find yourself working within a system that does not attune with your own values and beliefs. As you become more skilled in managing behaviour for learning you might feel that the school's approach is undermining your teaching style, or you might feel that the system offers insufficient support, or that you are not given sufficient independence by your mentor. Any one of these reactions is understandable but the school is a community in which you are a privileged guest and you should seek to integrate as fully as possible with its *modus operandi*. However, your own professional development can certainly be enhanced by careful reflection on the contexts in which you are working and perhaps through discussion with other trainees and your college tutor. Good teachers give students choices and make clear to students the consequences of the choices they make. In an ideal world you would hope that the use of sanctions would be a small part of your work but there will be several occasions when you feel that a student is deserving of some consequence. The purpose of your intervention is to manage behaviour for learning so you need to think very carefully about the actions you take.

PRACTICAL TASK PRACTICAL TASK PRACTICAL TASK PRACTICAL TASK PRACTICAL TASK

In the table below there is a list of sanctions which are typically deployed in schools. For each one, identify the student behaviour that could invoke it and then consider the possible advantages and disadvantages of the teacher's action. Some commentary has been added to encourage your thinking.

Sanction	Student behaviour	Possible advantage/disadvantage
'See me at the end of the lesson.'		
Work to be repeated to a higher standard		
Verbal warning/ reprimand		
Written report to Head of Year		
Contact with parent/ carer		
Detention		Detentions at break, lunchtimes and after school are commonly used in schools. They are highly inconvenient to staff and often require considerable administration. What is the intended outcome?
Exclusion from the classroom		This should be a very rare event and in many schools is discouraged and only acceptable in extreme situations to avoid confrontation in front of the whole class.
Withdrawal of privileges		
Stern/disapproving look		Effective teachers are skilled at using non-verbal techniques. Sometimes the eyes can work wonders and get a student back on task without a word being spoken.
Moving student to another desk		
Issuing a bad conduct mark		

Figure 7.1: List of sanctions

Teacher techniques

As a trainee teacher you are expected to know some of the techniques for managing behaviour for learning. You will learn these in a variety of ways: from your own reading, in workshops and by the careful observation of effective teachers. There are some techniques which have been identified by several researchers into effective teaching. They have been extensively written about, feature in many INSET sessions and form part of the ever-expanding literature on behaviour management. You may try some of these and find no or little success; others may work beautifully. The techniques themselves work best when other key aspects of pedagogy are present. But the classroom is above all else an environment where interpersonal relationships have pride of place. Students recognise when a teacher is knowledgeable, well prepared, the lesson has a clear learning focus and shared objectives and the teacher cares: they respond positively to a climate of learning. The techniques discussed in the next few paragraphs are certainly field-tested and effective but only if the foundations of good teaching are well established.

- **Tactical ignoring:** sometimes as a teacher you have to ignore some students' behaviour because if you respond then the flow of the lesson will be interrupted and your intervention will be more disruptive than the student's behaviour. This is never an easy judgement to make. Nor does it mean that you cannot speak to the offending student at a later stage.
- **Thank you:** acknowledging those who are on task can often encourage those who are still thinking about getting down to work to follow suit.
- **Redirecting:** rather than pointing out to students what they are not doing, you can simply reassert what 'we' are doing. 'Ismael and Alice, we are looking at the diagram on page 3, OK?'
- **Room to change:** it is often useful to draw a student's attention to what you would like them to do, then move away saying you'll check in a minute or two to see if they are on task. This gives the student a chance and room to do it without a stand-off or confrontation developing.
- **Location:** if you always teach from the front of the room you are wasting opportunities. Move around the room. Often, your proximity to a student or a group can encourage on-task behaviour and you don't need to say a word. (In taking different perspectives you also scan the room and may see things which were not visible in teaching from the front.)
- **Non-verbal signals:** effective teachers use a wide range of strategies which you may not be aware of as you observe them working with a group of students. You may be amazed at how a teacher uses eye contact to attract a student's attention or with a gentle smile indicates approval. Students are receptive to body language so you need to adopt a positive but not overbearing posture which exudes confidence. The appropriate use of a 'thumbs up' can send a strong message of approval as can a subtle nod; or the symbolic shaking of the head to indicate unacceptability. Sometimes to gain the attention of a whole class teachers can use signals to gain listening order: for example, standing at the front of the classroom with an outstretched arm pointing to the whiteboard can indicate your readiness to move to another activity. Some teachers count down from five to one (the five is loudly issued but not shouted and the following numbers are spoken with decreasing volume) and teach the class that at number one there is a listening silence.

Personal feelings

It is a cliché to observe that people have different reactions to different experiences. It can be quite challenging as a teacher when things do not go according to plan or when a student speaks to, or behaves towards, you in a manner which you find totally unacceptable. For some it could mean a really tearful moment; for others it could mean a groundswell of anger and frustration. And on a daily basis, of course, we have days when we feel a bit under the weather or the journey to work has been a stressful one with heavy traffic and delays. Teachers need to have a good sense of themselves and have to work hard at managing their emotional state so that it does not interfere with the business of teaching and learning. This is not to suggest that teachers are automata without feelings, delivering some sterile, bland curriculum in a highly prescriptive way, but you do need to look hard at yourself and use your 'emotional intelligence'.

Confrontation/challenging behaviours

These words evoke some of the horror images referred to in the introduction but you probably do want some advice on this area. One thing to bear in mind is the very language we use when we talk about student behaviour. It is important to agree definitions. For example, some writers talk about unacceptable behaviour, some use the phrase challenging behaviour and some refer to confrontational behaviour. There is, of course, a sliding scale from a student's refusal to follow a simple instruction to threatening the teacher's physical well-being (a very rare event indeed!).

As teachers we cannot control all the frustrations and pent-up emotions of our students, but we can try to equip them with the skills to express their anger effectively. If you encounter an angry student try these ideas:

- **Don't match the student's anger with your own. This leads to escalation. The student needs you to be calm as a palliative to their own anger.**
- **Be consistent in your response: express that you are not happy at being shouted out, respond to the behaviour and be specific.**
- **Offer the student a chance to talk about how they are feeling. You might suggest a cooling off period before they tell you more. Offer to be a listener; do not be judgemental.**
- **Point out the positives in their behaviour which you have seen previously: use this as a way to give genuine praise and work towards a resolution.**
- **Give space and room: do not invade the personal space of the challenging student.**
- **Speak calmly, clearly and ask questions which show a genuine wish to understand the problem.**
- **Deal with the behaviour and not the student.**
- **Remember that the challenge is probably not directed at you personally.**
- **Assistance should be available from other staff in the school. (Note: as a trainee you are under the supervision of a designated mentor who is legally responsible for your welfare. Technically, you are never responsible for the students in your classroom; that responsibility lies with the school that is hosting your training.)**

Being able to recognise and understand your reaction to unacceptable behaviour enables you to be more objective, respond appropriately and use one or more of the techniques already discussed to re-direct students and avoid confrontation. If this is an area where you feel you need further ideas, you will find some useful material in Paul Blum's *The Teacher's Guide to Anger Management* and in Michelle MacGrath's *The Art of Teaching Peacefully*.

It is important in these challenging moments to be able to control your own emotions so that they do not impede your ability to act professionally. This is easier said than done of course because the 'moment' is highly charged. Different actions trigger different responses in people, as you well know, but you should begin to think through your own sensitivities so that you can manage them accordingly. Are you likely to overreact to a student who fails to extend the common courtesy of using 'Sir' or 'Miss'? Would a student ostentatiously chewing in your lesson invoke a major incident? Would you be very offended if you overheard a student using offensive language to their neighbour? How would you react if a student commented on your hairstyle or your clothing? Would you 'lecture' a student you found smoking because you are a non-smoker yourself? Would you be affronted if a student asked about your family or made a so-called witty comment about your ancient car?

IN THE CLASSROOM

A trainee teacher is having considerable difficulty with a Year 10 Set 1 English group who are studying *Othello* for GCSE. The students are enjoying the play, and were particularly attentive while watching extracts from a film version starring Lawrence Fishburne. As soon as the trainee teacher tries to lead a whole-class discussion, the students disregard the classroom conventions (and school policy) of orderly response. Students shout out answers and comments without waiting for permission. The trainee is unsure how to recover the situation without destroying the students' enthusiasm and obvious engagement with the text. There is nothing malicious in the students' behaviour but the trainee feels that there is a distinct lack of order: the students are manipulative but never rude.

Understandably, the trainee decides that the next lesson will be more orderly and decides that the discussion about the film will continue but it will be done differently. In fact, the trainee decides that the classroom rule of students seeking permission to speak by raising their hands will be strictly followed. The trainee rightly plans to limit the discussion (it will only last for 20 minutes) and decides that the students will be told that a written task will follow the discussion.

Unfortunately, and rather predictably, the next lesson does not go as anticipated because the students simply refuse to accept the classroom rule about raising their hands and the trainee becomes increasingly wearied and irritated. The discussion becomes fragmented and disjointed because the trainee spends time and verbal energy trying to establish the 'new order'. Eventually, the trainee moves to the written task to restore acceptable levels of behaviour and tells students that they can expect more writing in future lessons unless their attitude and behaviour improve. The students do engage in the written task and the quality is good.

REFLECTIVE TASK

Referring to the classroom story, try the 'miracle question' technique. Imagine a fairy godmother is able to grant one wish to the trainee who is working with this Year 10 group! What would the trainee ask for?

To frame the question for the fairy godmother, the trainee needs to think carefully about the desired outcomes. There are some suggestions below.

Desired outcomes:

- **The students will answer questions and join in the discussion in an orderly way which gives everyone a chance to make a contribution.**
- **The students will listen carefully and politely to the contributions from others and learn from them.**
- **The students will respect the teacher's role in structuring the discussion and follow the established protocols.**

- **The discussion will enable the students to learn through reflection and debate.**
- **The students will be able to accept different views and opinions.**
- **The discussion will last long enough for key learning objectives to be achieved.**

The idea of the miracle question technique is to enable a problem to be changed into an achievable goal. Often, because of the intensity of the classroom with so many things happening simultaneously and a steady stream of interactions, the trainee may not be able to analyse the problem beyond the immediacy, for example, of irritation and disappointment with the non-co-operative students. The miracle question is a chance for fresh thinking and an opportunity to see a positive future. From this vision, it is possible to derive the possibilities and also to really see what the problem is.

So, what wish should this trainee put to the fairy godmother?

Scaling

Another way to address classroom management issues which are causing you concern is to use a *scaling* technique. The trainee with the Year 10 English group might feel that chaos was the key feature of the lesson and that their authority has been undermined. Worse still they might have genuine dread at the thought of the next lesson: how can I restore my professional credibility? The truth is often hard to see when you are overwhelmed by emotions. It can be really helpful to analyse the situation, perhaps with the help of a mentor. Scaling is a simple strategy. Think of a scale of 1 to 10 with 1 representing the lowest point and with 10 representing the highest point. You then attach a brief description to each point on the scale, decide where you are on that scale and consider steps to move you gradually up the scale: you are not trying to make a giant leap but small manageable steps towards a better situation. This is a really positive way to address concerns and helps you to see the wood for the trees!

PRACTICAL TASK PRACTICAL TASK PRACTICAL TASK PRACTICAL TASK PRACTICAL TASK

Refer again to the classroom story about teaching *Othello*.

There are three stages to this task:

(a) Look at the following scale which has been part completed. Can you attach description to points 7, 8 and 9?

(b) Now consider where on the scale you would place this Year 10 English class.

(c) Then, working with a mentor or another trainee, suggest one or two strategies which could be attempted to move the class one point up the scale in the conduct of whole class discussion.

Point 10 is of course the ideal, but no teacher can move a class from point 1 to point 10 in some great miraculous leap!

1. The students shout out, don't listen and much of the talk is irrelevant and designed to upset the teacher and prevent learning.

2. The teacher tries to follow the classroom rules but the students ignore them.

3. The teacher keeps having to stop the discussion to remind students about the rules for discussion; occasionally they are followed.

4. The students know the rules but break them because they want to be talking; the teacher has to be very firm on the rules and is unhappy that students are not learning and using them.

5. The students engage well with the topic and make lively contributions but it is rather chaotic, and certain students are dominating the discussion.

6. The teacher is taking a back seat for parts of the discussion because students are talking to/with each other in a fairly sensible way.

... 7, 8, 9 – Describe these points on the scale.

10. The class discuss the film in a mature way following all the conventions of debate and verbal exchange; the teacher is able to take a back seat and only occasionally intervene as a facilitator to move the discussion forward.

Every Child Matters

The Children Act 2004 has, at its heart, five outcomes to ensure the health and well being of all children. The five outcomes are:

1. be healthy;
2. stay safe;
3. enjoy and achieve;
4. make a positive contribution;
5. achieve economic well-being.

Everyone in all settings (including the trainee) must consider how the activities of their classroom, their attention to good relationships and their development of a positive class-room climate contribute to securing these five outcomes.

Promoting positive behaviour for learning and creating a climate for purposeful learning touch, to a greater or lesser degree, on each of the five outcomes.

Consider the chart below which has been adapted from the grade descriptions for evaluating *Every Child Matters* (ECM) outcomes (Ofsted 2005).

Be healthy	Students are able to recognise what situations contribute to their personal stress levels and are beginning to develop an understanding about how to deal with this
Stay safe	Students feel safe from bullying, racism and other types of discrimination. They are able to demonstrate concern for the safety and well-being of others, both other students and staff
Enjoy and achieve	Students are well motivated and engage well with the learning process. They attend school regularly and are punctual for lessons. Students understand rule reminders and respond positively to requests and gentle reprimands
Make a positive contribution	Students understand the importance of good personal relationships. They understand that with rights come responsibilities and they are able to apply this to their work in the classroom
Achieve economic well-being	Students have enough self-confidence to be independent learners yet are still able to work co-operatively in a team. Students are able to cope with change and are actively engaged with the learning process. They are beginning to develop problem-solving skills

Figure 7.2: *Every Child Matters*

REFLECTIVE TASK

Read through this chapter again in relation to the chart above.

Consider which of the strategies and techniques that have been described will support you in securing one or more of the five outcomes. For example, praise that is personal, specific and genuine might contribute to being healthy, enjoying and achieving and making a positive contribution.

Think 'outside the box' in terms of your personal feelings and the way in which you model behaviour for students.

What other strategies and techniques might you need to develop and employ to ensure that you contribute to securing the five ECM outcomes?

This chapter has attempted to offer some guidance and support. There will be days when you feel that the your best plans for learning have fallen foul of things beyond your control, whether that be inclement weather or the distraction of a false fire alarm! Other days, your students will be responsive and engaged, you will see real progress and you will gain those rather intangible benefits ascribed to the 'buzz' of the successful classroom. As your competence and confidence grow you will become less conscious of managing behaviour for learning and the skilful blending of pedagogy and student and classroom management will be achieved almost without you knowing it. Good teachers, like good poets, borrow from one another: do not be afraid to try new ideas and new techniques acquired from other teachers or your own reading; do not be disappointed if what works one day is less effective on another. The successful teacher is innovative; the effective teacher is reflective and the very best make mistakes and learn from them.

A SUMMARY OF **KEY POINTS**

> **The management of behaviour is not a separate set of skills to be applied to students but an integral part of the teacher's role in enabling students to learn. That is why the chapter is entitled 'Managing behaviour for learning'.**

> **The climate of the classroom depends on key values and beliefs: paramount is that of mutual respect.**

> **Techniques and tips are part of the effective teacher's repertoire but in themselves will not deliver effective teaching and learning.**

> **Through reading, observation, discussion and practice your skills will develop.**

> **Students will occasionally exhibit really challenging behaviours and as a trainee you need to be confident not only to use your skills but also to call on the support of the school's staff and procedures.**

> **Everyone has a responsibility to contribute to securing the five outcomes of *Every Child Matters*.**

Moving on

The next step is to consider how you might measure the impact of your behavioural interventions, and the kind of qualitative and quantitative data you can collect. You might need to do this to demonstrate that the strategies you are using are having an impact not only on students' levels of confidence and their developing social, emotional and behavioural skills but also on their academic progress. This form of measurement is particularly important at the school level.

FURTHER READING FURTHER READING **FURTHER READING** FURTHER READING

Blum, P. (2001) *A Teacher's Guide to Anger Management*. London. RoutledgeFalmer. This book offers a range of tips, techniques and strategies and is written by a successful practitioner.

Cowley, S. (2001) *Getting the Buggers to Behave*. London. Continuum. This book is a bestseller and attracted considerable attention when it received a very positive endorsement from Tim Brighouse. It has spawned a series of books for teachers.

DfES (2005) *Learning Behaviour. The Report of the Practitioners' Group on School Behaviour and Discipline*.

MacGrath, M. (1998) *The Art of Teaching Peacefully.* London. David Fulton.

Marland, M. (2002) *The Craft of the Classroom*. 3rd ed. London. Heinemann Educational Books. This book is a very accessible and practical survival guide with ideas which are still applicable today.

Rogers, B. (1997) *You Know the Fair Rule*. London. Prentice Hall. This book contains lots of good advice and strategies for making management easier and also good fun.

Watkins, C. and Wagner, P. (2000) *Improving School Behaviour*. London. Paul Chapman. This book is based on detailed research and offers insights and ideas in a very readable style.

For further information on managing behaviour for learning, visit **www.learning matters.-co.uk/education/learnteach/chapt7.html**

PART 3
PROFESSIONAL KNOWLEDGE:
ACROSS THE CURRICULUM

8
Teaching literacy across the curriculum
Rob Batho

Professional Standards for QTS

Q13, Q14

To be awarded QTS to teach a subject at Key Stage 3, you must know and understand the cross-curricular expectations of the National Curriculum and be familiar with the guidance set out in the Secondary National Strategy. You must also be able to use the cross-curricular elements, such as literacy and numeracy, set out in the Secondary National Strategy, in your teaching, as appropriate to your specialist subject.

You may find it helpful to read through the appropriate section of the handbook that accompanies the Standards for the Award of QTS for clarification and support.

Introduction

Anyone who is reading this book is likely to have sophisticated literacy skills but may not know how they acquired them or be able to identify them in order to teach them to others. This lack of understanding is not unusual and is not confined to literacy. Think of riding a bike or swimming. Imagine how difficult it would be to explain how to do one of those activities, for which you have tacit understanding, to someone who hasn't a clue. Part of the difficulty is remembering how you acquired those skills in the first place. More than likely you would have had some tuition and, most importantly, support and advice as you practised, spluttered or wobbled your way to success. To attempt to achieve such success and learn those skills only through trial and error and immersion in experience, without tuition, guidance or support can often lead to failure and an unwillingness in the learner to try again. The same can be said for literacy; all of its skills can be taught and can lead to more effective and efficient learning. As a good reader yourself (and probably writer and speaker too), you may not realise how important it is for weaker readers to be taught and given support in developing their reading skills and strategies, and that the same applies to writing and speaking and listening.

The purpose of this chapter on literacy across the curriculum is to encourage you, as a beginning teacher, to be alert to the specific literacy demands and skills of your subject so that you are in a position to support students in your class to develop their own literacy skills and by so doing improve their ability to understand your subject and to communicate that understanding to others.

The chapter will consider briefly the nature of and the context and reasons for literacy across the curriculum in secondary schools before focusing on strategies, supported by evidence from research, which can assist teachers in improving the literacy skills of students in all subjects. It will also offer practical tasks to help improve your understanding of literacy within the school context, and finally, summarise the key points of the chapter and suggest further reading.

The context

In 1998 the National Literacy Strategy and the National Numeracy Strategy were introduced to improve standards of literacy and numeracy in primary schools. These initiatives were built on and developed into the Key Stage 3 National Strategy with the introduction of the English and mathematics strands in 2001 and science, foundation subjects, ICT and behaviour and attendance in subsequent years. In 2005 the Key Stage 3 National Strategy was renamed the Secondary National Strategy to reflect its worth across Key Stages 3 and 4. Literacy is one of the cross-curricular elements of the Secondary National Strategy.

The need to improve literacy in schools arose out of evidence indicating poor standards of literacy in England and Wales. For example, the DfEE report *A Fresh Start* (1999) reports that:

- **an estimated seven million adults in England cannot locate the page reference for plumbers in the *Yellow Pages*;**
- **of the 12 OEDC nations surveyed in 1997 for levels of adult literacy, only Poland and Ireland emerged with a lower level than Britain.**

Look at the Professional Standards for QTS at the beginning of this chapter. Those 'cross-curricular expectations' refer to numeracy and ICT as well as to literacy, and the expectations for literacy are discussed below. The guidance in the Key Stage Strategy which is referred to can be found in the *Framework for Teaching English* (DfEE 2001a) and some of it will be considered later in this chapter. But what is also being clearly stated in the two Standards quoted is that it isn't sufficient for you to simply know and understand the cross-curricular expectations but that you demonstrate through your teaching that you can teach aspects of literacy as befits the literacy demands of your specialist subject.

What is literacy?

Before going any further, it is important to define the boundaries of what is meant by *literacy* in the context of literacy across the curriculum. Until the latter part of the twentieth century, literacy was defined as simply reading and writing, but since the late 1980s it has been argued (Graff 1987, Meek 1991, Cairney 1995) that there is a plurality of literacies which includes such areas of knowledge as the visual arts and the media. While accepting that argument, in this chapter literacy is defined as reading, writing and speaking and listening to maintain parity with the National Curriculum (DfEE/QCA 2000) and the *Framework for the*

Teaching of English (DfEE 2001a). Moreover, David Wray (2001), when writing about literacy in the secondary curriculum, gives a definition of literacy which suits the purpose of this chapter:

> Literacy is the ability to read and use written information and to write appropriately for a range of purposes. It also involves the integration of speaking, listening and critical thinking with reading and writing and includes the knowledge which enables a speaker, reader or writer to recognise and use language appropriate to different social occasions
>
> (Wray 2001, p. 12).

Literacy is not being viewed as a mere set of basic, functional skills to meet societal demands such as filling in forms or reading newspaper headlines; it is rather seen as a means to enable individuals to apply their literacy skills, knowledge and strategies to a range of texts and situations and, as Eve Bearne (1999, p. 202) puts it, 'being able to read the small print as well as read between the lines'.

Literacy and subjects

The view that language and literacy are the responsibility of all subject teachers is one which is advocated in the expectations of the National Curriculum:

> Pupils should be taught in all subjects to express themselves correctly and appropriately and to read accurately and with understanding.
>
> Pupils should be taught the technical and specialist vocabulary of subjects and how to use and spell these words. They should also be taught to use the patterns of language vital to understanding and expression in different subjects. These include the construction of sentences, paragraphs and texts that are often used in a subject.
>
> (DfEE/QCA 2000, p. 40)

In the Rationale to the *Framework for Teaching English* (DfEE 2001a), literacy and language are also viewed as the responsibility of all subject areas:

> Language is the principal medium of learning in a school, and every teacher needs to cultivate it as a tool for learning. Teachers have a genuine stake in strong language skills because language enables thought.
>
> (DfEE 2001, p.15)

It will make more sense to students if they consider specific literacy matters within the context of the subject where it naturally occurs (e.g. a science report in science, an historical enquiry in history). Each subject, in the way it is structured and formulated, will make certain and specific literacy demands on students beyond some that may be common to most or all subjects (and which the English department may well attend to). As Christine Counsell (2001) explains:

> A subject...is a way of working with certain kinds of information in order to answer certain kinds of questions. A subject is not 'information'; it is knowledge. Any knowledge has a structure...The way a subject uses words, sentences and

texts will be dominated not just by its types of information but by the questions and issues that each subject confronts.

(Counsell 2001)

Sheeran and Barnes (1991), when discussing writing in subject areas, take much the same view:

Cognitive and communicative ground rules are the essential definers of any discipline ...Specialist subjects consist of both implicit and explicit rules and organising principles governing both academic cognition and the social presentation of knowledge in the form of writing.

(Sheeran and Barnes 1991, pp. 55 and 101)

The Qualifications and Curriculum Authority (QCA 2001) in their publication *Language at Work in Lessons: Literacy Across the Curriculum at Key Stage 3*, underline the importance of all subject teachers being in involved in language work because teachers who currently incorporate a focus for language in their subject believe that it will:

- **help pupils manage their learning in a subject more confidently and effectively;**
- **enable pupils to make good progress with the subject's increasing conceptual complexity and the specialist language involved;**
- **give pupils the tools to articulate, explain and justify their ideas and understanding;**
- **enhance pupils' achievements overall.**

(QCA 2001, p. 5)

Having established the need for literacy teaching in all subjects, what then of the approaches and strategies which you could adopt to assist students' literacy development?

Approaches and strategies for teaching literacy across the curriculum

Research suggests that there are many such strategies and there is not the space here to detail them all. Neither is it the intention to consider separately reading, writing and speaking and listening, mainly because a number of the strategies require all four aspects of literacy to combine in support of one another. For instance, speaking and listening are essential to the discussion of reading and the sharing and planning of writing; and writing a specific text type for the first time is best promoted through the initial exploration through reading of the conventions and patterns of such a text. However, what can be done is to approach and group the strategies in a way that should help teachers who are planning for literacy in their lessons. The approach to be adopted is an active one. It will also be expressed chronologically in terms of the cyclical sequence for teaching from the planning stage, through the lesson introduction, the main part of the lesson, the plenary and the ensuing evaluation and assessment which feed back into future planning (see Figure 8.1).

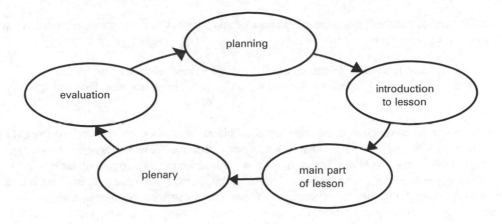

Figure 8.1: The teaching cycle

Wray (2001), when discussing literacy in relation to teaching and learning, makes the point that:

> It is useful for secondary teachers to recognise that many of the processes involved in supporting literacy are also involved in developing learning.
>
> (Wray 2001, p. 50)

Planning

In planning for literacy, you first of all need to identify and select which aspect of literacy needs developing, and in many subject department schemes or units of work that selection will already have been done, very often where the objectives for learning have been adapted or taken from the *Framework for the Teaching of English* (DfEE 2001a). Departments might also have adapted their schemes of work to include literacy using the QCA's schemes of work in combination with their publications *Language for Learning* (QCA 2000) and *Language at Work in Lessons* (QCA 2001) which demonstrate, through worked examples, how literacy objectives (taken from the Strategy's *Framework*) can be employed effectively in planning and classroom practice. Once the literacy objective has been identified, then you can consider the strategies which you think will most help students meet that objective in the lesson. That range of strategies will be explored in the sections to follow.

REFLECTIVE TASK

Think of a Year 7, 8 or 9 lesson in your subject which you have recently seen taught, and ask yourself what was the main literacy demand of that lesson. Did it concern reading, writing or speaking and listening? Find a copy of the *Framework for the Teaching of English* (DfEE 2001a) and identify an objective for that year and for that aspect of literacy. Jot it down together with ideas for how that objective could have been addressed in the lesson in order to assist students' competence with that aspect of literacy. You might then like to share your ideas with your subject mentor or tutor.

Lesson introduction

During the introduction you should clearly state and explain to students what the *literacy objective* for the lesson is in order that they can know what is to be expected of them. Wray

(2001) emphasises the importance of teachers setting clear literacy objectives in contributing to high quality teaching:

> High quality teaching can be characterised by several factors, one of which is clarity of purpose. Making the literacy objective of a lesson explicit helps do this.
>
> (Wray 2001, p. 50)

A further strategy which is often introduced at this stage, but which should also precede most tasks, whether they be to do with literacy or not, is the *activation of prior knowledge*. Langer (1981), following her development of a method for identifying and classifying prior knowledge in students, found that, when reading, those students who engaged in activating their prior knowledge learned and retained more than those who did not. She argued that activating prior knowledge helps students make new learning more meaningful. Activating prior knowledge can provide students with a bridge between their existing knowledge and the new and it can also assist the teacher in early assessment of students' knowledge as a basis for further planning. If this activation does not happen then, as Wray (1999) points out, learning is: 'rote only, and is soon forgotten once deliberate attempts to remember it have stopped' (p. 54). Practical activities which activate prior knowledge can range straightfor-wardly from you asking the students what they know, to the following:

- **brainstorming around the subject to be focused on;**
- **predicting what might happen next, building on previous knowledge and/or experience;**
- **word association from key word, picture or artefact from the subject to be focused on;**
- **filling in a mind-map, or grids (further details later).**

Main part of the lesson

What is important in the main part of the lesson is that wherever possible it should be directly and explicitly linked to the introduction. The teaching process should generally follow a movement which begins with teacher explication and demonstration to the whole class, through a series of activities which are often collaborative to support students' learning, to students working independently. This teaching process owes much to the ideas of Vygotsky (1962), who suggested that learners learn best when they start learning with an expert (could be teacher, parent, other adult or peer), who they first watch and observe, before gradually, under the guiding hand and eye of the expert, they take over some parts of the work, and then as confidence and competence grows, they take over more and more until they finally take over the task completely and work unaided. Lewis and Wray (2000), in their work on literacy in the secondary school, have translated this process into four distinct stages:

1. Demonstration.
2. Joint activity.
3. Supported activity.
4. Individual activity.

Demonstration

Particularly if this task is to involve a new type of writing or the reading of a text not met before, it often helps students if you speak aloud your thoughts so that they can gain an insight into the mental processes. Bereiter and Scardamalia (1987), who researched the writing process and composition, emphasise the importance of the teacher modelling writing composition:

The thinking that goes on in composition needs to be modelled by the teacher, who can thereby show the problem-solving and planning processes that...pupils are often unaware of...and so that they can benefit from observing and discussing each other's mental efforts.

(Bereiter and Scardamalia 1987, p. 174)

Similarly when students are expected to read an unfamiliar text (a subject text book, a reference text [which could be electronic], a pamphlet, etc.) you could use an enlarged version (via OHT) of part of the text and demonstrate the reading skills needed.

PRACTICAL TASK PRACTICAL TASK PRACTICAL TASK PRACTICAL TASK PRACTICAL TASK

WRITING NON-FICTION

To explore this idea of using an unfamiliar text, find a piece of non-fiction writing connected with your subject (it could be a chapter from a book, a magazine article, a leaflet, etc.) which you could use with your students. Now, using the *Literacy Across the Curriculum* training folder (DfEE 2001b) turn to page 9 in the unit on Writing Non-Fiction, and try to identify first of all the category (e.g. recount, explanation etc.) that your piece best fits. Following that, use the Conventions grid on page 10 and attempt to describe the main conventions of your piece, and then compare your suggestions with those for your category which are given in Handout 2.4 at the end of that section.

Joint activity

This is where 'The expert and the learner share the activity' (Lewis and Wray 2000, p. 27), and in terms of the writing and reading activities referred to above, it could be where, having demonstrated the writing of the first couple of sentences of a type of writing, you ask students to suggest the next sentence or so and discuss the suggestions as you write them on the board. Or, with reading, having demonstrated certain skills, you ask students to offer their readings.

Supported activity

In this stage of the process you, the teacher as expert, should maintain careful observation of the students and a readiness to assist but ask the students to work on the activity, sometimes with a partner or as part of a small group or with other support (writing frames, diagrams, instructions, etc.). It can also be the stage, again for reading or writing, where you work closely with one particular group of students in order to support and monitor their progress.

Individual activity

Some students may attain this stage earlier than others. You need to be sensitive to students' progress and needs in the early stages of support.

PRACTICAL TASK PRACTICAL TASK PRACTICAL TASK PRACTICAL TASK PRACTICAL TASK

GROUP TALK

Think back over some lessons you have observed recently and jot down the different types of student groupings (paired, small group [4–6], large group [6+], mixed ability, etc.) you observed. How were the groups organised? What would you say was the function and purpose of such groupings? Now look through the Management of Group Talk section of the *Literacy Across the Curriculum* training folder (DfEE 2001b) and compare your responses, focusing particularly on 7.2 Choosing the size and composition of groups, 7.4 Strategies for organising group talk and 7.8 Golden rules.

Plenary

The plenary is a vital stage in the lesson. It is the point where you and the students can reflect upon, review and consolidate what has been learnt so far; a point where the learning objectives for literacy, stated at the opening of the lesson, can be revisited. This is a time which can develop a student's metacognitive intelligence (one of seven different intelligences identified by Howard Gardner [1993]), the ability to reflect upon and take control of one's learning. (For more information on multiple intelligences see Chapter 4, p 39.)

Evaluation and assessment

This is another important area, where you need to both evaluate the effectiveness of the lesson on students' literacy development in order to inform future lesson planning, and to assess individual students' literacy learning so that class and individual literacy targets can be reviewed and set. You can achieve this informally, during (through talking with, listening to and observing students) and after the lesson (through reading and marking students' work).

A word or two on marking written work for literacy. When you set a piece of written work, indicate which aspects of literacy will be commented on or 'marked'. This requires you to prioritise and be selective. For example, if one of the objectives for the lesson has been to learn and spell key vocabulary, it would be appropriate to tell students that those key words will be assessed both for understanding and spelling (rather than marking every spelling mistake). Similarly, if the literacy objective had been understanding how to introduce paragraphs in a particular type of writing in a subject, comments on the success or otherwise of the paragraph opening would also be appropriate. An important element to consider when responding to students' work is that of praise and positive reinforcement. On this subject, Lewis and Wray (2001, p. 51) make the point that low levels of literacy are often associated with poor self-esteem and advocate teachers giving positive rather than negative feedback to students on their reading, writing and speaking and listening. Debra Myhill in her book *Better Writing* (2001), which is based on the research she carried out into writing in schools, gives the advice to teachers when assessing writing to 'isolate and praise what is effective as well as weaknesses' (p. 98).

The EXIT model and further strategies

The EXIT model

The EXIT model (Extending Interactions with Texts) grew out of the work of David Wray and Maureen Lewis on the Nuffield Extending Literacy (EXEL) Project. The purpose of the EXIT model was to present a 'description of the processes involved in learning with texts' (Lewis and Wray 2000) and thereby to suggest certain strategies which are directly linked to the model. Lewis and Wray identified ten mental activities involved in learning with texts and devised a ten-stage process as follows.

1. Elicitation of previous knowledge.
2. Establishing purposes.
3. Locating information.
4. Adopting an appropriate strategy.
5. Interacting with text.
6. Monitoring understanding.

7. Making a record.
8. Evaluating information.
9. Assisting memory.
10. Communicating information.

(Lewis and Wray 2000)

As can be seen, the sequence complements in part the sequence for teaching from the earlier part of this chapter, with its allusions to activating prior knowledge, stating the learning objective and evaluating the learning. Each part of the sequence can be linked to certain strategies. As mentioned earlier, there are far too many to be listed here but it is worth referring to a few.

One particularly effective group of strategies which would appear within 'Interacting with text' in Lewis and Wray's EXIT model and which has been in use in schools for many years is termed DARTS.

DARTS

DARTS stands for Directed Activities Related to Texts and they were activities first devised in 1984 by Lunzer and Gardner to further and encourage active approaches to reading. Since DARTS inception, teachers have added to and amended activities, but helpfully, Geoff Dean (2000, pp. 110–111), following many others, has categorised them into:

*   **reconstructive activities;**
*   **processing activities.**

With reconstructive activities, the text has been altered in some way and the students have to reconstruct it and it includes such activities as cloze procedure, which involves students filling in words which have been deleted from a text; sequencing, where the text has been cut up into segments and the students have to reorganise them and give a reason for their decisions; or prediction, where students are given a text where the ending of it or the ending of a section is missing and they have to predict the next part based upon their reading and understanding of their reading so far.

Processing activities require the students to work with unamended texts and include such activities as text marking, where students are asked to apply a specific focus or question to the text and to respond by highlighting or annotating the parts of the text that refer to the focus or question; and questioning, where they are asked to generate questions about the text being studied for others to attempt to answer.

Most DARTS activities lend themselves to collaborative work, where students work in pairs or groups, and can be seen as especially useful in supported activity in the main part of a lesson.

Another effective strategy for use with texts can be the use of grids to help in terms of activating prior knowledge, establishing a purpose and making a record. Lewis and Wray advocate the use of two in particular: the KWL grid and the QUADS grid (Lewis and Wray 2000).

KWL grid

What do I *know* about this topic?	What do I *want* to know about it?	What have I *learnt* about it?

It can be seen that this grid helps the students to organise their approach and to record their findings and is based on 'three cognitive steps – accessing prior knowledge, determining what needs to be learnt, recalling what has been learnt' (Lewis and Wray 2000).

QUADS grid

Question	Answer	Details	Source

This grid acts in a similar way to the KWL without so much emphasis on the activation of prior knowledge but with more emphasis on recording information. Students are required initially to formulate a question about the topic they are exploring, to find (via books, internet, etc.) and record the answer, but also to record any relevant details connected with their research question as well as the source of the information.

Writing frames

It was through the EXIT project that Lewis and Wray suggested that the use of 'frames' could act as a support for students when they are engaged in writing (particularly non-fiction) in any subject. A 'frame' in this context is simply a bare outline of a text such as the one below (Figure 8.2: Lewis and Wray 2000, p. 93):

UK and Kenya – a comparison

Although .... and .... are different they are

alike in some interesting ways.

For example they both ....

....

They are also similar in ....

....

They also have the same ....

....

Figure 8.2: Example of a writing frame

Writing frames are helpful in structuring text, providing examples of ways to begin both whole texts and paragraphs and how to connect the different parts of a text, but, as Roger Beard points out:

> they are intended to be used as a kind of prompt, eventually to be dispensed with, as children begin to adopt the features of the genre for themselves.
>
> (Beard 2000, p. 113)

Spelling

The ability to spell is not innate; it is a skill which can be learned. There are various strategies which can be employed to help students improve their spelling. It is first of all important to recognise that there are three basic reasons why students may be poor at spelling.

1. They have underdeveloped visual memory – they can't remember how words look.
2. They have underdeveloped auditory analysis – they have poor awareness of the constituent sounds of words (phonological awareness).
3. They have underdeveloped intellectual awareness – they lack the understanding or ability to use knowledge of the way words are derived or structured or follow spelling conventions.

It follows that the spelling strategies which you advocate for your students (individual and whole class) should attempt to address these weaknesses singly or together as does the popular 'look – cover – say – write – check' method.

Make spelling active. When a student asks you for a spelling, you should resist the temptation to give the spelling immediately but instead ask the student to try spelling it.

IN THE CLASSROOM

In Jane Marston's science class one student, Alex, put up his hand and asked her how to spell immediately. Jane asked Alex to try spelling it.

'I-M-E-D-I-A-T-E-L-Y,' Alex uttered.

'Very good, Alex,' responded the teacher, 'You have ten out of the eleven letters right. There's one missing; what d'you think it might be?'

'Is it another M, Miss?'

'It is Alex, well done.'

The lesson in this story is that even if the student doesn't get the whole word right you should praise them for the number of letters they do get right before asking them or indicating where the error lies. You should ask the class how to spell words which are vital to the subject they are addressing in the lesson, and you should encourage students to keep a spelling log book which contains words which are important in their subject and which they can easily refer to.

PRACTICAL TASK PRACTICAL TASK PRACTICAL TASK PRACTICAL TASK PRACTICAL TASK

VOCABULARY

Find out and make a list of the key vocabulary for your subject in Year 7 and see how you might incorporate some of those words into a scheme of work for that year.

Using the teaching environment to support literacy

Medwell (Medwell *et al*. 1998 in Lewis and Wray 2001, p. 49), in the *Effective Teachers of Literacy* project, found that it was important to create 'literate environments' in the classroom. It is yet another way for the teachers in the school to show how valued literacy is in that community. The teaching environment could be any site in the secondary school where teaching and learning take place, including classrooms, IT suites, gymnasia and drama studios, but also other sites such as the school's entrance hall and corridors. All are sites which teachers could use to support and emphasise literacy within and across subjects. You, as an individual subject teacher, could ensure for instance that wall displays are changed regularly to coincide with current literacy objectives for different classes (e.g. key terminology and vocabulary); or that good examples of students' writing are displayed attractively and effectively; that key books are displayed and that literacy materials and resources such as dictionaries are easily accessible by students.

PRACTICAL TASK PRACTICAL TASK PRACTICAL TASK PRACTICAL TASK PRACTICAL TASK

LITERACY WALK

During a break, take a walk around the school and look to see how the school environment (classrooms, corridors, reception areas, halls, etc.) supports students' literacy development. Make a note of good examples and practice in your school and be prepared to share it with others. For example:

- **in which areas are there examples of advice for students as to how to improve an aspect of their literacy?**
- **in which areas are there good displays of books?**
- **in which areas are there good displays of recent students' written work?**

Literacy and students with English as an Additional Language (EAL)

The inclusion of students learning English as an Additional Language is a key principle of the National Curriculum 2000. Literacy competence and confidence are essential for students with EAL if they are to access all subjects in the curriculum. Virtually all of the strategies for developing literacy outlined above will be helpful to those students because they encourage teacher support, scaffolded activities, collaborative working, the activation of prior knowledge and planning for talk. In order to be of greatest assistance to their students you will, in addition, need to know the language and literacy background and identity as well as the previous educational experiences of your students. You should also have high expectations of your students and plan for them all to be involved. (For more information on teaching students with English as an Additional Language, see Chapter 13.)

Literacy across the curriculum and the role of the English teacher

If your subject is English, all that has been discussed so far in terms of strategies and approaches will apply to your classroom practice, but it is not your responsibility to teach all aspects of literacy that will be covered across the curriculum. I hope that it is now clear that each subject has a responsibility for identifying its own literacy demands and teaching those accordingly. With English as your subject, what you can do to help support literacy across the curriculum is to teach some of those generic aspects of literacy which will support students' literacy in other subjects. For instance you can teach pupils many of the conventions of English spelling; strategies for spelling; paragraphing; punctuation; understanding and writing the main text types; reading strategies; the roles and skills of group discussion, etc.

A SUMMARY OF **KEY POINTS**

The foregrounding and teaching of literacy is an essential responsibility of all teachers, whatever their subject, if they are to fully develop and sustain the learning of all their students. The following are, I believe, the key points from the chapter which will lead to your success in improving the literacy skills of the students you teach.

> **Understand the literacy demands of your subject.**

> **Plan your lessons to include literacy objectives and the development of students' literacy.**

> **Teach literacy skills. Don't assume that their literacy will automatically improve by simply doing more reading or writing.**

> **Model and demonstrate good literacy practice.**

> **Provide support and guidance for students' reading, writing and speaking and listening.**

> **Respond constructively to students' literacy in their reading, writing and speaking and listening.**

Moving on

In your subject, which aspects of literacy, reading, writing or speaking and listening do you think give your students the most difficulty? Ask some of your students and your subject colleagues for their views. Now decide what seems to be the single most important aspect, and with a colleague consider how you might address the problem in your planning and teaching with a particular class that you teach.

FURTHER READING FURTHER READING **FURTHER READING** FURTHER READING

DfEE (2001a) *Framework for Teaching English: Years 7, 8 and 9.* London. DfEE. The document which contains all of the objectives for literacy for Key Stage 3 as well as advice on planning and guidance on inclusion.

DfEE (2001b) *Literacy Across the Curriculum.* London. DfEE. This is the training folder for all subjects at Key Stage 3 and it contains discussions and teaching advice on all aspects of literacy from writing non-fiction to spelling and from active reading to managing group talk.

DfES (2002) *Literacy in…* series. A series of booklets and video extracts exmplifying good practice in literacy teaching in art, PE, MFL, design and technology, history, geography, music, RE, citizenship and careers.

DfES (2004) *Literacy and learning.* London. DfES. A further series of subject-specific booklets and CD-ROMs which incorporate the Literacy Across the Curriculum materials and give practical ideas on how to devise effective objective-led teaching which focuses on learning through talk, from text and through writing.

Lewis, M. and Wray, D. (2000) *Literacy in the Secondary School.* London. David Fulton. This contains information on the EXEL project together with discussion and advice on teaching strategies to improve students' literacy.

Myhill, D. (2001) *Better Writing.* Westley. Courseware Publications. Good advice on teaching writing based on recent research.

QCA (2000) *Language for Learning in Key Stage 3.* London. QCA. Useful advice on mapping the objectives in the QCA schemes of work for various subjects.

Website

www.standards.dfes.gov.uk/secondary/ This site contains materials for literacy across the curriculum and literacy and learning (look in 'Resources and Publications') as well as other material relating to the Secondary National Strategy.

For further information on teaching literacy across the curriculum, visit **www. learningmatters.co.uk/education/learnteach/chapt8.html**

9

Teaching numeracy across the curriculum
Kate Mackrell

Professional Standards for QTS

Q13, Q14

To be awarded QTS to teach a subject at Key Stages 3 and 4, you need to be familiar with the cross-curricular expectations and guidance contained in the National Curriculum and the Secondary National Strategy. You also need to be able to incorporate these expectations for numeracy into your teaching of your specialist subject.

You may find it helpful to read through the appropriate section of the handbook that accompanies the Standards for the award of QTS for clarification and support.

Introduction

When the first edition of this book was being written in 2002, the Key Stage 3 strategy was very new, and an important part of that strategy was the Numeracy across the Curriculum initiative. This initiative has now been implemented, with each school expected to have a numeracy policy and subject departments expected to collaborate in enhancing student numeracy both for its own sake and as a contribution to other subjects. The focus of attention at Key Stage 3 has hence shifted away from numeracy as other initiatives such as 'Leading in Learning' are being developed. Much of the current focus on numeracy is now at Key Stage 4, with continued emphasis on the key skills, of which numeracy is one. However, numeracy continues to be critically important to students at Key Stage 3, and, particularly for trainees who teach subjects such as science, geography or design technology in which mathematics is used extensively, must be taken seriously.

The aim of this chapter is hence:

- to help trainees whose main subject is not mathematics to successfully incorporate the mathematics necessary to their subject in their teaching;
- to encourage those trainees whose main subject is not mathematics to see the development of student numeracy as enhancing both their subject and the development of other cross-curricular skills;
- to help mathematics trainees to be aware of the issues faced by non-mathematics teachers in incorporating numeracy in lessons and to begin to distinguish their own role in encouraging numeracy across the curriculum.

In this chapter, the following questions will be considered.

- What is numeracy?
- Why focus on numeracy across the curriculum?
- What are the objectives of numeracy across the curriculum?

- What maths is relevant to your specialist subject?
- How can you make sure you know the maths you need?
- How can you plan to incorporate numeracy in your lessons?
- What's important in delivering such a lesson?

You will require access to three DfES publications:

- *Secondary National Strategy Framework for Teaching Mathematics: Years 7, 8 and 9* (referred to as the Framework in the remainder of this chapter);
- *Numeracy Across the Curriculum Notes for School-based Training* (referred to as the NAC notes);
- the video from *Numeracy Across the Curriculum Support Materials for School-based Training.*

These should be available through your training provider and are widely available in secondary schools. The first two are available to download at: **www.standards.dfes.gov.uk/ secondary/**

What is numeracy?

Numeracy is not just about being able to do calculations: it is about being able to use mathematics effectively outside the mathematics classroom. This includes for example the ability to use simple formulae, understand basic probability and create and interpret graphs. A detailed definition is given on page 9 of the Framework.

It is probably more useful to think of numeracy skills as being mathematical skills used in a real context rather than as a particular group of mathematical skills, as it can be argued that numeracy encompasses all of the mathematics at Key Stage 3 (Perks and Prestage 2001).

Why focus on numeracy across the curriculum?

Do you feel bogged down at the thought of including numeracy in your subject teaching? Surely teacher training is tough enough without throwing maths into it!

REFLECTIVE TASK

Spend some time writing about how you feel about mathematics. Do you enjoy it? Have you found it hard? Boring? How confident are you with everyday maths? How do you feel about incorporating mathematics into your subject teaching?

You have probably just pinpointed a major problem with numeracy: many people dislike maths, become anxious when required to do any maths and lack confidence in their ability. Many people also have very negative images of mathematicians and these likewise (and perhaps particularly for girls) can get in the way of learning. Here are some common misconceptions:

- maths doesn't involve creativity;
- maths is about rules to be memorised;
- boys are better at maths than girls;
- some people can do maths but some can't.

Also, being 'innumerate' is socially acceptable in a way that being 'illiterate' isn't. Hence there can be little incentive to become competent at mathematics.

Does this matter? I get very anxious about the idea of diving off a board 20 feet above the water and hence I avoid having to do it and have not developed the skills needed to do it successfully. Impact on my life? Negligible.

The effects of maths avoidance and lack of skill are not negligible. Mathematical skills are increasingly needed in employment: research has shown that poor numeracy skills have more impact on employment prospects than poor literacy skills (Basic Skills Agency 1997).

Why can't problems with numeracy be solved in mathematics classrooms?

Mathematics classrooms have indeed changed considerably: concerns about both adult numeracy and the relatively poor performance of English students in international studies of mathematics achievement led to the introduction of the National Numeracy Strategy at Key Stage 1/Key Stage 2 in 1998 and the Key Stage 3 Framework for Teaching Mathematics in 2001. This has involved the introduction of a detailed programme of study for each year and a change in teaching strategies, with emphasis on reasoning and questioning and a high proportion of oral and mental work.

However, all learning is situated in a context (Lave 1988): in mathematics classrooms students learn how to do mathematics in mathematics classrooms. They do not and cannot learn how to do mathematics in other settings until they are in that setting. For example, students who are competent at drawing graphs in a maths lesson may not be able to draw similar graphs in a geography lesson, despite the fact that their mathematics teacher has taken care to introduce graphs taken from many different contexts. This can lead to a great deal of frustration on the part of teachers of other subjects: it is easy to assume that the students are unintelligent or that their mathematics teaching is poor.

In order for students to make the links between the mathematics of the mathematics class-room and the mathematics required in other subjects it is important that teachers of other subjects are also involved in the mathematical development of the students.

The Numeracy across the Curriculum initiative

The Numeracy across the Curriculum initiative, initiated in secondary schools in 2001, has the aim of addressing this problem. The main focus of this initiative is to set up collaboration between mathematics and other subject departments to enable teachers to make explicit links with mathematics in different subject areas and to achieve consistency in approaches and expectations. The main focus of this initiative was to set up collaboration between mathematics and other subject departments to enable teachers to make explicit links with mathematics in different subject areas.

What are the objectives of Numeracy across the Curriculum?

The fundamental objective is that standards in numeracy will be raised and that learning in other subjects will be enhanced. A full list of numeracy objectives is given in the handout *Numeracy across the Curriculum Objectives* available with the NAC notes. This contains a breakdown by year of the objectives given on page 9 of the Framework.

These priorities have been identified:

- **to improve accuracy, particularly in calculation, measurement and graphical work;**
- **to improve interpretation and presentation of graphs, charts and diagrams;**
- **to improve reasoning and problem-solving.**

In order to achieve these objectives, schools will have designated a numeracy co-ordinator and ideally, the curriculum for mathematics and other subjects will have begun to be organised so that topics required for other subjects are first taught by the mathematics department. Schools should also be developing a numeracy policy which:

- **sets out an agreed approach to:**
  - **the teaching of agreed numeracy skills;**
  - **vocabulary, notation and units to be used;**
  - **use of calculators and other ICT;**
  - **methods for calculation;**
  - **algebraic techniques;**
  - **the representation of graphs;**
- **indicates areas of collaboration between subjects and processes for facilitating collaboration;**
- **gives links with using and applying mathematics;**
- **gives advice from the mathematics department on common difficulties, errors and misconceptions.**

What maths is relevant to your specialist subject?

The maths necessary to different subjects will vary: geography, science and design technology rely on mathematics extensively (for example, can you imagine design technology without measurement, or science and geography without graphs?), whereas there are no specific demands for mathematical skills in studying English.

Mathematics which is not strictly required can also be used to enrich subject teaching. A good example is found in the excerpt from the history lesson on the NAC video, where pie charts are used to enhance student learning about the daily life of a monk.

Here are some further enrichment examples from English and MFL.

- **Exploring the metrical pattern of poetry when using a poem as a model for writing.**
- **Exploring average sentence length in samples of various newspapers' front pages over time and considering whether any generalisations can be made.**
- **Number games such as Countdown conducted in the target language.**
- **Looking at the structure of the number system via the different words used for number in different languages.**
- **Money: conversations around shopping and internet shopping, currency conversions.**
- **Conducting surveys and presenting data in the target language, interpreting data from the target language country.**
- **Using mathematical language (e.g. square, rectangular) in describing objects.**

REFLECTIVE TASK

Identify the mathematical content necessary to your subject and begin to identify areas where maths could enrich your subject. Some sources of information are listed below:

- **the QCA/DfES schemes of work (and teacher's guide) for your subject;**
- **your subject department;**
- **page 23 of the Framework;**
- **the Mathematics Association publication *Numeracy across the Curriculum*;**
- **unit 3 of the NAC;**
- **a search on the internet on your subject and mathematics.**

Mathematics in your subject will also support the thinking skills described in the Leading in Learning initiative. Many activities will focus around handling data which involves all three of the NAC priorities listed above, enables your students to become researchers in your subject, and involves each of information-processing, reasoning, enquiry, creative-thinking and evaluation. Unit 7 in the NAC notes gives an extensive number of ideas for handing data across the curriculum.

As well as identifying mathematics content (such as percentages), improving reasoning and problem-solving will require you to identify the relationship between your subject and mathematical thinking skills (which are the sorts of skills you used in creating maths GCSE coursework). Thinking skills in mathematics in the National Curriculum are known as 'using and applying' and are categorised as:

- **problem-solving (making decisions about problems and methods and monitoring decision-making);**
- **communication (formulating, discussing, interpreting and presenting findings);**
- **reasoning (finding solutions and giving justifications).**

Pages 20 to 22 in the Framework give a description of the generic thinking skills in mathematics: you may find it useful to read these pages, identify how these relate to the numeracy priorities and compare with thinking skills in your subject.

How can you make sure you know the maths you need?

You can't. As an experienced mathematics teacher, I still sometimes get asked questions that I can't immediately answer. What matters is that I have the confidence and the resources to go away and come back with an answer – or to open out the question so that the class can explore it and we can all learn something new. You need to ensure that you are confident with the specific mathematics that you need in a lesson, but be prepared for unexpected questions to arise that you may not be able to respond to immediately. You can set an excellent model for students in your handling of unexpected difficulties if you openly discuss the issue and plan strategies to find out the mathematics needed.

What may be more important than knowing the mathematics in great detail is to check whether or not you have any misconceptions about maths. All of the statements below are true – some may surprise you. Look at the meaning of any unfamiliar mathematical words in the mathematics glossary on the Standards website.

Misconceptions in maths are common: even if you feel confident about mathematics you may find you have some. It's very important that you don't pass these on to students.

- Multiplying doesn't always make numbers bigger.
- Putting a nought on the end of a number to multiply it by ten doesn't always work.
- Sometimes adding two numbers can give a bigger result than multiplying them.
- To convert square metres to square centimetres you don't multiply by 100.
- If the price of an item is increased by five per cent and then reduced by five per cent the final price will not be the same as the original price.
- On the other hand, if the price of an item is reduced by a certain percentage and then VAT is added, the result will be the same as if the VAT is added before the price is reduced.
- If a set of data is grouped into five class intervals, the mean could fall into any one of the intervals.
- If you toss a coin twice the probability of throwing two heads is not 1/3.
- Two cuboids with the same volume will not always have the same surface area.
- If you double the lengths of a shape you will not double the area and the volume.
- Division sometimes makes numbers larger.
- When the area of a shape increases the perimeter can sometimes decrease.
- Dividing any number by zero does not give zero.
- The order in which you combine numbers using +, -, x or ÷ sometimes matters.
- There are nine times as many students as teachers in a school. P represents the number of students and T represents the number of teachers in the school. Hence $9T = P$.

(Adapted from Pope and Sharma 2001)

Detailed explanations of a variety of misconceptions may be found at **www.cimt.plymouth.ac.uk/resources/help/miscon.htm**

One aspect of the Key Stage 3 strategy is an emphasis on skills in mental calculation. The chances are that you were not encouraged to acquire such skills at school. If, for example, you work out the cost of eight calculators at £6.98 each you probably don't multiply 6.98 x 8 but instead use some sort of shortcut, and you might feel guilty about not working it out 'properly'. Such 'shortcuts' are called strategies and are encouraged by the Numeracy

Strategy. Useful examples of such strategies can be found on pages 82–111 in the Framework supplement of examples.

How can you plan to incorporate numeracy in your lessons?

Observe a mathematics lesson, ideally one in which mathematics relevant to your subject is being taught. Make notes of the teaching strategies used, in particular the use of questioning and mental and oral work and of the students' responses. Now observe a lesson in your subject in which mathematics is used. Contrast the teaching strategies and pupil responses with those in the mathematics lesson.

1. Identify the required mathematical skills, together with relevant misconceptions and common difficulties

Be specific about what mathematics you need: for example in the geography lesson on the NAC video, students need to find the area of a particular type of trapezium: they do not need to be able to use the general formula for the area of a trapezium. The history lesson requires awareness that many students find it difficult to use a protractor correctly and that a common misconception is that angles should be measured from the edge of the protractor, rather than from the line marked 0°. Hopefully information about misconceptions and difficulties will be contained in the school numeracy policy: if not, talk to a member of the mathematics department.

2. Identify prior learning

This is quite important in mathematics teaching: you need to ensure that you are building upon mathematics with which the students feel confident. Information about what mathematics the students have been exposed to should be in the mathematics departmental schemes of work. It is also worth looking at the yearly teaching programmes in section 3 of the Framework. Mathematical exposure is not the same as mathematical learning, however: find out as much as you can about the mathematical attainment of individual students. In particular you need to identify students who have particular difficulty with maths: they may not be the same students as the ones who find your subject difficult.

3. Decide on learning objectives

You may find at this point that there is a mismatch between the mathematics required and the students' prior learning. As the Numeracy across the Curriculum initiative becomes implemented fully, the mismatch between required mathematical skills in other subjects and prior learning in mathematics should be minimised so that you do not need to ever introduce new mathematical techniques for the first time to a class: your objectives will normally involve using mathematics in the context of your subject. If the mismatch is too great, you will need to revise your plans to include mathematics which is more appropriate to the students' prior learning.

You may find it difficult to break a piece of mathematics down into measurable objectives or to see what would be an appropriate progression: here the Framework objectives, found in both the Key Objectives section and the yearly teaching programmes, may be useful. Your objectives will normally involve consolidation of mathematical skills and application of these skills within your subject. For example the history lesson on the NAC video might have included 'gain experience in simplifying fractions' and 'interpret pie charts to draw inferences about the life of a monk'.

Remember that the cross-curricular priorities focus on accuracy, interpretation and presentation and reasoning and problem-solving. Do your learning objectives relate to these priorities?

4. Decide on teaching strategies

It may be useful to read pages 6, 26 and 27 of the Framework and compare the teaching strategies suggested with those used in your subject. Most of these will be to some extent familiar to you as they are considered good practice in most subjects.

The emphasis in the Framework is on direct interactive teaching, mental and oral work and in promoting students' thinking skills. The lesson excerpts on the video give examples of these strategies. There is an emphasis on questioning: the students are never told what to do or how to do it, but are asked to reflect on their knowledge of mathematics in order to decide for themselves. Mental calculations are required and students are asked to explain how they worked out particular answers. In addition, notice that the mathematics involved is explicitly connected with the mathematics studied in mathematics lessons.

Discussion and questioning are key teaching strategies: students can be asked how they worked out their answers, whether or not their answers are reasonable and why they have chosen their methods or reached their conclusions. Students can be encouraged to discuss their strategies and share ideas.

The Framework also promotes a three-part lesson structure (see pages 28–31): in the first part of a lesson, the oral and mental starter, students might review some of the mathematics to be used later (this review will usually be necessary at some time in the lesson). The geography teacher might have reviewed the method used to calculate the area of a trapezium in this part of the lesson. The main teaching activity would include combinations of teaching input and pupil activies, as seen in the video extracts. The final plenary could include reflections on the use of mathematics within the lesson and the conclusions which the use of mathematics has enabled.

It's important to use the same approach as the maths department in dealing with specific topics. A temptation is to show the students a shortcut, as illustrated in the following story.

IN THE CLASSROOM

As part of their study of rivers, students in a geography lesson were converting some numbers from fractions to percentages. The teacher noticed that the students were using a variety of methods, most of which were unfamiliar to him and many of which did not seem very efficient. The teacher decided to address the class about this and said 'I know a better method for doing this – first you ... and then you ...' The students left the class feeling confused: though able to use the shortcut in that particular lesson, none of them understood why it worked or when it could be used. The consequence was, as noted in subsequent mathematics lessons, that their basic understanding of percentages deteriorated. It would have been better for the teacher to have listened to them explaining their methods.

A major consideration will be the approach you use to calculation: you need to consider whether to use mental, written or calculator methods and plan accordingly. Note that students may well be much better at mental arithmetic than you expect: by Year 7 students are expected to add and subtract two-digit numbers such as 73 and 49 mentally. If students can reasonably be expected to work out calculations mentally, telling them to use a calculator may deprive them of an opportunity to practise their skills in mental calculation. On the other hand, if the required calculations are lengthy and difficult, students may lose track of the purpose of the lesson by focusing on calculation alone. See units 5 and 6 of NAC for a consideration of calculations and calculator use.

5. Decide on assessment strategies

Appropriate assessment will enable you to gauge whether or not you have met your learning objectives and will also provide feedback which enables students to improve. Much of this you will achieve through observation and questioning during the course of your lesson. It is usually not appropriate to set a series of problems (even well related to your subject) which you can tick, cross and give a mark out of 20. While you should point out and comment on issues to do with accuracy and errors in mathematical techniques much as you would point out spelling errors in student work, the focus of your assessment should be on how well the mathematics has been used in the context of your subject. It's important to remember the general research findings about formative assessment (Black and Wiliam, 1998): students make better progress if they are aware of your assessment objectives and if you give feedback only with no mark. (For further information on formative assessment see Chapter 6.)

What's important in teaching a lesson involving numeracy?

We're going to come back to your attitude to mathematics, because at this stage it's critical. It's easy to let your dislike, lack of confidence, or prejudices show: consider the message you are giving if you get flustered when you make an arithmetic mistake, or your voice becomes more lively when you finish the maths and can get on to the 'important' stuff in your subject or you say 'Here's an easy question, so let's hear from one of the girls' (I've heard this said!). It's crucial to convey that mathematics is an important part of your subject, and an aspect of your subject that all students can participate in: remember that much of the problem with numeracy is not just lack of attainment but negative attitudes.

IN THE CLASSROOM

A drama teacher was working with a group to stage a play, and they were discussing how to design the set. A student, remembering maths homework in which they'd drawn scale drawings of their rooms, suggested they could make a scale drawing. Should the teacher respond with:

'No, let's do something a bit more imaginative, and anyway you can't expect me to do anything like that – I'm not a maths teacher.'

'Mmm, has anyone got any other ideas?'

'Good idea. How could we start?'

Your lack of confidence with mathematics is likely to be the biggest issue. Hopefully you will have gained some confidence through ensuring that you can in fact deal with the maths and that you have planned appropriately, but you may still be fearful of making a mistake, or feel daunted that some students will be better at maths than you are.

IN THE CLASSROOM

A science teacher had been transposing a formula on the board, and a student pointed out that he had made a mistake. Which do you think would be the most helpful response?

'No, I haven't.'

'Oh, uh, well it was deliberate, uh, just testing you, uh – time to set the homework!'

'Yes, I might have. Let's check it through. How did you spot it – and well done!'

Many students will be better at mental arithmetic than you are: can you add and subtract two-digit numbers in your head? Remember that what you have to offer is your understanding of how maths is going to enhance your subject – and let them teach you some of their strategies!

Another issue is that of creating a supportive atmosphere. All students should feel that their contribution is of value and should not worry about making mistakes. Notice that in the geography lesson when a student gives an incorrect answer the teacher indicates that it is almost right and invites other students to correct it.

IN THE CLASSROOM

In comparing the proportions of various pictures an art teacher asked the class for their measurements. One student gave a measurement that was, to the teacher, obviously inaccurate. Which response will be most helpful?

'No, that's wrong. Go and do it again.'

'I'm not sure that that's quite accurate. How did you get it?'

Students should also not be put under pressure to do mathematics that they find too difficult. If you see any signs of anxiety, such as a lack of response when you ask questions, or a deterioration in behaviour, it's best to back off and do something else. Talk to someone in the mathematics department about what you observed and, with their help, plan a different strategy. On the other hand it's important that students are challenged. With reflection on your experience you will begin to achieve this balance.

For the mathematics trainee

Your responsibilities with regard to numeracy across the curriculum are rather different: it's expected that almost everything that you do as a teacher will be enhancing pupil numeracy, and you will receive detailed training on teaching mathematics as required by the Secondary Strategy as part of your subject specialist work.

There are two aspects of numeracy across the curriculum which should inform your teaching, however. First, you should bring in contexts from across the curriculum and make explicit the links between mathematics and other subjects: you might for example talk about the way in which scale drawing is used in design technology in the course of a lesson. Second, you should help teachers of other subjects to effectively promote numeracy within their subjects: you might for example tell the design technology teacher what approach the maths department takes to scale drawing and what difficulties are experienced by students.

PRACTICAL TASK PRACTICAL TASK PRACTICAL TASK PRACTICAL TASK PRACTICAL TASK

Working with a group of other trainees, which includes a mathematics trainee if possible, plan a cross-curricular day to focus on the theme of enhancing numeracy across the curriculum. Plan a lesson for your subject in detail, paying attention to the requirements given above. If possible, teach and evaluate your lesson.

A SUMMARY OF **KEY POINTS**

> **Numeracy is about using maths effectively outside the maths classroom and is an important skill for all students.**

> **The Numeracy across the Curriculum initiative, part of the Secondary National Strategy, is designed to improve numeracy skills across the curriculum and also enhance the teaching of other subjects through collaboration between subject departments.**

> **To incorporate numeracy in your teaching, you need to identify the mathematics involved in your subject, ensure that you have confidence in your knowledge of this maths and plan to build on students' prior knowledge and understanding of mathematics.**

> **Key teaching strategies are the use of discussion and questioning, in which students are encouraged to explain their methods and reasoning.**

> **A supportive classroom atmosphere, in which students are not afraid to make mistakes, is important.**

Moving on

Find out about the academic literature on situated cognition and mathematics. A useful paper is:

Boaler, J. (2000) Mathematics from another world: Traditional communities and the alienation of learners. *Journal of Mathematical Behavior*, 19 (4): 1–19 available at **www.stanford.edu/ ~joboaler/JMB_2000.doc**

This paper contains an introduction to situated cognition in mathematics and connects this perspective to students' experiences in learning mathematics in six English schools. It will enable non-specialists to see some of the issues in traditional mathematics teaching, which can lead to insights about how to more effectively incorporate numeracy in their own subjects. It also contains an extensive bibliography for further reading.

FURTHER READING FURTHER READING **FURTHER READING** FURTHER READING

Ledwick, M. (2001) *Numeracy Across the Curriculum in Secondary Schools*. Leicester. Mathematical Association. A resource to assist in the planning and implementation of this initiative.

Perks, P. and Prestage, S. (2001) *Teaching the National Numeracy Strategy at Key Stage 3*. London. David Fulton. A very useful discussion of the ways in which the KS3 numeracy strategy may be implemented.

For further information on teaching numeracy across the curriculum, visit **www.learning matters.co.uk/education/learnteach/chapt9.html**

10
Teaching ICT across the curriculum
Cathy Wickens

Professional Standards for QTS

Q13, Q14

To be awarded QTS you must know how to use ICT effectively, both to teach your subject and to support your wider professional role. You should know and understand how to use ICT as an integral part of your teaching using the National Curriculum Programmes of Study and the relevant national frameworks and schemes of work. You must be able to use ICT effectively in your teaching providing opportunities for learners to develop their ICT capability, including e-learning.

You may find it helpful to read through the appropriate section of the handbook that accompanies the Standards for the Award of QTS for clarification and support.

Introduction

In a new century where information and communication technology (ICT) capability is prized as never before, we are duty bound to design a curriculum for all students which will allow them to be educationally 'street-wise' with today's technology. This chapter seeks to demonstrate that the use of ICT in teaching and learning can help students learn more effectively and enjoyably with the same avid concentration and commitment that they have for computer games.

In September 2000, the new orders for the National Curriculum stated that all students in England were to be given opportunities to apply and develop their ICT capability through the use of ICT tools to support their learning in all subjects (with the exception of physical education at Key Stages 1 and 2). It is not the intention of this chapter for the reader to feel constrained by the statutory orders of the National Curriculum or the criteria for Initial Teacher Education. Rather that through classroom examples and results from research it will demonstrate how the use of ICT can enhance and enrich the learning experience across the curriculum and form the basis for lifelong learning. Practical tasks and ideas for the use of ICT in school will enable those embarking on the teaching profession to demonstrate a developing pedagogy of ICT.

Claims

There are many claims for what ICT can do in support of teaching and learning. For example ICT can help:

- **motivate learners and raise levels of attainment;**
- **reduce the teacher's workload;**
- **link school, home and the rest of the world.**

Some of the key research

The research has a shorter history than other subject areas but there is growing evidence to confirm that there is a correlation between good resources, good teaching and student attainment. *Ways Forward With ICT*, Moseley *et al*. (1999), although a primary focused report, has some very important conclusions demonstrating that ICT contributes to teaching and learning where:

- clear subject-focused objectives had been identified;
- the teacher could use the ICT to deliver those objectives;
- the teacher ensured that students had ICT skills that were sufficient to enable them to achieve the subject-specific objectives;
- students were given sufficient access to ICT to achieve learning objectives.

The findings from the ImpaCT2 report (Becta 2002), which evaluated the impact of the ICT in Schools Programme and the Secondary School of the Future Report (Becta 2001), the purpose of which was to analyse the relationship between ICT and secondary school standards, certainly support these claims. The first three bullet points above are concerned with teaching at its best; when not meeting these standards the report shows that teachers underestimate the capability of students although the students are generally enthusiastic about using computers and they perceive using ICT as useful. Seymour Papert's book *Mindstorms* (1980) gives an account of his vision of how computers might be used in education using the Logo language as an example. His work supports that of the Swiss psychologist Jean Piaget, who spent decades studying and documenting the learning processes of young children. Piaget believed that students excel by actively building and constructing for themselves the specific knowledge they need, rather than having a teacher dictate numerous facts. Therefore I would suggest that ICT lessons which are largely skills-based are unlikely to meet the subject specific learning objectives.

Visit **www.futurelab.org.uk/research/lit_reviews.htm** for further reading.

First steps

Knowing where to start developing your own ICT capability depends very much on your own situation but personal access to modern ICT is crucial. Explore the facilities in your own institution and visit the professional development area of Teachernet at **www.teachernet. gov.uk/wholeschool/ictis/cpd/**

For those working towards Qualified Teacher Status, you will need to demonstrate:

- that you know how to use ICT effectively in teaching the subject for which you are qualifying to teach, and to support your wider professional role;
- that you are able to teach the cross-curricular elements of the National Strategy;
- that you use ICT effectively in your teaching for learners to develop ICT capability including opportunities for e-learning.

The evidence for these competencies will come from a range of sources such as your teaching file or classroom resources. Keeping a file of the practical tasks in this chapter which are relevant to you will be further evidence that you have met the standards. The Professional Standards for the award of QTS do not specify a list of required ICT skills although there is an ICT skills test as part of gaining QTS – see **www.tda.gov.uk/skillstests/ practicematerials/ict.aspx**

As a simple base line you should ask yourself if you can:

- **word-process;**
- **use a spreadsheet for simple calculations and graphing;**
- **use a database;**
- **communicate effectively using ICT;**
- **use the internet.**

The following sites are a useful starting point for your own professional development.

- www.brighton.ac.uk/sms/ **tutorials for the main Microsoft Office applications.**
- www.netskills.ac.uk/onlinecourses/tonic **is an online tutorial for use of the internet.**

PRACTICAL TASK PRACTICAL TASK PRACTICAL TASK PRACTICAL TASK PRACTICAL TASK

Produce and use a template for lesson planning using a word processor. Email a copy as an attachment to a colleague. Visit the Teaching and Learning section of Teachernet at **www.teachernet.gov.uk/ teachingandlearning**/. Look for examples of lesson plans in your own subject area which use ICT for teaching and learning.

When is it appropriate to use ICT?

A word of warning. One of the biggest mistakes made using ICT is when its use does not support the learning, the presumption being that just because the students are using ICT its use is appropriate. It is also easy to fall into the trap of using ICT as, for example, a reward for good behaviour, 'I'll let you go onto the internet if you finish your work', or awarding higher attainment for work that has been produced using ICT when the content is weak.

IN THE CLASSROOM

A student was asked to word-process a handwritten essay so that the teacher could use it for display.

Comment – A word-processor should have been used to allow for amending and refining during the drafting stage, and additional features such as thesaurus and spell checker would have made the use of ICT an integral part of the learning.

A group of Year 10 business studies students were researching on the internet for their coursework and were given a worksheet to write their results on.

Comment – The students should have been copying and pasting information as they found it into a word-processing package so that they could use it using ICT in subsequent activities, thus learning to share, exchange and present information in a variety of contexts. An extension to the learning could have been a discussion on the implications of copying information from web-based sources and plagiarism.

It should also be noted here that as part of the *Every Child Matters* agenda for staying safe, all use of the internet should be carefully monitored and pupils made aware of online safety. See **www.safekids.com/kidsrules.htm** for easy-to-understand rules for pupils and **www.kidsmart.org.uk/** for guidance and resources.

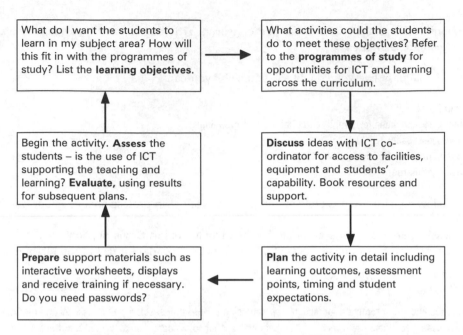

Figure 10.1: The planning process for an ICT activity

From Figure 10.1 it can be seen that at the planning stage the learning objectives need to be addressed in the activities, so that they can then be demonstrated in the learning outcomes.

Building on the ICT strand of the National Strategy, in 2004 ICT across the curriculum (ICTAC) was launched as a major initiative with support materials for all subjects. The focus is on developing ICT capability, described as:

> the technical and cognitive proficiency to access, use, develop, create and communicate information appropriately, using ICT tools. Learners demonstrate this capability by applying technology purposefully to solve problems, analyse and exchange information, develop ideas, create models and control devices. They are discriminating in their use of information and ICT tools, and systematic in reviewing and evaluating the contribution that ICT can make to their work as it progresses.
>
> (DfES 2004, p. 7)

The support packs demonstrate that teachers are not expected to teach ICT as a subject; rather they are to support the strands of the ICT National Curriculum programmes of study, as appropriate for their subject. Visit the ICTAC website at: **www.standards.dfes.gov.uk/ keystage3/respub/ictac**

If we look at the distinctive features of ICT we can then begin to unpack the contribution that information technology can offer within the learning environment.

The four main features are:

- **provisionality;**
- **speed and automatic functions;**
- **capacity and range;**
- **interactivity.**

Provisionality

Work can be revised easily with ICT. For students working to extend their literacy skills or prepare a presentation this is an important feature. Word-processors can be 'thought processors' allowing ideas to be revised without the chore of a total rewrite. A number of applications can take the tedium out of traditional methods of working and open up opportunities for higher-order thinking skills and interpretation. Art and music software, for example, encourages experimentation without the fear of losing what has already been created.

IN THE CLASSROOM

A Year 8 history class was set the challenge of producing a newspaper front page with the start of World War One as its lead story. Initial research was done using a variety of sources (not all IT-based) and a class discussion was held in order for them to highlight the main issues. They worked in groups of about four students with each child initially as a journalist word-processing their own article and then taking on different roles such as editor. They were encouraged to use features such as double line spacing, thesaurus and spell checker for drafting, and writing frames were used to structure their arguments. The completed articles were imported into a desktop publishing package where images, graphics, etc were added with audience in mind.
www.warwick.ac.uk/staff/D.J.Wray/Ideas/frames.html

PRACTICAL TASK PRACTICAL TASK PRACTICAL TASK PRACTICAL TASK PRACTICAL TASK

Find an article or section of text that you want to use with your students. Consider how the use of formatting could make the text accessible for all students.

For example:

- **change the font to one such as *Comic Sans* – you will notice in the example that the 'a' is cursive (how students write it) and for many it is easier to read than usual print;**
- **altering font colour and size;**
- **use 'find and replace' for words which some may find difficult to understand;**
- **embolden key words.**

NB If the original text is in a book, try using a scanner which can read text and import this into a word-processing package. If it is web based, use copy and paste.

Speed and automatic functions

Collecting large amounts of data and processing it rapidly are tasks that computers are very good at. The graph-plotting capability of spreadsheets allows students to examine quickly a number of ways of displaying data, allowing them to look for patterns without having to re-plot the data manually. Graphics and computer aided design (CAD) packages engage students with design concepts. Their ideas can be developed quickly, modelling solutions and producing sophisticated outcomes. Data logging, for example using electronic sensors, allows for higher order thinking skills as students can progress into analysis of the data rather than being involved in the tedium of collecting it. Automatic control systems can be created from a range of electronic sensors and output devices such as motors, lights and loudspeakers. As with data logging this gives immediate feedback as changes can be observed as they happen. Sense and control functions often feature strongly in design and technology, and music, but I would like to contest the notion of one area of ICT 'belonging' to a particular subject. For example, a short input on how information is processed at a supermarket checkout with credit cards and 'reward cards' as the focus would work very well in a citizenship curriculum, which is not usually associated with control technology. Students could discuss and reflect critically on the economic, legal and ethical issues associated with personal data being used to monitor shopping habits. (For further information on formatting text for accessibility see Chapter 12, p 146.)

PRACTICAL TASK PRACTICAL TASK PRACTICAL TASK PRACTICAL TASK PRACTICAL TASK

Set up a spreadsheet for one or more of the classes that you teach to monitor their performance. Input test results, levels and any other data you have on the students. Use the functionality of the program to perform tasks such exam percentages, searching for students at a particular level using graphing to compare data to predict results. Most secondary schools in England use a database called SIMS (School Information Management System); ask the SIMS manager if you can access historical data such as end of key stage results and Cognitive Ability Testing for your students. Visit **www.nfer-nelson.co.uk** to find more information on how you could use this data.

IN THE CLASSROOM

A physical education department used fitness data (bleep tests) on their students to allow them to monitor their own progress over a key stage. Students entered the data into a database and analysed their own results using increasingly complex queries. Identities were kept anonymous on the charts for the whole year group. Students began to take an increased interest in their own performance as they could watch it improve over time.

Modelling (answering the question 'what if?') is a difficult concept for students, especially as the examples used are often too difficult for the students to engage with. Making the example tangible (as in the next story) allows the students to visualise the possibilities and discuss the issues (for example, why people would want a low fat sandwich). Use of an interactive whiteboard for whole class or small group teaching can similarly engage students with the learning. Allowing students to physically touch the board, and encouraging them to hypothesise and evaluate as changes happen, concurs with the constructivist model of teaching. See **www.mirandanet.ac.uk/pubs/smartboard.htm** Visit the National Whiteboard Network for online guidance at **www.nwnet.org.uk/pages/software_guidance /interactive_whiteboards.html**

IN THE CLASSROOM

A Year 8 design and technology project used a failing sandwich company as a focus for a range of problem-solving tasks. The students were faced with the scenario of a sandwich company whose best-selling line – cheese sandwiches – were not selling as they should. This was a substantial project, part of which entailed looking at how food products are researched and developed. They weighed the ingredients for their sandwich using accurate electronic scales and then modelled the nutritional analysis of their 'new' sandwich looking at the marketing possibilities (e.g. low fat) and implications for cost of production and the final label. The worksheet in Figure 10.2 supported the latter part of the activity.

Modelling the nutritional analysis of your sandwich

	Cheddar Cheese	White Bread	Butter	
Weight in grams	24.5	55	10	
Protein per 100g	26	7.8	0.5	Amounts per
Carbohydrate per 100g	0	50	0	100g found in
Kcal per 100g	400	230	750	food tables
Fat per 100g	34	1.7	82	
Protein per weight used	6.37	4.29	0.05	Formulae used
Carbohydrate per weight used	0	27.5	0	to calculate amounts
Kcal per weight used	98	126.5	75	
Fat per weight used	8.33	0.935	8.2	

NUTRITIONAL ANALYSIS OF THE
SANDWICH

PROTEIN	10.71
CARBOHYDRATE	27.5
KCAL	299.5
FAT	17.465

Sum function used

Now you are ready to **model** - the example above has been modelled to produce an 'under 300 kcal' sandwich for someone on a calorie-controlled diet. You could try a different one e.g. reduced fat.

Extension - now that you have learned the skill of modelling on a spreadsheet to find the nutritional analysis, see if you can use the same method and sheet to work out the cost of production for your sandwich using the prices below.

Cheese - £5.26 per 1 kg   Butter - £0.57 per 250g   Bread - £0.25 per 250g

Can you suggest a retail price?

There are additional costs (labour, buildings, transport etc.) - £0.25 per sandwich that you must consider. What will your profit be?

All of you will manage to complete the first spreadsheet with formulae and **most** of you will be able to model e.g. an under 300 kcal and a reduced fat sandwich. **Some** of you will have successfully completed the extension task.

Figure 10.2: Worksheet for nutritional analysis of sandwich

Capacity and range

This feature is concerned with the diversity of ways in which information can be presented, the ability to communicate with people all over the world and the immediacy and availability of information which is up to date, sometimes to the minute, and can bring life to research into current issues better than traditional research methods.

IN THE CLASSROOM

A teacher of a Year 9 MFL class found a class of similar age students in France for her students to correspond with using email. The project began very well with the students writing half of their message in the target language and half in their own language. The theme of the first few letters tended to be all about themselves, but subsequent correspondence became difficult for both classes as they were struggling with vocabulary. The teachers realised that they had to work to common themes so that the students' correspondence was an extension activity of the learning taking place in the classroom. Other subject areas became interested to such an extent that it became a cross-curricular project with a focus on festivals and a celebration of cultural diversity. They looked at festivals that were common (such as Christmas and Easter) and those that were unique (for example, Guy Fawkes and the French Pepper Festival). Three more schools joined the project from Portugal, Germany and Slovakia.

The following are the types of activity that have subsequently taken place:

- recording songs in music;
- shared assembly on Europe Day – 9 May;
- exchanging recipes for use in food technology;
- videos of events;
- digital images of art work;
- a display created in each school, a 'Point Europe', regularly updated with information from all the partners.

Look at **www.epals.com/** to find partners for your students.

The feature of capacity and range can work against a teacher if the lesson isn't well planned. Students can lose valuable time, for example, by scrolling through a clip art gallery rather than doing a focused search or surfing for information from the internet in an understandable format. One of the features of Microsoft Word is that when the 'enter' key is pressed at the end of a web address it becomes a live link (it changes to blue, is underlined and when the cursor points at it there is the familiar 'pointing hand' denoting a link). Therefore interactive worksheets can be easily produced which students can use 'live' to links which have already been checked for suitability. This is not to say that students should never be offered the opportunity to do a 'free search'. The use of 'key words' and Boolean logic to refine a search on a CD-ROM or in a search engine is an important concept for students to engage with and is relevant to all subject areas. However, we would never offer students the entire works of *Encyclopaedia Britannica* or a vast library to search for information without some guidance and it is the same when using computer-based research.

Interactivity

The interactive way in which information can be processed and presented enables teacher and students to explore prepared or constructed models and simulations. They can search for and compare information from other sources, presenting it in a variety of different ways, using a range of technologies thus making it accessible for different audiences. Interactivity actually encompasses many of the other features of ICT, pushing the boundaries of what is possible with the use of technology. The audience and the author are almost indistinguishable as the roles become blurred. Examples can be found particularly in multimedia work and web authoring. The integration of text, graphics, sound, video and hyperlinks allow for the reader to take 'excursions' into the narrative, exploring, researching, exchanging information and learning as they do so.

Visit the Hackney's Highwire City Learning Centre at **www.highwire.org.uk**

IN THE CLASSROOM

A group of Year 7 students and staff went away for an enrichment week of cross-curricular activities. Each day the students took digital photographs of their experiences and in the evening they word-processed a diary of events. The images and text were then placed on the school website, not only as a record to refer to later but also for family and friends to see what they were up to. The site allowed interaction with those at home by sending messages, which were checked and then read to the whole group in the evenings.

Kettlethorpe High School, Wakefield: **www.kettworks.com/**

REFLECTIVE TASK

Building on the vision of our changing schools, as outlined in *Transforming the Way We Learn* (DfES 2002), and growth in internet access from home, school, public libraries and community centres, many activities can now be continued or developed outside normal school hours. In addition, an increasing number of schools have developed their own virtual learning environment such as **http://moodle.org/** to use e-learning, to extend discussions, exchange ideas, enhance group work, post support material, use blogs, create wikis and allow students to submit work. Explore the Moodle site for examples of what others in the profession are doing and consider the implications for your own practice.

The contribution ICT can make to SEN students and inclusion

Various references have already been made to how ICT can be used to support SEN students but as this is such a huge topic it cannot be dealt with adequately in this chapter. Guidance for specific needs can be found at the Becta website, **www.becta.org.uk/**, which provides strategic techniques to help with particular difficulties. There is no doubt, however, of the contribution that ICT can make to inclusion. Portable writing aids, communication aids and devices, portable computers, screen magnification software, and appropriate keyboard alternatives can help to support inclusive practice. (For further information on supporting SEN students, see Chapter 12.)

www.nagcbritain.org.uk/index.html – the National Association for Gifted Children.

www.nasen.org.uk/ – the National Association for Special Educational Needs.

Access

Sufficient access to appropriate and up-to-date ICT for any student is of course an issue for all students. The *ImpaCT2* report (Becta 2002) reassuringly confirms that connectivity is reaching government targets, with all secondary schools having internet access. However, it also demonstrates a strong relationship between access to the internet at home and socio-economic status, with those advantaged students spending four times longer using ICT at home compared with at school. An ICT activity doesn't mean that all of the students need to be sitting in a computer suite interacting with a monitor; in fact this is often a sign of poor practice if this is all that occurs. However, it does mean that all of the students need to have sufficient time to achieve the learning objectives and this does entail careful planning, keeping abreast of new technologies and not being afraid to have a number of activities happening in the classroom at one time. Remember that e-learning can include the use of mobile technologies such as phones, PDAs and MP3 players. You could stimulate active use of them, such as encouraging pupils to download the BBC breakfast TV daily video podcast (**news.bbc.co.uk/1/programmes/breakfast/**).

Assessment

The curriculum model of ICT in schools can vary from ICT being taught as a discrete subject to being totally subject-integrated. Whatever your model there will be a member of staff who has responsibility for the co-ordination of ICT within the curriculum as well as assessment. However, teachers are often asked to assess students' work for both their own subject area and for ICT. The National Curriculum in Action website at **www.ncaction. org.uk/subjects/ ict/index.htm** uses students' work and case study material to show what the National Curriculum in ICT looks like in practice. The examples given show:

- **the standard of students' work at different ages and key stages;**
- **how the programmes of study translate into real activities.**

PRACTICAL TASK PRACTICAL TASK PRACTICAL TASK PRACTICAL TASK PRACTICAL TASK

Using students' work from an ICT activity that you have planned, assess the work for your own subject area then look at the work again for its use of ICT. Select what you would consider to be high, middle and low achieving pieces of work and discuss these with the ICT co-ordinator in your school. How did the levels of attainment compare with:

- **the levels in your own subject area;**
- **the Key Stage 3 strategy target levels?**

Were there any other issues that the discussion raised such as suitability of the task, gender bias and access to technology?

ICT for professional purposes

You will notice that a large number of the websites suggested in this chapter include discussion forums for teachers to exchange and share ideas with other professionals. Join one of these forums, read what your new colleagues are doing and be adventurous in your own teaching. Listen to your students: what are they doing with new technologies? Remember that ICT isn't just about working with computers.

A SUMMARY OF **KEY POINTS**

- > **There is no substitute for good teaching. It is crucial that you always question whether the planned activity supports the learning objectives for the lesson.**
- > **Never underestimate the ICT capability of students.**
- > **Plan lessons to maximise the use of ICT so that time is not wasted, for example with trouble-shooting equipment, unnecessary searching for sites or formatting without a purpose.**
- > **Develop strategies for linking home, school and the outside world.**
- > **Do not be complacent about your own capability, take advantage of any training that is offered and keep abreast of new technologies.**

Moving on

The ever-changing world of ICT inevitably means that keeping abreast of current changes is a constant challenge. However confident you are with your use of ICT to support teaching and learning, you may like to take one subject-specific innovation and investigate its impact, for example on creativity or gender basis.

FURTHER READING FURTHER READING **FURTHER READING** FURTHER READING

www.becta.org.uk The British Educational Communications and Technology Agency provides information, advice and dialogue relating to ICT in education, and is an excellent resource for research plus links to other affiliated sites.

www.nc.uk.net/ The government's definitive curriculum site for teachers. It contains not only the National Curriculum but also a wealth of support material especially in support of recent initiatives, plus downloadable files and links.

www.tes.co.uk A monthly insert in the *Times Educational Supplement* called Online contains useful classroom ideas, book reviews and ICT news.

For further information on teaching ICT across the curriculum, visit **www.learning matters.co.uk/education/learnteach/chaptl0.html**

Chapter glossary

Boolean logic The internet is a vast computer database and its contents must be searched according to the rules of computer database-searching. Much database-searching is based on the principles of Boolean logic. When using internet search engines (the most common method of searching), the user is often unaware that this is happening but can be disappointed with the search results. Constructing a logical search using 'or, and, not' (or +, -, = signs) with the search words can refine the search and make the 'hits' much more successful. Visit the following two sites for further information: **www.education-world.com/a_tech/ tech001.htm** and **http://computer.howstuffworks.com/boolean.htm**

Capability ICT capability is characterised by an ability to use effectively IT tools and information sources to investigate and research, develop ideas, communicate, analyse and evaluate. It is not concerned with the acquisition of skills but the teaching of these skills may form part of the learning process towards capability. See also Allen *et al.* (2000, p. 2).

ICT IT is to ICT as literacy is to books, journals or screen displays. The focus of IT is on students' capability with ICT. For this reason IT is the title used for the National Curriculum subject qualifications.

Key skills The six key skill areas which are embedded in the structure of the National Curriculum – communication, application of number, information technology, working with others, improving own learning and performance, and problem-solving.

Logo A programming language plus a philosophy of education developed in the 1960s by Seymour Papert. It was designed as a tool for learning and its features – modularity, extensibility, interactivity, and flexibility – follow from this goal.

11
The 14–19 curriculum: aims and values
Richard Pring

The developing 14–19 phase

There is some arbitrariness in any division of education and training into separate phases, not least that of 14–19. But such a phase is now assumed in government policy both in England and Wales. Indeed, developments post-14 would seem to justify this. It is the end of Key Stage 3. Young people start preparing for their GCSE examinations. Choices are made about subjects. Those choices determine what subsequent courses and employment they might follow. Certain National Curriculum subjects can be discontinued – modern languages and the humanities. Career guidance commences. Work experience becomes a requirement. And for those who are deemed to need a more practical and vocationally oriented learning experience, opportunities are now available for 14- to 16-year-olds to take part of their studies in colleges of further education.

Furthermore, although school is compulsory only to the age of 16, a large majority remain in some form of education and training beyond that. And it is government policy that all young people should remain in education or training until 18 or 19, and that 50 per cent should continue into higher education.

Therefore, there are major developments which are having a profound effect upon the educational and training arrangements for all 14- to 19-year-olds. These include:

- **development of specialised diplomas, with a vocational orientation, which, from 2008 onwards, can be taken instead of more traditional 'academic' subjects;**

- compulsory work experience for all 14- to 16-year-olds;
- opportunity for young people on more practical courses to undertake part of their studies in colleges of further education where there are the facilities and expertise;
- 'entitlement' of all young people to pursue the full range of 'academic' and 'vocational' subjects;
- corollary 'entitlement' to discontinue what were compulsory subjects in order to pursue what they are entitled to;
- establishment of local arrangements between schools, colleges and private training providers to ensure that this entitlement is available.

These developments are quite revolutionary. They undermine the autonomy of schools as they enter into partnership with other providers of education and training. They put demands upon the careers advice and the counselling which all young people need in order to make appropriate choices. They require teaching expertise and skills which are not generally available within the profession. They require, especially with the new Diplomas, major staff development. They necessitate a different 'framework of qualifications', as new courses are developed, new modes of assessment created and new progression routes into further education, training and employment established.

In anticipation of these developments, a working group under the chairmanship of Michael Tomlinson produced a Report in 2004, *14–19 Curriculum and Qualifications Reform*, which tried to produce a unified system of qualifications. This, to the almost universal dismay of teachers, universities and employers, was not accepted by the government. Instead, the government proposed what in effect is a divided system post-14, namely, the traditional 'academic' route for some and a more practical, 'vocational' route for others through specialised diplomas. Although the word 'vocational' is used less and less in official documents about the diplomas, each of the 15 new diplomas will have a vocational orientation. The first five will be ready in 2008; the others come on line in 2009 and 2010.

Educational aims

The 2005 DfES White Paper *14–19 Education and Skills* briefly set out educational aims in terms of helping all young people to realise their potential, part of which will be to give greater 'stretch' to the more able (stretching is emphasised over 60 times in the White Paper). That, and an enormous number of other government papers, also emphasise the need to make young people more employable both for their personal sakes and for the sake of society. Such an aim is, of course, crucially important, but employability must be tempered by broader humanistic considerations. And talk of realising potential is unhelpful – there is as much potential for bad as there is for good. Indeed, despite the radical changes envisaged for education and training, little attention has been given to the aims of education and the values which should shape that system.

However, to educate is to teach and nurture those qualities and understandings which are judged to enrich life and to foster a distinctively human form of life. For example, the government, in setting the standards and content of a National Curriculum, in determining which subjects are compulsory, in requiring certain forms of assessment, in prioritising certain modes of learning, in requiring work experience, is implicitly shaping what is judged to be an educated person. Economic usefulness is one aspect of that human flourishing, but only one, and its value has to be seen within a broader moral context.

Therefore, the Nuffield Review (a three year, independent review of 14–19 education and training in England and Wales) started with the question:

What counts as an educated 19 year old in this day and age?

REFLECTIVE TASK

REFLECTIVE TASK

Consider this question yourselves. How would you characterise an educated 19-year-old today? What are the contemporary demands placed upon young people by society (including employment and higher education)?

In defining an 'educated 19-year-old', what *educational* values should prevail? 'Intellectual excellence' (traditionally excluding the majority of young people, but remaining a yardstick against which a majority is still assessed as ill-educated)? Practical usefulness (emphasising capability and economic usefulness, but relegating in status the intellectual virtues and aesthetic qualities once cherished)? Character formation (possibly embracing new definitions of citizenship)?

Those who doubt the significance of these questions might be referred to the diminishing importance of the humanities and the arts in the idea of a general education post-14, not only in the newly developed diplomas, as learning is increasingly geared to economic usefulness ('realising our potential' through the acquisition of the skills needed for a highly competitive economy). The arts and the humanities fit uncomfortably in the division of courses into academic and vocational. On the other hand, practical learning no longer plays a significant part in the prevailing idea of general education, as standards are increasingly defined in terms of written accounts even when those standards concern practical activities. Under the cover of a 'new language', education and training are being redefined. Different aims and values are being promoted. A different conception of human flourishing is presupposed. The essentially moral language of education (concerned with human fulfilment and personal development) has been trumped by other forms of discourse derived from other areas of public life. That language is increasingly one of *curriculum delivery* rather than of teaching, of *inputs related to outputs* rather than of the struggle to understand, of *efficiency gains* rather than of changing pedagogy to meet more challenging teaching tasks, of *audits* rather than of professional judgement, of *performance indicators* rather than of the standards internal to the activity, of *economic relevance* rather than of human fulfilment, of *clients and customers* rather than of apprentices to a form of life and a way of thinking.

It is difficult to deliberate about the aims of 14–19 education when the very language of morality has been subverted by the language of business management. In resolving this set of difficulties, one needs to address two major considerations.

The first lies in some view of what it means to be fully or distinctively human. Bruner (1966), in his pioneering social studies course, *Man: a Course of Study*, identified three questions which should shape the curriculum, namely, 'What is it that makes us human?', 'How did we become so?', and 'How can we become more so?' Education would seem to be about the development – whether through character formation, practical capability or increased understanding – of those qualities which make us distinctively human.

The second major consideration lies in the social context in which we nurture the growing humanity of young people. To flourish requires living within a particular community and making a contribution to it. Hence, the qualities, knowledge and skills need to be relevant to living within and contributing to that community – the capacity to appreciate the problems which beset it, the skills which enable one to prosper within it, the knowledge which empowers one to challenge those in authority, the moral qualities which help develop a fairer and more inclusive society.

21st-century curriculum

The Nuffield Review (2004), having raised these concerns, issued a four-page document which suggests what should constitute a '21st-century curriculum', embodying the learning achievements which might arise from the distinctively human qualities of all young people irrespective of their different talents, abilities and backgrounds. These might be summarised as follows.

1 The pursuit of excellence
Excellence refers to the attainment of standards. Those standards are defined in relation to the purpose of the activity – which could be in intellectual pursuits, art, sports, project management, making artefacts, etc. There is a need to include a wider range of standards by which young people might get a sense of achievement and be seen to excel.

2 Knowledge and understanding
Education is associated with the initiation into those forms of knowledge or understanding through which we make sense of the physical, social and moral worlds we inhabit – and which are systematically introduced through various subjects. Such initiation can be at different levels.

3 Moral responsibility
All young people have the potential to be responsible about how they conduct their lives, form relationships, decide upon future employment, treat the environment, etc. Such responsibility operates within a context of virtues which need to be nurtured. It is important, therefore, to see schools and colleges as moral, not just learning, communities.

4 Practical capability
A liberal tradition of education has too often ignored the world of practice – the world of industry, of commerce, of earning a living, of practical usefulness. There has been a disdain for the practical intelligence – indeed, for the technological and the useful.

5 Appreciation of big issues which affect all (e.g. environmental change)
The critics of a general education based almost exclusively on subjects point to the way in which the 'big issues' get squeezed out. For example, environmental change and racism are 'big issues' which should be addressed in the education of all young people 14–19. But the 'big issues' cannot avoid ethical questions and the adoption of a moral stance.

6 Basic and wider skills
Essential to everything are 'basic skills' – competence in reading, writing, listening and communicating. Added to those must now be competence in ICT. Also there is now an acknowledgement of the 'wider key skills' concerned with interpersonal relations and the organisation of one's own life and future.

7 Ideals which inspire

To educate is to open up what is humanly possible, and thereby to inspire and to enable young people to extend themselves beyond the immediate and the mediocre. In so many ways (through literature and drama, through example and narrative) they can be exposed to ideals which they find worth pursuing, and enable them to persevere when life gets tough.

8 Economic viability

A main thrust of educational policy has been to ensure that young people acquire the qualities, skills and knowledge required to meet the needs of the country and of their own economic viability. Such development is open to all at different levels and in different modes, responsive to the changing economic face of the regions in which they live.

9 Social responsibility

The current interest in citizenship, following the Crick Report (1998), emphasises the positive part young people should play in creating and sustaining a healthy society. But that part requires active participation, meeting practical challenges and engagement with the community. Citizenship as an educational aim demands attention to the school as a community.

To summarise: reform of 14–19 needs to raise questions about the qualities, skills and knowledge which are to be nurtured, if all young people are to have a fulfilling life. That requires a curriculum and a form of life in the school or college or training provider which is wider than an initiation into the traditional subjects (although not rejecting them either) and that no longer thinks in terms of academic or vocational. Rather it would include:

- **the opportunity for all young people to excel in some way;**
- **the knowledge and understanding essential for intelligent living, with the possibility of progressing to more specialised studies;**
- **moral commitment and responsibility;**
- **practical capability;**
- **appreciation of big issues which affect us all;**
- **basic skill;**
- **ideals which inspire;**
- **economic relevance;**
- **social responsibility and citizenship.**

Inclusion

Fundamental to government policy (and to the principles of the 21st-century curriculum outlined above) is that these educational ideals should apply to all young people, irrespective of ability, social background or religion. But any policy and practice aimed at greater inclusion must recognise the social reality of classrooms and the wider society in which young people live. Broader questions about 'adolescent well-being', which impinge upon the aspirations and behaviour of young people and which cannot be ignored in any arrangement for their education and training, are currently being explored by the Nuffield Foundation (2004). Evidence gathered by the Institute of Psychiatry (see Meltzer and Gatwood 2000) on time trends in adolescent mental health indicated that the mental health of adolescents in the UK declined over the previous 25 years. Meanwhile, a UK enquiry was launched in 2004 to investigate rising levels of self-harm among young people – further evidence that many young people are finding it increasingly difficult to cope with the demands of everyday living.

This negative aspect of the social context affects profoundly how teachers see their role and find difficulty in carrying it out. They speak continually of the rising violence and indiscipline. In 2003/4, there were 10,000 permanent exclusions from schools, and over 200,000 who had one or more fixed periods of exclusion (MacBeath 2006). A large proportion of those permanently excluded is lost from the system and has a strong likelihood of subsequent imprisonment. Of the rising prison population, 18,000 are aged 20 or below, and seven tenths of these were reconvicted. The proportion of pupils in referral units rose by 25 per cent between 2001 and 2003 (Ofsted 2004, quoted in MacBeath).

Any development of the 14–19 system must take this dimension into account – in particular, the implication for the diversity of provision (including the use of voluntary bodies and the youth service), the resourcing of those with special needs, the training of and support for teachers, the more personalised organisation of learning, and the criteria of accountability. As the MacBeath Report says:

> As schools widen their intake and as teachers meet more disturbed and damaged children the need for pastoral care increases commensurately. This becomes particularly acute in disadvantaged communities where the issues are compounded by poverty, violent communities and turbulent domestic circumstances.
>
> (p.25)

Elsewhere the Report says:

> Practitioners in particular, conceived the educational system to be too inflexible to accommodate a broad range of needs, governed by the demands of the National Curriculum, by high stakes testing, parental choice and the strictures of Ofsted. All of these constrained any radical departure from the 'official' programme of study and its preferred pedagogy, based largely on whole class instruction.
>
> (p12)

Across a number of indicators, young disabled people experience poorer outcomes: namely, membership of NEET (Not in Employment Education or Training) 27 per cent of the 16–19 year olds with disabilities are in NEET, compared with 9 per cent of the non-disabled (Haines 2006); 21 per cent aged 16–19 having no qualifications; and much less likely to proceed to higher education.

The idea of an educated 19-year-old, as that has been argued for, embraces those with special educational needs and those with disabilities. At the same time, those same aims need to be reconceptualised to reflect the progress and achievement of young people, who, for whatever reason, are not able to progress as far or as quickly as other young people in some aspects of their learning. Alternative approaches to learning should 'embody greater opportunities for them to participate fully in society as adults'. That is, however, not always easy, for as Haines says, citing Miller *et al*. (2005):

> The standards agenda depends too much on measures of success defined by summative assessment and external verification. The effect is that there is less incentive to differentiate the curriculum and use formative assessment that can benefit young disabled people's learning.

Implications for 14–19 provision

Learning and curriculum

In the light of a defensible answer to the question 'What counts as an educated 19-year-old?', five aspects of 14–19 organisation of learning require attention.

Listening to the learner's voice

In improving learning, one needs to attend to 'the learner's voice'. Rudduck's (2005) work is concerned with the responsiveness to the student voice in the teaching itself, partly (if not mainly) because the articulation of ideas or of problems is crucial in the development of understanding. The very best work in the humanities has always understood this. Drama lessons, *par excellence*, enabled young people to articulate their feelings and understandings of human relations and predicaments. The Humanities Curriculum Project put discussion, informed and challenged by evidence, at the centre of the learning experience (Stenhouse 1975), as indeed did many projects. It is generally felt that the scope for discussion has diminished under the pressure to cover content related to the ever more detailed targets measured by tests. A lively tradition of oral work in the classroom, reflected in Chapter 10 of the Bullock Report (1975) and once an integral part of the examination of young people, is now almost forgotten.

More radical, however, is the example of the voice of the young person *becoming the curriculum* – not just an aid to the learning of someone else's curriculum. This is by no means an alien concept in youth work, where so often those who have opted out of school, or have been excluded from it, find a place where their voice is taken seriously and where a better understanding of the world in which they live is made sense of (Davies 2005).

Practical and experiential learning

The antithesis between 'academic studies' on the one hand and, on the other, practical and experiential learning (wrongly confused with 'vocational') is deeply embedded in our culture. Yet the central importance of hands-on learning and learning from experience is reflected in the *14–19 Education and Skills* White Paper. It is reflected, too, in a wide range of innovative practices, both past and present. The Technical and Vocational Education Initiative (TVEI), launched in 1983, integrated theory and practice through making and designing which transformed the experience of learning for many young people across the ability range (see Dale 1990), but it ended with the National Curriculum and with a regime of accountability which put much more focus upon writing than upon 'doing'. The more recent emphasis upon practical modes of learning is usually associated with the less able and the disengaged, which does a disservice to a way of knowing which benefits all young people.

Potential of information technology

Frequent reference is made in the evidence to the benefits (some say revolutionary benefits) of advances in information technology – the use of the internet as sources of information and the communication made possible by email.

Wider key skills and qualities

ASDAN is a non-profit-making examination board, whose qualifications are recognised for funding purposes by the DfES. Its new Certificate for Personal Effectiveness, Level 2, is seen as equivalent to one GCSE graded A-C. It is now taken in over 100,000 centres by over 20,000 young people 14–19, and illustrates the ways in which, first, a range of key skills, seen to be essential for success in employment, in higher education and in citizenship, can be taught and assessed without distorting the skills and qualities themselves, and, second, how the system of awards can accommodate a radical and student-centred innovation (**www.asdan.org.uk**).

Subjects

The idea of a subject as a 'building block' in the curriculum is contentious. Certain core subjects are seen traditionally to be the basis of a more 'academic curriculum', whereas many, who are concerned about the 'relevance' of the curriculum and the need to engage more young people in learning, argue for a curriculum more based on practical activities or on work-related experience. But this should not be seen as an 'either-or' debate, and subjects at their best represent ways of enquiring into, and of understanding, the world which have withstood critical scrutiny and the test of time. They, therefore, provide the resources upon which teachers and learners need to draw.

However, the subjects themselves, and the selection of material within each, need to be justified in terms of how they contribute to the aim of education spelt out above – and for all young people, not just the intellectual elite. For example, the humanities (history, drama, geography, literature, etc.) do particularly address the human story – what, in the words of Bruner, makes us human, how we became so and how we might become more so. That is why they should remain central to the educational experience of all young people.

Assessment and qualifications

According to the Tomlinson Report (2004), students are overburdened. They are currently expected to sit for over 100 public exams, around 40 in the last three years. This clearly affects the nature and the quality of learning, since much of the assessment is 'high stakes' both for learners (in terms of selection for post-16 provision, choice of courses, and employment) and for providers (in terms of league table places, recruitment and funding).

There is a need to rehearse the different purposes of assessment, and in the light of those purposes, to see, first, what is necessary and, second, what assessments need to be in the public domain, thereby 'raising the stakes'. The following are the main purposes:

- 'assessment for learning' (see Black and Wiliam, 2005) through giving accurate feedback to the learner;
- diagnosis of learning difficulties;
- statement of national standards (which contribute to but are not the same as support for learning);
- account of a student's achievement at the end of a stage in education;
- selection of students for particular purposes (e.g. university entrance);
- accountability of the various providers and of the system as a whole.

One major difficulty in the present overburdening and highly expensive system lies in the confusion of these purposes and the use of instruments of assessment which, though appropriate for some purposes, are inappropriate for others – often with considerable financial and personal costs.

Hence, the national examinations normally taken at 16, 17 and 18 unsuccessfully try to combine the different functions of *setting standards* (disputed by professional and academic experts within the respective areas), *giving an account of individual and institutional attainment* (but thereby narrowing what is to count as personal and institutional achievement), and *discriminating between students for selection purposes* (in which they are deemed to have failed by universities themselves). What they in fact do are: first, set, in increasingly detailed way, what teachers must teach irrespective of their professional judgement; second, give a 'certificate of failure' to the many young people who otherwise might continue with their formal learning. They fail to provide 'assessment for learning', to motivate the disengaged to remain in education or to give the kind of information which helps universities and employers to select.

The way forward would be, first, separating 'assessment for learning' from 'assessment for accountability'; second, relying more on moderated teacher assessment (see Mortimore 2006); third, reconsidering of the continuation of public examinations for all (GCSEs) at 16; fourth, restoring relations between external assessment and curriculum development; fifth, finding ways of differentiating the most able for purposes of selection, thereby eliminating the proliferation of expensive tests now being created by separate universities.

Teachers

The pamphlet *Curriculum for the 21st century* referred to (Nuffield Review 2004) emphasised the need to see the teacher as a curriculum developer, not just as a curriculum deliverer. It is important to see the teacher as one who is immersed in that which he or she has to teach, for it is not just the facts or formulae which have to be 'transmitted' but a love of that which has to be learnt. And that applies as much to the practical and the vocational activities as it does to the traditional subjects.

Good history teachers have a deep grasp of the historical issues; they have learnt to think and to enquire in a distinctively historical mode; they believe in the importance of what is being taught. The learner is being introduced 'to a conversation between the generations' – to arguments and understandings, to distinctive ways of seeing the world, to a social tradition of critical enquiry which itself has a history. The teacher is trying to get the learner onto the inside of a way of thinking, indeed a form of life, to which he or she already belongs and is committed. At their best, professional associations, such as NATE (National Association for the Teaching of English) or the Geographical Association or the Historical Association help sustain this identity. The teacher is a mediator of the cultural understandings we have inherited to a new generation of learners.

This applies, too, to the teachers of so-called vocational subjects – to the teachers of joinery and construction, of hospitality and hairdressing. The learner is being introduced to an activity which has its standards of accuracy and relevance, and which the teacher believes to be important and seeks to impart through example and correction. There is a wider dimension (aesthetic and economic, moral and social) to vocational areas, with which the learner needs to be acquainted. To acquire the 'vocational skills' can be an educational experience where this more holistic dimension is conveyed.

However, the specialised diplomas raise problems about the preparation and qualifications of teachers. First, few qualified teachers in schools have the experience of the skills relevant to teaching the specific vocational content. Second, those people who do have such skills and experience (e.g. bricklayers, hairdressers, engineers) may not have the degree-level background to qualify as teachers. Third, those who teach these skills in further education

(FE) are not qualified to teach 14–16 in schools – and, indeed, may not want to. There are anomalies – inevitable in a rapidly changing system of education and training. Teachers qualified to teach in schools can teach in FE with no further training – their QTS carries an implicit ability to teach 'vocationally', whereas PCET (Past Compulsory Education and Training) lecturers can teach 14–16 in the colleges, but not in schools, even though many sent to college have 'challenging behaviour'. In addition, there is a shortage of qualified staff even in FE in some diploma areas (e.g. a major college closed a plumbing course because of shortage of staff).

PRACTICAL TASK PRACTICAL TASK PRACTICAL TASK PRACTICAL TASK PRACTICAL TASK

In your placement school, who has responsibility (in terms of overview) for 14–19 education? Talk to the person (or people) responsible about the changes in this phase and the school's development plans. Has the school started to think differently about the purposes of education and training at Key Stage 4 and above, for example?

Provision

There are intensive debates about the aims of learning and about the best ways to improve the learning experiences of everyone. This is made possible by a range of government policies and initiatives – for example, the encouragement, and now requirement, of 14–19 Partnerships (see Arnold 2006), the quite massive Building Schools for the Future Programme, the Networked Learning Communities, the development of Centres of Vocational Excellence, and many others. At the same time there are opportunities for new curriculum developments, especially in science and mathematics, arising out of the criticisms of major reports (see Smith Report 2004).

Indeed, it is difficult to reconcile the apparent tensions between, on the one hand, the apparent managerial language of accountability and of 'public service reform principles' (which exudes from government papers with their specific targets and high-stakes testing) and, on the other hand, the increasing freedom which schools and colleges, supported by government initiatives and by examination boards, seem to have to explore imaginatively different ways of addressing the learning needs of all young people.

Summary

Radical changes are affecting the 14–19 curriculum, approaches to learning, assessment, teaching and institutional provision. These changes are affected by underlying aims and values. There are differences of aim, reflecting different underlying philosophical views and values. At the same time, there is an increasing opportunity for schools, colleges and teachers to shape these changes. But that means going back constantly to the aims of education. What ought to be the 'educated product' of our educational and training system?

FURTHER READING FURTHER READING **FURTHER READING** FURTHER READING

Papers about the current reforms of 14–19 education and training – and details of events and conferences – are available at: **www.nuffield14-19review.org.uk/**

PART 4
PROFESSIONAL KNOWLEDGE: INCLUSION

12
Special Educational Needs
Geraldine A. Price

Professional Standards for QTS

Q1, Q3, Q6, Q10, Q12, Q18, Q19, Q20, Q21

To be awarded QTS you must have respect for the differences in learning and development experienced by students and seek to promote the self-esteem of those who find learning difficult. You need to be aware of the variety of ways in which support staff can be used to promote inclusion and must be able to demonstrate the ability to differentiate the curriculum effectively, drawing upon a developmental approach to enabling progression.

You may find it helpful to read through the appropriate section of the handbook that accompanies the Standards for the Award of QTS for clarification and support.

What is inclusion?

The Green Paper (DfEE 1997) entitled *Excellence for All Children: Meeting Special Educational Needs,* and the DfEE document *Meeting Special Educational Needs: A Programme of Action* (1998) embraced the principle of inclusion and set out in the educational arena the government's aim of social inclusion. The concept of inclusion is more than another word for integration. It embodies Human Rights and Equal Opportunities. Its general principles encompass:

- *Valuing diversity:* all students should be valued. This extends beyond a simplistic view of Special Educational Needs (SEN) and disability. It extends beyond the notion of geographical integration, which is concerned with where students with SEN are placed.
- *Entitlement:* all students are entitled to receive, with a suitable peer group, a broad, balanced and relevant curriculum.
- *Dignity:* all students, and their parents, are entitled to be treated with respect and have their views taken into account.
- *Individual needs:* inclusive practice should not create situations within which individual needs are left unmet.

An historical overview

Research, policy and practice in the education of students with SEN have moved through three broad stages since the turn of the twentieth century:

- segregation;
- integration;
- inclusion.

In a sense these stages embody philosophical, sociological and political thinking over the years. It is important, therefore, to understand what has gone before in order to grasp the principles of inclusive learning environments and to be sensitive to the underlying issues that inclusion embraces. A closer examination of how the terminology in this field has evolved demonstrates changes in attitude towards those with SEN.

Terms such as handicap, impairment and disability need clarification if we are to understand the evolution of Special Education.

- *Handicap* is defined by the Oxford English Dictionary as 'any encumbrance or disability that weighs upon effort and makes success more difficult'.
- *Impairment* is a characteristic, feature or attribute within the individual that is long-term and may be the result of disease, injury or congenital conditions.
- *Disability* is the loss or limitation of the ability to take part in normal life on an equal level with others. This disability may be 'a physical or mental impairment which has a substantial and long-term adverse effect on his ability to carry out day-to-day activities' (Disability Discrimination Act 1995).

At the heart of these definitions is the *inability* of the individual who is regarded as presenting problems for society.

Segregation

At the turn of the twentieth century, emphasis was placed upon a student's **handicap** to determine appropriate schooling. The education of students with handicaps was in the hands of the medical profession to a large extent. Categories of handicap and the educational placement of individuals relied upon the medical model of diagnosis and treatment. In the early twentieth century, educational placement was resolved by segregation, according to the individual's handicap. Early special schools were established for those with sensory handicaps, such as deafness and blindness.

The system of categorisation relied heavily upon the concept of defect.

> ... segregated classes and schools that were to be the repositories for all the varied kinds of students that could not fit into the regular class without creating problems for the system ...
>
> (Sarason and Doris 1979)

Some of the labels used at that time may appear bewildering and offensive today. Terms such 'deaf and dumb', 'deaf mute' and 'cripple' reflected prevailing attitudes to disability and impairment.

The debate still rages about the efficacy of special schooling. The predominantly medical model used for the segregation of students was placed under the spotlight. The educational value of special schooling came under fire. Major changes in the curriculum of mainstream schools have occurred, and the introduction of a National Curriculum, with its highly prescribed content, in a sense mitigated against the continuation of special schools. It was suggested that the curriculum in most ESN (Educationally Sub-Normal) special schools was a watered-down version of that provided in mainstream schools. Those who defended the special school system would point to the adaptation of the curriculum to meet the particular needs of the students. There is no doubt that the dedicated staff in these schools possessed specialist qualifications and were often the expert practitioners. However, special education went through a period of turmoil with a ground-swell of feeling that segregation of students needed to be scrutinised in terms of its educational value. New concepts of handicap were emerging which placed less emphasis upon the *individual* defect. More focus was given to the *educational environment*. This paved the way for integration.

Integration

The 1981 Education Act was a landmark in special education and the embodiment of new, radical thinking. The concept of **integration** was embraced. It was concerned with making mainstream schools 'special' and transposing the special education ethos into the mainstream setting. In retrospect, it was essentially about bringing SEN children into the mainstream setting and making physical adaptations to the buildings where necessary; differentiating the mainstream curriculum – to account for a continuum of needs (Warnock Report 1981). Integration, therefore, was embodied in the notion of 'bringing them (the students) into their premises but on the schools' terms' (Gross 2002, p.234).

The drive also came from a desire to ensure that all students, regardless of their SEN, should have the opportunity to participate in the wider context that the mainstream school provided and to be 'included' with their peers. Such moves towards integration spawned their own mechanisms for funding, which remain to some extent today.

Integration is regarded as a 'within-child' model. This implies that the difficulties lie within the student. This model aimed to ensure that students were able to fit into the educational system.

Inclusion

Inclusion embraces aspects of integration but goes beyond this. Inclusive learning and teaching environments will demonstrate flexibility and differentiated learning in order to respond to individual needs. In line with the principles set out in the SEN and Disability Act (SENDA) (DfES 2001, chapter 10) as a teacher, you will be expected to provide suitable learning challenges for *all* students, by planning effectively to overcome potential barriers to learning and by responding to diverse learning needs.

The term 'inclusion' takes the notion of integration one stage further, and is more to do with changing the educational system to suit the needs of students, rather than making sure that students can fit into the system.

> Inclusion implies a radical reform of the school in terms of curriculum, assessment, pedagogy and grouping of pupils. It is based on a value system that welcomes and celebrates diversity arising from gender, nationality, race, language or origin, social background, level of educational achievement or disability.
>
> (Mittler 2000, p. 10)

Every Child Matters

Every Child Matters (2003) set out the government's vision for procedures and frameworks for future provision of SEN children and students. Its intention was to bring together multi-disciplinary services and to reform children's services at local, regional and national levels. The government's Green Paper entitled *Removing Barriers to Achievement* (2004) built upon the 1997 Green Paper *Excellence for All Children*, and the resulting Programme of Action which followed in 1998. This set out the framework for procedures and was followed by SENDA (2001) and the new SEN Code of Practice.

Children's trusts

These trusts provide integrated services whereby Education, Health and Voluntary Services work in multidisciplinary teams. The aim is to bring about early intervention and to embed inclusive practices in every school.

Removing Barriers to Achievement

> All children have the right to a good education and the opportunity to fulfil their potential. All teachers should expect to teach children with special educational needs (SEN), and all schools should play their part in educating children from their local community.
>
> (DfES 2004:5)

Removing Barriers to Achievement was published in 2004 in response to concerns that many SEN students had to wait too long before their needs were met. There were growing concerns within the teaching profession that classroom teachers were ill-equipped to meet the needs of the range of SEN in schools and the potential influx of students with complex difficulties in mainstream schools. Thus, one of the main aims of *Removing Barriers to Achievement* was to demonstrate how the barriers could be broken down by *personalised* learning for *all* students.

Personalised learning

> We need to provide a personalised education that brings out the best in every child, that builds on their strengths, enables them to develop a love of learning, and helps them to grow into confident and independent citizens.
>
> (DfES 2004:16)

Personalised learning is not new. It is an approach to SEN which has been at the heart of teaching and learning for the last 50 years. It means that teachers devise a curriculum and lessons in such a way that the needs of each student are met. Teachers are required to have high expectations for all their students and provide opportunities for learning by utilising a wide repertoire of teaching approaches. Equally, students are expected to take a more active role in their learning and be part of the planning and evaluation of their progress and performance.

Brain matters: neuroscience and education

How the brain works has always been of interest to the general public, as witnessed by the popularity of programmes on television which inform the viewers of fascinating facts about how your brain works. Over the past five years, there has been increasing interest in bringing together the two disciplines of neuroscience and education which have hitherto had little dialogue. What do they have to offer each other? Will brain research, which is conducted in experimental, controlled conditions, be able to inform the naturalistic setting of the classroom?

Neuroscience is the study of the inner workings of the brain and draws upon aspects of physiology, biology and chemistry. The quest to unravel the structure of the brain, its workings and its organisation has been a driving force in research in neuroscience. Much has been found out about brain functioning but much is still to be explored. How the brain is wired up and how it fires up has become a fascinating topic.

However, unrealistic claims were made initially about the impact of neuroscience research upon education. The inevitable backlash has suggested that 'neuro-myths' (Bruer 1997) have emerged. The oversimplification of the research findings has led to psycho-babble discussions about the way in which this knowledge can be used by educationalists.

Brain-based education

It has been suggested that classroom practices, curricula and pedagogy should change in response to the unfolding knowledge of how the brain works. An example of this is the Learning Style movement in schools, whereby students are taught according to their individual learning style preference. This has gained ground, and the impact of VAK (visual, auditory and kinaesthetic) systems has ben due in part to a growth industry of training educationalists to change the teaching and learning environment to respond to the way in which the brain takes in information. However, there is little research evidence to support the effectiveness of this in terms of increased performance.

Two findings from neuroscience research may have implications for education:

- **The plasticity of the brain.**
  - **This refers to the brain's ability to rejuvenate and reform during a lifetime. It suggests that the brain can be retrained. For example, Guinevere Eden conducted a study with adult dyslexic people who had experienced difficulties with reading. She carried out a controlled experiment to find out if the reading pathways in the brain could be retrained using a specific reading intervention programme. She demonstrated that the blood-flow channels in the brain were changed, and the participants increased their reading skills. This has importance for those in the field of SEN. It becomes imperative to choose the most effective intervention programme, linked to scientific evidence of brain changes. However, research into this is in its early stages.**
- **Critical periods for learning.**
  - **Early research by neuroscientists has demonstrated that the brain has sensitive periods of development and that it is crucial, therefore, to use this knowledge to maximise when students are taught different skills in school.**

Brain myths

It is apparent that what neuroscience has to offer education may bring about changes but research is still in its early stages and there is insufficient evidence at the moment to make radical changes to the curriculum and the teaching and learning environment. Oversimplification of what is complex and technical research in the sphere has led to many brain myths. One such example is the 'gendered brain' (Goswami 2004). The populist notion has emerged that there are two kinds of brain and that male and female brains work differently. If this is true, it could have implications for the way in which schools are organised. It would certainly fuel the debate for single-sex classroom environments which would more effectively differentiate learning to suit a specific brain type.

Nevertheless, a more cautious optimism may be the way forward. Two high-profile research studies have had an impact upon classroom practices. Madeleine Portwood's trials in Durham schools have demonstrated that performance and behaviour can be improved by giving students Omega 3, a type of fish oil. Insights into how the brain deals with number knowledge are of interest to mathematics teachers. However, it is the research conducted by Brian Butterworth and his team into possible deficits in certain areas of the brain which could help a better understanding of dyscalculia. This research could, in the long term, help teachers develop more effective and incisive identification and assessment tools. Early identification will then lead to early intervention, which is one of the main aims of *Every Child Matters*.

What are special educational needs?

'Special educational needs' is a catch-all term. It is used frequently in schools and often, depending upon who is using the term, it has different significance. However, you must be aware that it is a term that is embedded in current educational thinking and is defined in statutory legislation.

> A child has *special educational needs* if they have a learning difficulty which calls for *special educational provision* to be made for them.
>
> (Education Act 1996, Section 312)

The Education Act gives a clear definition of what can be considered a learning difficulty and what is meant by special provision. This provides us with shared working definitions to ensure that students can be identified and that there is a uniformity of provision nationally for the different categories of needs. The Act makes reference to 'significantly greater difficulty in learning' and the impact of disability on learning. Educational provision for SEN students is regarded as the provision which is *additional* to (or *different* from) that which is offered generally to all students.

All newly qualified teachers should read the *Code of Practice* (DfES 2001) which is available in all schools. This is a guidance document that will inform your practice on issues such as:

- the Formal Assessment Procedure leading to a Statement of SEN;
- characteristics of different categories of SEN;
- meeting the needs of different categories of SEN;
- monitoring students' progress;
- additional resources needed in mainstream schools.

What are the SEN categories?

The term 'special educational needs' (SEN) has undergone many face-lifts over the years. It may even be feeling somewhat schizophrenic because of the many name-changes it has had over the last 30 years. Nevertheless, the reason why it is constantly under scrutiny is because of its importance in the educational arena. Coping with the range of SEN may seem daunting to a trainee or a newly qualified teacher, and grappling with new terminology

– Emotional and Behavioural Difficulties (EBD), ADHD, Dyspraxia, Asperger's Syndrome, to name but a few – may be overwhelming.

Nevertheless, it is important to recognise the various categories of SEN so that you can plan your lessons to ensure that you:

- **set suitable challenges for *all* students;**
- **respond to 'diverse needs';**
- **provide access to the National Curriculum.**

The Code of Practice exemplifies the following broad categories:

- **Cognition and Learning Difficulties:**
  1. **General Learning Difficulties**
  2. **Specific Learning Difficulties, e.g. Dyslexia, Dyspraxia;**
- **Emotional, Behavioural and Social Difficulties (EBD);**
- **Communication and Interaction Difficulties:**
  1. **Speech and Language Difficulties**
  2. **Autistic Spectrum Disorders, e.g. ADD/ADHD/Asperger's Syndrome;**
- **Sensory and Physical Difficulties:**
  1. **Hearing Impairment**
  2. **Visual Impairment**
  3. **Physical and Medical Difficulties.**

What is 'graduated response' to SEN?

'Graduated response' is a phrase that is used in the Code of Practice and signifies a staged response to the needs of students with SEN. This approach encapsulates the concept of a continuum of needs and is a method of optimising resources available within the classroom and the school to meet differential needs. It is also a way of ensuring that the individual is at the heart of the process. The procedure has been divided into two main parts: School Action and School Action Plus.

School Action

This is the initial stage of support for students. Schools are required to examine their resources to meet the individual needs of a student. Thus, classroom resources are a key feature in the support. Intervention at this level is a question of how the school and its human resources can provide an environment that enables the student to move towards independent learning. Collaboration between subject teachers and the SEN department is conducted to devise the most appropriate, differentiated environment for the student's SEN from within subject and school resources. An Individual Education Plan (IEP) is initiated so that long-term and short-term targets can be monitored carefully to measure progress.

School Action Plus

If a student is making little progress, despite school intervention, and is performing 'substantially below National Curriculum levels expected for students of a similar age' (DfEE 1999), schools may need to consider seeking advice from outside agencies, such as support services provided by the LEA and other agencies. For example, a school may consult the psychological services to conduct a detailed, specialist assessment of the student's needs to inform further planning and to consider a range of different teaching approaches.

The subject teacher's role

As part of your professional duties you will be monitoring the progress of students in your care. As the person at the coalface, so to speak, you will have opportunities to observe how students learn and to monitor and record their level of achievement in your classroom. You are, therefore, in an ideal position to identify individual strengths and weaknesses. It is your responsibility to initiate the School Action stage of identification of needs. Your concerns about a student who does not appear to be achieving as you would expect will be discussed with your head of department or the school's SENCO (SEN Co-ordinator). At this stage, it is important to record and to gather evidence of the student's progress.

Gathering evidence

This will be done as part of your normal duties and will consist of some, if not most, of the following:

- **observation of the student's response to interactive oral work;**
- **class/group files for comparative purposes;**
- **mark book records;**
- **National Curriculum levels;**
- **attainment levels within the National Literacy Framework;**
- **samples of the student's work output.**

You may also want to look at school records for standardised assessment in reading, spelling and non-verbal reasoning. (For further information on assessment see Chapter 6.)

If you are concerned that a student's behaviour is a barrier to learning, it is important to keep records of:

- **the *type* of behaviour which is cause for concern, for example, anti-social behaviour directed at peers in the form of defiling others' work; or verbally abusive responses to peers and/or the teacher;**
- **the *frequency* of the behaviour;**
- **when the behaviour occurs – to examine patterns of behaviour and triggers. For example, a student may demonstrate disruptive behaviour when working in groups. The behaviour may occur on specific days in which case it may be necessary to look at his/her timetable to find out if there is any significance to the occurrence;**
- **the degree of severity – this can be subjective but will always be made in the context of the school's rules concerning acceptable behaviour.**

What is an IEP?

An Individual Education Plan (IEP) is a working document which is shared by the teacher, the student and the parent. It sets outs to record the provision 'which is additional to, and different from, the differentiated curriculum' for all children in the school (DfEE 10/99).

A good IEP should adhere to the following guidelines:

- clearly written with measurable targets wherever possible;
- three or four focused, short-term targets;
- appropriate teaching strategies;
- additional provision, e.g. the use of a laptop in specified lessons; or the additional support of an LSA (Learning Support Assistant) in specified lessons;
- criteria for success so that the student, the parent and teacher can measure when a target has been achieved;
- review procedures clearly stated.

What is a Statement of Special Educational Needs?

You will come across 'Statemented' students in your class. This means that these students have a Statement of their Special Educational Needs. A Statement is given to students with severe and complex difficulties that cannot be met within the school's resources. This Statement is a legally binding document issued by the LEA after a consultative process with the school, parents and outside agencies. The Statement specifies the student's SEN and sets out the type of provision needed to meet the individual's needs. This Statement must be reviewed annually.

As a newly qualified teacher you will be given guidance from the special needs department on the best ways to meet the student's needs in your classroom.

Inclusive teaching and learning environments

Creating an inclusive learning environment in your classroom will ensure that all students, regardless of their SEN, can make the most of their potential and can experience success in their learning. Inclusive environments will ensure that the barriers to learning are minimised.

> Pupils with SEN should have the same opportunities as others to progress and demonstrate achievement.
>
> (DfEE 1997, 1:24)

This means that you will be expected to differentiate your teaching. Differentiation is about ensuring that the way you teach and what you teach matches the individual student's needs. *How* you teach will take account of differentiated learning.

> If a child cannot learn the way you teach, you must teach the way s/he learns.
> (Chasty 1990, p. 269, cited in Pumfrey and Elliott 1990)

Considering the variety of SEN categories, mentioned previously in this chapter, which you could encounter in your classroom, planning differentiated work and providing differentiated delivery may appear to be daunting, if not overwhelming, for the NQT. It is vital, therefore, that some general principles are adhered to so that you can develop good practice which can then be modified to meet the more complex needs of some students.

General teaching strategies for SEN

Responding to students' diverse needs and overcoming potential barriers to learning will help to ensure that you provide equality of opportunity for learning. You should bear in mind the following when planning your lessons for students with SEN.

- *A multisensory environment*: this means that you need to give careful consideration to the fact that students learn in different ways. Some are visual learners, some auditory learners and some learn by doing (kinaesthetic learners). Thus, the way in which you present information to your students and the way you expect them to interact with the information and knowledge should tap into as many of these senses as possible.

- *Staged support*: in planning your lessons you must work out different levels of knowledge and understanding for a topic. You must consider what a student should know, and what a student must know within curriculum topics. In other words you will be differentiating basic knowledge from more in-depth knowledge. By asking yourself these fundamental questions you will be able to work out how you can develop competence and skills to match the student's SEN.

- *Provide structure*: this means that you will devise tasks for classroom activities and for assessment purposes whereby you have broken down the process of learning to provide practical, step-by-step procedures while the student is gaining confidence and skills.

- *Provide success*: this may seem obvious and a goal to which all teachers aspire. You must remember that success is very individual but essential for building up self-confidence as a learner. This is especially the case with secondary school students with SEN who may have experienced failure in the past and as a result have become de-motivated or anxious about new learning situations. If you examine what the student can do, you can use her/his knowledge and skill as a springboard so that s/he feels secure in the initial stages of learning a new concept and then gradually moves to new challenges. Providing success is more than the metaphorical pat on the back. Secondary school students with SEN are sensitive to praise and can often see through the empty 'well done' phrase dished out too often. If praise is to be effective and credible, you must let the students know what they have done that is successful. Thus, *targeted* praise is essential. For example, 'good work' is vague and does not let the student know what s/he has done which was good. You must target a skill which the student has used so that s/he learns to use skills and knowledge effectively. In this way you will help students to become aware of their own learning (metacognition), and you will help them to generalise skills to new learning situations. Targeted praise would then become: 'This lab report is well presented in a scientific way.' Thus, you have spelled out for the student that the way s/he has written is appropriate for the type of task.

- *Model the skills*: if you expect your students to be able to take and make notes by the end of Stage 4, demonstrate a variety of ways of presenting information as you are introducing new concepts and information. However, if this is to be effective it is vital that you make your modelling explicit and point out to the students that you have demonstrated the different ways of writing down information. In this way you can model how to use flow charts, bullet points, etc.

- *Effective management of TAs*: remember that TAs should be used to help develop a student's independence, not to create a dependency culture. Ask yourself the question: what do I want these students to do as a result of this lesson/series of lessons (learning outcomes)? A long-term target for a student may be that you want him/her to be able to read your worksheets in class. In the short-term, getting a TA to read for the student may seem the best solution. This may well get over the decoding difficulties which the student is experiencing. You might consider using the TAs' time more creatively by getting them to record frequently used worksheets on audio tape so that the student can be more independent and still has access to your texts while developing decoding skills. This is a scaffolded approach to teaching and learning. Directing TA time to the re-presentation of frequently used texts (see guidelines on p 146) may provide differentiated worksheets which are more accessible for students with SEN.

Manageable solutions

What do students find difficult to cope with in lessons?

You can greatly improve the quality of the learning experience in your classroom and ensure that you consider student diversity by examining the main components of lessons with which SEN students in general have difficulty.

Potential sticking points in lessons for SEN students

- Verbal instructions.
- Written instructions.
- Reading.
- Writing.

Verbal instructions

- Think about *when* you are going to give the instructions. SEN students often tire easily in lessons – students are often at their most receptive at the beginning of your lesson. Do not leave giving out vital homework instructions to the end of the lesson as the bell is sounding. This will distract those with ADD/ADHD, for example, and they will not even 'hear' your vital instructions.
- Try to stagger the amount of information you give – setting up the lesson with all the instructions at once is placing extra pressure upon those with specific short-term memory difficulties, for example.
- Provide alternative formats – some students do not take in information if it is only given verbally and may need the back-up of a flow chart of simple instructions. (This is multisensory and differentiated learning.)
- Allow some students to tape record verbal instructions which they can play back when memory goes into overload and so that you help them with language processing. This will enable them to hear the instructions again and again without constantly asking you to repeat – less frustrating for them, for you and for the rest of the group.

Written instructions

- Beware of one channel of taking in information, for example the auditory channel is one way of taking in information by listening. If all-important instructions are only given in written form this makes it more difficult for the auditory learner. It will also create difficulties for those whose reading skills are hesitant or weak.
- Provide alternative formats – some students do not take in information if it is only given in written format and may need the back-up of a flow chart of simple instructions. (This is multisensory and differentiated learning.)
- Do not put vital instructions only on the board. Often SEN students are not quick enough to take down these instructions and miss out what you want them to do. Provide some typed instruction cards to distribute among groups. In this way you will not single out SEN students who may be sensitive to having 'different' work from their peers.
- Keep the instructions clear and *simple*. Often NQTs try to give too many instructions and make the instructions unnecessarily complicated, thinking they are helping SEN students by expanding upon the information. Clear, boxed information with practical sub-headings will direct the student and help those with language processing difficulties to make sense of written instructions.

Example:

> **What you have to do**
> Write THREE note points about . . .

> **How to make a start**
> Use your classroom handouts to highlight relevant information.
> Use the textbook to find out more information.
> List all your information. .
> Decide upon the best order to present your notes.

REFLECTIVE TASK

Choose one of your teaching groups, preferably one with some students with SEN! Examine a week's lesson notes and reflect upon how you gave instructions to the group by filling in the following table.

Describe instruction	What worked	How I would change this in the future
Verbal instructions Timing Amount of information given Use of alternative back-up instructions Use of teaching assistant		
Written instructions Timing Amount of information given Use of alternative back-up instructions Use of teaching assistant		

Worksheet production

Secondary school students have grown up in a world of computer graphics and sophisticated animation. Often teachers try to emulate these features and try to produce entertaining worksheets. This may be admirable but, if such worksheets are simply provided for visual impact, they may sadly miss the target for SEN students who experience difficulties and worries about accessing texts and worksheets. Worksheets which are too fussy and contain too many graphics and unrelated pictures are confusing for a student who is trying to make sense of the written word. These students will use pictures and graphics to help them to unravel the text so you must ensure that anything you use is complementary and is an alternative, visual method of presenting the written text or prose, not something which you have zapped in from a clipart program because it brightens up the worksheet.

Guidelines for writing worksheets
- **Use of Comic Sans font is easier on the eye for those with reading difficulties.**
- **Key vocabulary in bold text.**

- Use of colour – key words, for example, could always be in red. This ensures that these words stand out and those with hesitant reading skills can be taught to skim more effectively.
- Layout of written text – uncluttered information is easier to access for those with literacy difficulties. If you put boxes around information you will help the students to 'see' that certain information is linked and goes together.
- Visual representations in tandem with prose.
- Talking worksheets – these are ways of providing a multisensory environment. Your worksheets can be accessed by the 'read back' facilities of a number of computer programs.

PRACTICAL TASK PRACTICAL TASK PRACTICAL TASK PRACTICAL TASK PRACTICAL TASK

Design a worksheet for use with a class that contains students with reading difficulties. Incorporate at least three of the above features. Trial this with your class and find out which features of your design provided the best help.

Writing

Modelling how to go about the writing *process* for your subject is important for SEN students. You will provide them with glimpses of 'how the expert goes about the task', and will ensure that you are tapping into different learning styles. Showing students examples of the finished product, e.g. a lab report, may help students to 'see' the way the written work is presented but does not help students to understand the process involved in writing for different subject purposes.

Guided practice is essential for all students but the way in which you manage this for SEN students is critical. You must embody the principles of inclusive learning environments. Thus, you must ensure that you provide structured practice to meet the individual's needs and his/her stage of learning. It is important to provide opportunities which start at the point of need and extend the student's learning.

Writing frames are an excellent example of this. You can provide as much or as little as is needed to get the student started with writing. Key words, phrases or starting sentences are graduated ways of developing writing. Report writing for scientific purposes, giving an account of a field trip in geography etc. all lend themselves to writing frames. (For further information on writing frames see Chapter 8, p.96.)

A word of warning is needed, however. Remember that writing frames are a means to an end and should not be regarded as the pinnacle of achievement for those who are experiencing writing difficulties. Rather they should be considered as a stepping stone – or scaffold – to success. Eventually, the frame should be withdrawn so that the student can work independently.

Managing students with emotional and behavioural difficulties (EBD)

Students who find it difficult to concentrate for periods of time, who cannot seem to sit still in the classroom, who are verbally or physically abusive to their peers and/or their teachers or whose behaviour is considered anti-social, soak up a considerable amount of a teacher's time and energy. It is vital that instructions, both verbal and written, and tasks are carefully planned and designed so that learning is in small steps. Ensure that academic tasks are broken down so that attention span is constantly stimulated. (For further information see Chapter 7 Managing behaviour for learning.)

Managing the working environment for these students is essential so that opportunities for poor and unacceptable behaviour are minimised. By adopting the solutions in the previous section, you will begin to provide a more secure learning environment for EBD students.

In addition to these generic solutions, consideration should be given to the following:

- *Make explicit your classroom ground rules*. You must demonstrate some flexibility in what you expect these students to achieve while not compromising your authority with the class as a whole. One of the most effective ways of doing this is to draw up a learning and behaviour contract with the student and discuss this with him/her. This individual approach will give you a chance to show the student that you are prepared to be firm but fair in dealing with his/her particular situation but that there are lines which you will expect the student not to cross. However, remember that teenagers will not necessarily show any appreciation for your considerations!
- *Be consistent*. You must always deal with disruptive behaviour consistently. This provides the EBD student with a sense of security and reinforces the rules for classroom behaviour. It strengthens your discipline by demonstrating fairness – an attribute highly regarded by all children.
- *Keep calm and try to avoid losing your temper*. This seems such an obvious statement but one which has to be worked on when dealing with difficult classroom behaviour. Some students seem to take pleasure from trying to get their teachers angry. Remember they are past masters at argument, shouting out and causing disruption. Counter this behaviour with even, quiet speech and measured actions. Try not to retaliate when these students shout abusively but rather mentally count to ten and go over to their working area so that you minimise the upheaval. This type of restraint which is non-invasive can be most effective not only with the specific student but also your standing with the class in general.
- *Give consideration to the specific praise and rewards for individual students*. These will be effective if the EBD student really perceives the rewards as something which is valued in the culture. What you might regard as a reward may be of no value to the teenager. Discussing rewards with the individual can ensure greater success.

A SUMMARY OF **KEY POINTS**

- > Read the Code of Practice for SEN to familiarise yourself with the different categories of learning needs and some general guidance for teaching.
- > Examine your lesson planning to incorporate both a variety of modes of delivery of information and a range of activities to meet differing learning styles and abilities.
- > Ensure that you weave in the principles of good practice to provide a differentiated curriculum that enables students to participate in the academic tasks you set, mindful of realistic targets for individual students.
- > Inclusive learning environments will be multisensory, provide structure and, where necessary, give opportunities for 'small step' learning (staged support).
- > Make opportunities for modelling and guiding the learning process.

Moving on

If you wish to deepen your understanding and knowledge of any category of SEN, it is worth visiting specialised websites such as the British Dyslexia Association site,

www.bdadyslexia.org.uk, or the Dyslexia Action site **www.da.org.uk**. Explore the notion of scaffolded learning to provide classroom support for all learners. Look out for Master's level training courses. There are many modular courses in the generalised category of inclusion and some for professionals who wish to specialise in a specific category, for example, specific learning difficulties (SpLD). Local universities are a rich source of information.

FURTHER READING FURTHER READING FURTHER READING FURTHER READING

Ainscow, M. (2003) Using teacher development to foster inclusive classroom practices. In T. Booth, K. Nes and M. Stomstad (eds) *Developing Inclusive Teacher Education*. London. Routledge Falmer.

Cheminais, R. (2000) *Special Educational Needs for Newly Qualified and Student Teachers.* London. David Fulton. This is a practical, easy-to-read guide for newly qualified teachers. It provides brief descriptions of the various categories of Special Educational Needs and there is a section on planning for progression.

Mittler, P. (2000) *Working Towards Inclusive Education: Social Contexts*. London. David Fulton.

Qualifications and Curriculum Authority (1998) *Supporting and Target Setting Process: Guidance for Effective Target Setting for Pupils with Special Educational Needs.* London. DfEE/QCA. This document is also practical and gives a wealth of information about how to tackle the teaching of those with different Special Educational Needs.

Stakes, R. and Hornby, G. (2000) (2nd ed.) *Meeting Special Needs in Mainstream Schools: A Practical Guide for Teachers.* London. David Fulton. This is an accessible guide for busy, newly qualified teachers. It provides information to help you develop strategies for classroom management.

Wearmouth, J. (2000) *Special Educational Provision: Meeting the Challenges in Schools*. London. Open University Press.

www.bdadyslexia.org.uk British Dyslexia Association website.

www.dyslexiaaction.org.uk Dyslexia Institute is now known as Dyslexia Action.

For further information on inclusion: special educational needs, visit **www.learning matters.co.uk/education/learnteach/chaptl2.html**

Chapter glossary

Attention deficit disorder (ADD) or attention deficit hyperactivity disorder (ADHD). Students who have been diagnosed with these disorders are recognisable in class because they can only concentrate for very short periods and often fidget and move around the class. They are often distracted by 'working' noise in the classroom and may behave inappropriately.

Asperger's syndrome is a form of autism. Many students who are identified are at the higher academic level of the autistic spectrum. They are often characterised by their difficult or unusual behaviour and their lack of social skills may cause problems in the classroom.

Auditory learners Some students may identify themselves as 'auditory learners'. These are students who believe they remember information more effectively if they listen to the teacher or work in groups where they can listen to verbal accounts.

Autistic spectrum disorders There are many disorders which are associated with autism. The degree of severity is the way in which many are distinguished. ADD, ADHD and Asperger's Syndrome all form part of this continuum. Other associated disorders are speech, language and non-verbal communication disorders. Students who fall within this continuum have varying degrees of difficulty in social interaction.

Dyslexia/specific learning difficulties Dyslexia is best described as a combination of abilities and difficulties which affect the capacity to process symbolic information in either alphabetic, numeric or musical notation. Acquisition of literacy and basic numeracy is also affected. Most dyslexic students have weaknesses with working memory, sequencing and organisation. Some may be creative and demonstrate a discrepancy between oral and written performance in class.

Dyspraxia Dyspraxic students often appear clumsy and have difficulty in planning and carrying out complex movements. This sometimes affects their handwriting and motor control. They often take much longer than their peers to produce written work in class. Some dyspraxic students have difficulties co-ordinating the muscles needed for speech production.

EBD Emotional and Behavioural Difficulties.

Kinaesthetic learners Some students may identify themselves as 'kinaesthetic learners'. These students believe they like to learn 'by doing'. They learn best by experiential learning.

General learning difficulties Students with general learning difficulties will experience all-round difficulties in conceptualising and have been labelled as 'moderate or mild learning difficulties' or 'slow learners'.

Hearing impairment Students with a hearing impairment may experience some degree of hearing loss. Some students may have a severity of loss and require extra resources to access the curriculum. In severe cases the teacher will be expected to wear a radio microphone to enable the student to access verbal information.

Meares-Irlen/scotopic sensitivity syndrome This is a perceptual problem caused by light sensitivity. Students identified with this difficulty will have experienced difficulties with reading. Problems appear to be worse with black print on a white background. This has implications for the use of black markers on white boards. Often the mild difficulties can be remedied by the use of an appropriate coloured overlay on text and photocopied handouts on coloured paper to suit individual needs. Some students may have tinted/coloured lenses with spectacles. The colours of the spectacles' lenses and the overlays are not usually the same. Spectacles are useful for reading from a white board or overhead projector transparency.

Visual impairment Students with a visual impairment may experience some degree of sight loss. Some students may have a severity of loss and require extra resources to access the curriculum, such as brailled text or special software for computers to enable the student to use a word processor.

13
English as an Additional Language
Sue Walters

Professional Standards for QTS

Q1, Q5, Q11, Q11, Q15, Q16, Q19

To be awarded QTS you must have high expectations of all of your students and a commitment to ensuring that they are all able to achieve their full educational potential; this includes students for whom English is an additional language (EAL). You need to have an appreciation of the role of social, cultural, religious and linguistic influences on learning and to be able to make effective personalised provision, as far as this is practicable, for all EAL learners. In doing so you need to be aware of assessment issues in relation to EAL learners and the way in which statistical data can be used to evaluate provision and raise levels of achievement. You also need to recognise and value the contribution that parents and carers play in supporting the learning and achievement of EAL students as well as the importance of promoting equality and inclusion in the classroom.

You may find it helpful to read through the appropriate section of the handbook that accompanies the Standards for the award of QTS for clarification and support.

Introduction

Many of the students that you will teach will be learners who bring with them into the classroom rich experiences in and knowledge of languages and dialects other than English. Many of these students will be learning English at the same time as they are learning your subjects *through* English. These students are generally referred to as students with English as an additional language (EAL), bilingual students or English language learners.

In England, in 2004, 11 per cent of students in mainstream schooling (and 8.8 per cent in secondary schools) were recorded as students with EAL (National Statistics 2004). As the figures in Table 13.1 illustrate, some areas of the country have a much higher proportion of EAL students than others. However, most schools will have some EAL students at some time and many more will have students who use and speak other languages and literacies outside the classroom.

Table 13.1: Percentage of students whose first language is known or believed to be other than English (National Statistics 2004, p.85)

	In maintained secondary schools	In maintained primary schools
England	8.8	11.0
North East	2.2	3.3
Yorkshire and the Humber	7.3	9.5
West Midlands	10.4	13.4
Inner London	45.3	50.2
South West	1.6	2.0

One of your roles as a teacher, as set out in the Standards, is to make effective provision for this group of students so that they have access to the curriculum and are able to achieve in your classroom alongside their monolingual peers. This may appear to be a daunting responsibility, one that you do not have the expertise for, especially in those cases when you need to plan for and support the learning of a student who has arrived in your classroom with very little English, or none at all, and who you need to include and teach at the same time as your other students. However, as this chapter demonstrates, by working with some clear principles in mind and utilising strategies that you are already familiar with in your teaching with monolingual learners you will be able to support EAL learners and provide the necessary teaching and learning opportunities for them to develop their language(s) and achieve in your classroom.

While there is only space to indicate some of the key principles and strategies that can be used to support EAL students here, there are many excellent 'how to' resources available as well as more information about the principles of good practice. Details of these are given at the end of this chapter.

Why EAL and not ESL?

In schools and in policy documents you will come across the term 'English as an additional language' (EAL) used to describe learners who need support with their English in order to access the curriculum. This term is used rather than ESL (English as a second language) because the term ESL suggests that the learner already speaks one other language and is now learning their second. However, many learners, including very young children, come into our classrooms with experience and expertise in a number of languages. For example, a learner such as Afia, a seven-year-old girl born in England whose parents both come from Bangladesh, knows and uses a number of languages and literacies in her everyday life. See Table 13.2.

Table 13.2: Afia's experience and expertise in a number of languages and literacies.

Afia at seven years old. She
speaks:
- Sylheti at home with her mother.
- Sylheti and English with her father.
- English with her older brother.
- English at school.

is learning to read:
- Arabic in her Mosque school.
- (and write) Bengali at home, taught by her mother.
- (and write) English in her English primary school.

watches and understands:
- TV soaps in English.
- 'Bollywood' movies in Hindi (and can sing many of the most popular songs).
- Bengali TV programmes via satellite television.

Learners like Afia bring to our classrooms a rich experience and knowledge of languages and the term ESL does not do justice to the range of languages and experiences that such learners bring with them.

It is worth noting here that Afia's languages and literacies, as do those of many of the EAL students in our classrooms, frequently remain invisible and not known about. You may have noticed that in Table 13.1 the wording was 'Percentage of students whose first language is known *or believed to be* other than English'. It is sadly the case that some schools fail to find out accurate information about their students' other languages and literacies or to build on or support these rich and important linguistic resources and skills. This situation flies in the face of research that consistently demonstrates that bilingual and multilingual students achieve more highly in school when they continue to use and develop both or all of their languages (Cummins 2000). As a teacher it is worth spending some time considering the ways in which you can use and build on your EAL students' expertise in other languages and literacies and how you may be able to provide ways of developing these languages alongside English.

Why are beginners in my classroom and not in a special EAL class?

EAL students, even when they are beginning to learn English, are educated alongside their peers in mainstream schools. Learning alongside their fully fluent peers in the classroom is the best place for EAL learners to learn. In this way EAL learners will hear and see good models of English being used and will have access to the very aspects of English language that they will need in order to learn and take part in the activities of their classrooms and to be an achieving learner in these contexts. If you have EAL learners in your classroom then planning to support their language development is a central part of your planning for learning in the classroom. This may sound very daunting but many of the things that you plan for and do in your classroom for your EAL learners will benefit all the learners and many of these strategies are ones you may already be aware of.

EAL students and who they are

EAL students are learning both the language English in our classrooms and the content of the curriculum through English.

EAL learners do not form a homogenous group of students. Table 13.3 (on page 154) indicates how they may differ.

EAL students bring a wide range of life and language experiences to our classrooms. Each student will have a unique profile. To be able to provide for such students we need to find out as much as we can about their learning, their languages, the literacies they are familiar with and so on, and we need to have a clear idea of what they can already do and what kind of support we need to provide for them.

Table 13.3: Ways in which EAL students may differ

Where they were born and where they have lived	In the UK or overseas. May have moved a lot between or within countries or may have always lived in the same place. May have parents from more than one country who speak different languages. May have come from a country/countries experiencing war or internal conflict. May have come from a very secure and settled background and this is their first move to a new place.
Their schooling experiences and learning styles	May have attended schools in countries where the following are very different to England: • the starting age • how classrooms are arranged • what is expected in terms of behaviour and showing what you know and have learnt • student–teacher relationships and where: • there are better or poorer or very different resources for learning • schooling has been severely disrupted due to conflict, war, etc.
The languages they speak and have expertise in	There is no simple relationship between home=one language, school=another language. Many EAL students will speak one language with one parent, another language with the other, perhaps a different language with siblings, other relatives. May have a language for spiritual practices that is different to the language they use socially with relatives. May have very different levels of expertise in their different languages.
Their knowledge of spoken and written English	This will vary depending on previous educational and social experiences. Some will be able to read English quite well or fluently but not speak it and vice versa. Some will know dialect or 'pidgin' forms of English. Some will be complete beginners in English.
Their spiritual and cultural practices	EAL students will come from all faith groups. Even when they share a religion/faith there can be large differences in belief and practice. Care needs to be taken not to assume that all Christians, or all Muslims, practise their faith in the same way. Children may be involved in learning outside school in community and religious classes. These may have very different learning and teaching practices to the mainstream English classroom, while not detracting from children's learning in their English school.
Their socio-economic status	Some learners (and/or their parents) will be from middle-class homes, the children of professionals (e.g. doctors, university lecturers, dentists), some learners will come from working-class backgrounds and/or from very rural/agriculture-based backgrounds. Learners and their families will thus have differing access to social, cultural and economic resources (like all learners in our schools).
The value placed on their mother tongue and the languages they use outside school	Some will speak languages that are highly valued in England (e.g. French, Italian, German) while others will speak languages that are undervalued (e.g. Bengali).
Their gender and ethnicity and other people's responses to these aspects of their identity	For example, assumptions and expectations exist in the UK about South-East Asian girls and boys. Assumptions are made about ethnicity and about families. In addition, many EAL learners are also minority ethnic students and experience name-calling and other forms of racism in and outside school.
The amount of time they have lived in the UK and will continue to live in the UK	Some EAL learners will have been born and lived all their lives in the UK; they will be EAL learners because they speak and use languages other than English in the home (and sometimes in the community). Some EAL learners will have just arrived in the UK and be settling into a new home and country. Some may have moved within the UK. Some EAL learners will only be living and going to school in the UK for one or two years (learners whose parents are in the UK on short-term contracts in universities, hospitals or in the private or agricultural sectors) while for others the UK is their permanent home and they will complete their schooling in the UK.
Their life experiences	Some EAL learners will have lived very secure and settled lives; others will have lived very mobile lives; others will be asylum seekers and refugees and may be living in the UK without their families. These learners may have recently experienced violence and trauma.
Their school and community setting	Some EAL learners will be attending school and living in communities where there are other people who share their languages, cultural and faith practices and ethnicity, while others will be the only or one of a few EAL students in their school. They may be the only child who speaks a particular language and may be the only member of a particular faith group. They may not live close to people who share their cultural and faith practices or ethnicity.

Assessment and EAL students – planning for learning and teaching

Finding out about experiences, practices and skills

Finding out as much as you can about the previous experiences (and continuing out-of-school language and learning experiences) of the EAL students in your class is part of your initial and ongoing assessment of these students. This information can be gathered from the students' parents, friends, siblings and from the students themselves.

Ongoing assessment

In addition to the above, you will need to keep some record of your EAL learners' language development in the classroom in order to plan and support their learning. There have been a number of well-used methods for doing this. However, in 2000 the government introduced the 'A Language in Common' framework (QCA 2000) which offered descriptors for EAL students' levels of English development which were in line with the descriptors used for all children's language development in the National Curriculum. There is a great deal of debate about using such descriptors. This centres around whether EAL students' language development can be considered in the same way as monolingual learners' English language development or whether a more subtle and appropriate form of assessment and description should be utilised which respects the language profiles and different learning paths of multi-lingual or bilingual learners. The government also introduced a new way of funding the support of EAL learners in the late 1990s, called the Ethnic Minorities Achievement Grant (EMAG). EAL learners were included with minority ethnic students and the focus was placed on achievement for these learners. The funding arrangements place an emphasis on statistical data regarding student achievement whereby schools are encouraged to track and compare the achievement of their minority ethnic and EAL students, thus preventing such students' underachievement going unremarked and unaddressed.

You may come across a number of different ways of assessing and recording EAL students' language development in your placements.

PRACTICAL TASK PRACTICAL TASK PRACTICAL TASK PRACTICAL TASK PRACTICAL TASK

Find out how your placement school assesses and describes EAL learners' progress and attainment in relation to the development of their English language.
How is this method of assessment and description used in planning and teaching for these students?
What are the strengths and weaknesses of the methods used?

Care should always be taken when an EAL student appears to be struggling in school to explore whether their learning needs are connected to their EAL learning needs or whether they also have some special need that requires support. Deryn Hall's *Assessing the Needs of Bilingual Students* (2001) is a useful resource for making such an assessment.

Social fluency and academic proficiency

As we already seen, an important aspect of providing for EAL learners is to assess their level of language expertise and development in order to be able to plan for their language development. Care needs to be taken not to base an assessment of an EAL learner's ability to use English in your classroom simply on their oral and social English. It is easy to hear an EAL learner chatting away fluently to friends and classroom adults and to assess that student as being fluent in English and not in need of EAL support, with the result that language support and planning are not provided. Any subsequent failure of the student to complete work or take part in classroom activities is seen as a lack of interest or a lack of ability, much to the detriment of many EAL learners. They are labelled as uninterested or of poor ability when all they lack is access to the language they need as a learner in order to achieve. This is why it is important for you as a teacher to plan for language development as well as teaching the content area of your subject. We will now consider this in more detail.

Inclusive practice and effective provision

A 'language conscious pedagogy'

EAL students are supported by using what Pauline Gibbons calls 'a language conscious pedagogy'. Each subject teacher is responsible for being aware of the language that is required in order to understand, to take part in classroom activities and to demonstrate understanding in their particular subject – and for planning for and providing support to EAL learners so that they can master this language.

> Language is integral to most of what happens in the classroom, but to a competent language user its role is like that of a window, through which we look at the content. It is transparent and although we may recognise that it is there, its transparency means that it is very hard to see. Focusing on content alone makes language the invisible curriculum in the school. And for children with poor English skills, the language becomes the block to learning. To put it another way, their window is made of frosted glass.
>
> (Gibbons 1991, p.12)

Maintaining this focus on language and providing for the language development of your students is key to their ability to engage with the curriculum and achieve as students. Let's consider how this can be done.

REFLECTIVE TASK

The following extract was recorded in a classroom in which the teacher was working with the class to prepare them to write a weather forecast. This extract comes from about ten minutes into the lesson. The teacher is standing in front of the class introducing the topic and the task to the students. She has written in a list down the left side of the board some of the phrases to be found in weather forecasts that the students have suggested but she does not write anything down on the board during this extract. There are no weather forecasts available in the classroom for the students to see.

Teacher: OK. Your weather forecast. The title will be weather forecast. You're going to have to write it in two bits. There will be a sub-heading for the first bit. It will be today ... and the second bit will be a title tomorrow. So be quiet please Jack. OK. I expect you to describe the weather for today. Made up. Remember you can choose one bad day and one good day and don't forget that the weather can change during the day.

Jaz (a student): Brightening up!

Teacher: Umm. Shh. Shh. No I didn't write that did I Jaz. Brighten up ... yeah because I couldn't get it up in the space so I wrote it below Jaz. Um so you might like to say today in the morning it will be blah, blah, blah. Shh shh shh sh! And then you might like to write later on in the afternoon it will become and you will describe how it will change. OK?

1. What might some of the difficulties be for a beginner EAL student in this classroom?
2. How might they be resolved?
3. What could the teacher be doing to support an EAL learner in this introduction to writing a weather forecast?

In the extract above:

- The teacher is not using any visual images to support what is being taught and what she hopes her students will be learning.
- The learner may be unfamiliar with the vocabulary, may not have much experience of reading and seeing weather forecasts (or may have experience of them in a very different cultural form) and has no opportunity here to see a weather forecast and thus what the teacher is talking about.
- None of the children is clear about whether the teacher is referring to the weather forecast that they see on the television or one they would find in a newspaper as this has not been stated at this point in the lesson.
- There is a list of phrases on the board but they are not written up in the way they would appear in a weather forecast.
- In her explanation of the writing task, it is hard for a beginner bilingual to know which of her words are:
  – the headings they are to use in their writing (and where to position the headings)
  – the phrases they can use in the body of the writing
  – instructions about the task that they need to listen to
  – words aimed at controlling the behaviour of other children.
- The teacher's use of 'blah, blah, blah' will be confusing unless the child is familiar with this expression and knows that it stands in for one of the phrases the teacher has previously written on the board.
- The range and flow of the language, with very little visual support, contextualisation or demonstration, is likely to mean that the EAL student (and other students in the classroom?) will struggle to follow, will feel overwhelmed by the wash of language around them and not be able to complete the task at any level although they may have a great deal of experience of writing in their other languages and perhaps of weather forecasts.
- It may also mean that if this is the dominant mode of teaching in the classroom the student will come to disengage from learning.

What could the teacher do? Well, the teacher in this situation could:

- Ask the children about where they see weather forecasts and what they are used for.
- Show the class a weather forecast (either one from the television or from a newspaper or from the internet) and discuss its features with the class. The EAL learner would be able to see what the teacher was talking about and may well be able to relate some of the contributions of their classmates to the text that was in front of them and to their own knowledge.
- Use pictures and other visuals to support the language/vocabulary being used.

- Spend some time looking at the particular form and features of a weather forecast and model how to write one herself with the children contributing to this process. The EAL student would have the opportunity of hearing and seeing how specific aspects of English were deployed in such a piece of writing.
- She could then write the title, the headings and the beginnings of sentences she suggests the children use on the board or on a worksheet and allow the children to practise using the language she is trying to teach them, perhaps in pairs.
- She could use a weather forecast in the student's other language(s) with the whole class to look for common features and to explore differences and allow the student to write a weather forecast in more than one language.

In addition, instead of asking the students to move straight into writing a weather report on their own, she could provide them with opportunities to practise using the language of a weather forecast in pairs and groups or as a class. The beginning bilingual in such a class could then be given a picture-matching activity in order to develop vocabulary and this could lead into an activity using simple statements to describe the weather. This can then lead to statements that describe the weather in the past, present or future, and so on.

In doing this, the teacher would be demonstrating the most important strategies that support language development. These are:

Start with what the learners already know:
Recap what you have already covered or taught or something that you did before. Refer to other contexts where this language/subject is found or has been used. Gain their interest through relating the activity to previous experiences. Help them make connections with previous learning and make it clear what is going to be learnt (and why – give a purpose). Ask them what they know about the topic from their own experience. Remember to focus on the language that is required as well as the topic.

Provide a rich context for what you are teaching or demonstrating:
Show the objects you are talking about or use examples. Use visuals – to indicate what you are talking about, to demonstrate a process visually. Model writing and reading. Direct attention to the language that is needed in order to engage with this topic. It may include specialist vocabulary (words change their meaning between subjects, e.g. 'face' means one thing in maths and another in an English lesson), the layout/genre of writing involved, the way connectives are used, and so on. Draw the learners' attention to the relationship between form and function. Be clear when you are 'teaching' the whole class, when you are talking to a group or a specific student, when you are dealing with administration or discipline. Using a student's name or using a phrase or gesture which makes it clear when you need them to listen is good for beginners – they will struggle with listening and filtering everything said in the classroom otherwise.

After introducing and/or demonstrating/modelling a topic or learning point, **provide many opportunities for students to comfortably practise and experiment** with the language and content that you have been teaching. This will probably involve pair or group work, can include a range of games and activities and may involve providing initial support through the use of writing frames or oral prompts. Provide learners with meaningful opportunities to use the language.

Move towards independence. Through providing many opportunities to practise and develop language and content knowledge in safe groupings, through activities that encourage language use and development (and with initial support provided by whole-class teaching/modelling, prompts and writing frames) learners are supported as they move towards being able to use a particular genre of writing or language item on their own without support. This is a gradual and iterative process.

You will have noticed that what the teacher could have done and the principles outlined above reflect much in the Secondary National Strategy. In this way the provision you make for your EAL learners is part of the provision you make for all the learners in your classroom.

In your planning, teaching and assessment you will also need to consider the following in relation to reading and writing.

Reading and writing

EAL learners share much with monolingual English speakers with regard to learning to write in English. However, they may need to learn a new script or change the direction they write in. They will almost certainly need to learn the relationship between the written symbols of the English system and the sounds the symbols represent. As a teacher you will need to be sensitive to this, allow time for such learners to orientate themselves and to learn from you about how writing is accomplished. You can provide your students with good modelling of writing. (You can also allow your students to write in their own language if they are able to do this as a way of recording information, writing up an experiment and so forth.) Most importantly EAL students, like monolingual students, will benefit from explicit instruction in the different text types and genres of English writing that they are required to engage with and use in school (as set out in the Secondary National Strategy).

In addition, when reading, beginner EAL students may not be able to call on many of the strategies that good readers use. They may not be able to identify the key words carrying the most information in a text. They may also have insufficient cultural or language knowledge to predict where a text is going or whether they have decoded a word they have read correctly. They also may also struggle with reading for meaning because they are unfamiliar with the cohesive ties that are used in English writing. For example, EAL students may not recognise the relationship between a reference word in a text and a referent and may have difficulties with substitutions and connectives in their reading and writing.

Reference words point (usually back) to something in the text (the referent):
'*Yasmin* flashed *her torch* round the room for the last time. **She** was about to switch **it** off when Yvette cried out.'
The words 'She' and 'it' here refer back to 'Yasmin' and 'the torch'.

Substitutions are when another word is used to substitute for a word already used; nouns, verbs and clauses can be substituted:
'Somebody lend me their *mobile*', shouted Max. 'I'm afraid I don't have **one**', said Billy.
'*Your behaviour is a disgrace*', muttered the woman. Chris thought that this was probably true but did not like to be told **so**.

Connectives are words and phrases that suggest addition, opposition, cause and time:

'Clean your bedroom **or else** you won't get to play on the computer. Make your bed **and** put away your clothes. **Then** tidy away all your toys. **After that**, clean up the mess you have made downstairs' [addition and time connectives[.

'We really like your work; **however** we do not have a position vacant at the moment. **As a result** we are unable to offer you anything until the end of the year' [opposition and cause connectives].

By being aware of the language you are expecting your students to use and to engage with, you can plan to include these kind of textual features in your classroom teaching by drawing attention to them and modelling their use in your work with the class as well as providing opportunities for students to practise using them. When asking your class to read the following are important:

- Give the purpose of the reading before the students read.
- Activate the students' prior knowledge – find out what they already know about the topic.
- Direct them to particular features of the text: build awareness.
- Model reading (think aloud).
- Allow uninterrupted time for reading.
- Think of way of covering what has been read so that beginner EAL students can stay part of the lesson.

Home–school relationships

You are probably already aware of the importance of home–school relationships to students' learning. The relationship between home and school is just as important, if not more so, for EAL students although establishing such a relationship may sometimes seem more difficult. To establish good home–school relationships with parents of EAL students be aware of the following issues:

- *Parents' working hours*: some parents may work in shops, restaurants, etc. where they have to be at work when children are picked up from school or when parent–teacher meetings happen. If a parent does not appear interested in their child's schooling then find out if this is the reason why you do not see very much of them and then find a mutually convenient time to meet.
- *Language*: Some parents do not feel able to cope with the English they need in order to talk to the teacher or understand what the teacher is saying and teachers feel inadequate in talking to parents when they don't share the language. Wherever possible try to provide some form of interpretation or translation for important meetings and conversations. This can be provided by an official interpreter (larger cities now provide such services), another parent, another family member (including a sibling if there is no one else). Always welcome any attempt to communicate and have a go using gestures, signs and so on.
- *School letters and forms*: In an ideal world it would be possible to have all school forms and letters translated into the languages that parents read. However, where this is not a possibility you should take care when you send letters and forms home that the font/writing is clear and easy to read. If you know that some parents are not familiar with reading in English and the information is important, then making a phone call to the home to pass on that information should follow sending a letter or a form. Where parents can read a little English then highlighting the important points (and where signatures are required) with a highlighter pen is useful. If a student needs to explain the form to their parents (and translate what is required) then make sure you give the student good, clear, oral explanation of what is in the text and what is required from the parents.
- *Don't hold children responsible*: When parents do not sign forms, return payments for school

photographs and so on, do not hold the student responsible. It may well be that the student has been unable to explain to their parents what is required. If you are in a situation like this as a teacher it is your responsibility to communicate with the parents and explain what is required, not the student's.

- *Parents' expectations*: As we noted earlier, EAL students do not form a homogenous group and neither do their parents. Parents will have diverse educational experiences of their own and may have different expectations of what a good school is. They may also have little idea of what their child is doing when they are in school because the system is very different to the system they are used to. This may be another reason why parents may not appear to be supportive. It can be remedied by providing information, in a way that can be understood, about how the school operates, what you are covering in the classroom and why.
- *Use and value parents*: The parents of EAL students will have a number of multilingual and multiliterate skills and experiences. Wherever possible use these. Parents and family members are also the most important people for helping you form a clear picture of the skills and abilities (in all their languages and literacies) of your EAL students and how you can plan for and support their language development.

Welcoming new students

This has been deliberately kept until the end of the chapter. This is because most advice provided to teachers about supporting EAL students focuses on this and just on this. It is hoped that what has come before this will support you as you effectively provide for your EAL students over the course of the first few years of their schooling and not just the first few months.

A few simple but very effective strategies for welcoming new students are as follows. They are things that you would do in your role as a form teacher rather than as a subject teacher but you might want to instigate some or all of these things for your particular subject area if they are not already in place:

Find a member of the class who will be their buddy – this will be someone who will take responsibility for showing the student to their classrooms, showing them what to do when certain bells ring and so on. The buddy doesn't have to share the new student's language(s).

Provide the new student with a bilingual dictionary so that both you and they can start to look up vocabulary. You can look up an English word and point to it and the student can read the translation in their other language.

Show new students the important places in the school (toilets, canteen, hall, school office, etc.): don't just give them a plan of the school.

Give students the language they will need in the first few days. For example, 'Can I leave the room/go to the toilet?'. You will be able to get simple introductory booklets with school language, etc. from your local authority's EAL service.

A final and most important point to make about EAL students is that if they are new to the English language they may very well remain silent for quite some time (up to a term or more) after joining your class. This is perfectly normal and is referred to as 'the silent period' by people who study second-language acquisition. Although a student may be silent it does not mean that they are not learning and taking in vast amounts of knowledge about English.

They are. Students should not be forced to speak; they will speak when they are ready. And when they do speak you will probably be surprised at the level and quality of their spoken English.

Moving on

Have a look at the vignettes from your subject area on the NALDIC website (see below) and consider how these could inform your planning and teaching. Also look at the publications, research and resource pages of this excellent website.

FURTHER READING FURTHER READING **FURTHER READING** FURTHER READING

Allandina, S. (1995) *Being Bilingual: A Guide for Parents, Teachers and Young People on Mother Tongue, Heritage Language and Bilingual Education.* Stoke on Trent. Trentham.

Cline, T. and Frederickson, N. (eds) (1996) *Curriculum Related Assessment, Cummins and Bilingual Children*. Clevedon. Multilingual Matters. Cline Cummins Assessment – pick the D. Hall chapter and any other with good ideas.

Gravell, M. (ed) (2000) *Planning for Bilingual Learners: An Inclusive Curriculum*. Stoke on Trent. Trentham.

Rutter, J. (1994) *Refugee Children in the Classroom.* Stoke on Trent. Trentham.

Useful websites

www.edu.bham.ac.uk/bilingualism Great reference list of books and articles.

www.literacytrust.org.uk Look for Professional resources under 'EAL', 'Multiculturalism'.

www.multiverse.ac.uk Exploring diversity and achievement.

www.naldic.org.uk National Association for Language Development in the Classroom. Lots of very useful resources and information; the first place to look.

www.nassea.org.uk Northern Assocation of Support Services for Equality and Achievement.

www.ofsted.gov.uk

www.qca.org.uk Look for the booklet *A Language in Common* – assessing EAL.

www.tes.co.uk Follow Staffroom link for EMAG forum.

14
Equality and diversity
John Clay and Rosalyn George

Introduction

Changing contexts: driving up standards

There have been significant changes in the educational climate over the past decade. The election of New Labour in 1997 heralded a range of new initiatives under the heading of modernisation. The White Paper *Excellence in Schools* (DfEE 1997) emphasised the need for education to offer 'equality of opportunity and high standards for all' (p. 3). This has meant, in practice, a renewed emphasis on literacy and numeracy and the setting of ambitious targets to raise attainment. The testing at 7, 11 and 14 that now underpins the primary and Key Stage 3 Strategies allows the system to monitor the outcomes at these different stages of schooling and this has been the mechanism used to 'drive up' standards. However, such an approach, which recognises and privileges the view that differences in attainment alone prevent individuals and groups from participating fully in the social, political and economic spheres, is highly problematic and contentious. Nevertheless, the focus on raising standards and promoting inclusion through education will therefore inform this chapter. As a consequence, equality of opportunity has been incorporated and subsumed within the wider agenda of inclusion.

Issues of equality and inclusion underpin the very foundations of the kind of society that we live in; how we relate to one another at the local, national and international level. Within this wider context, it is broadly accepted that education and schooling has a pivotal role in preparing future citizens to embrace the richness and potentialities of diversity and difference. Through an examination of the three central inequalities in education, namely, gender, 'race' and social class, we will explore:

- **what inclusion and equality mean in schooling and education;**
- **the legislative framework;**
- **the different patterns of achievement and expectations of pupils and students from within different communities, schooling and educational systems.**

Equality

In the context of education and schools, the terms 'equality', 'equal opportunity' and 'equality of opportunity' are used interchangeably as though they all mean the same. This is not the case and Hill and Cole (1999) succinctly sum up the differences. They maintain that:

> a distinction needs to be made between equal opportunities on the one hand, and equality on the other. Equal opportunities policies, in schools and elsewhere, seek to enhance social mobility within structures which are essentially unequal. In other words, they seek a meritocracy, where people rise (or fall) on merit, but to grossly unequal levels or strata in society – unequal in terms of income, wealth, life-style, life-chances and power. Egalitarian policies, policies to promote equality, on the other hand, seek to go further. First, egalitarians attempt to develop a systematic critique of structural inequalities, both in society at large and at the level of the individual school. Second, egalitarians are committed to a transformed economy, and a more socially just society, where wealth and ownership is shared far more equally, and where citizens (whether young citizens or teachers in schools, economic citizens in the workplace or political citizens in the polity) exercise democratic controls over their lives and over the structures of the societies of which they are part and to which they contribute. While equal opportunities policies in schools and elsewhere are clearly essential, egalitarians believe that they need to be advocated within a framework of a longer-term commitment to equality. Where they are not, the false assumption has been made that there is a 'level playing field', on which we all compete as equals.
>
> (Hill and Cole 1999, pp. 111–112)

Richardson and Wood (1999) argue that within the context of education:

> *equal opportunities* is concerned with ensuring that all pupils and students have genuine access to the curriculum, and that none are at an unfair disadvantage, because their distinctive experiences, concerns and identities are disregarded. The wider political task is to create and enforce legislation against unfair discrimination, both direct and indirect, in all major areas of social life, particularly in employment.
>
> (Richardson and Wood 1999, p. 15)

Some of the ideas embedded in these statements are complex, but, despite this complexity, can be translated into everyday issues and contexts that are relevant and meaningful to teachers and learners and will enable them to develop a deeper insight into the way our society is organised, how it operates and how this in turn impacts on schools and other educational establishments.

PRACTICAL TASK PRACTICAL TASK PRACTICAL TASK PRACTICAL TASK PRACTICAL TASK

Discuss with another trainee teacher the following key statements, which are intended to provoke debate and discussion.

- **The classroom can be seen as a microcosm of society.**
- **The education system and the school reflect and reproduce society's values.**
- **Knowledge selected for use in schools represents a particular view of the society, the perceived needs of individual, and the intrinsic value and logic of the knowledge itself.**
- **Behaviour that leads to discrimination against others is learned and sometimes taught by commission and omission.**
- **Challenging inequalities (and supporting young people to do the same) is the responsibility of the teacher through the formal, informal and hidden aspects of the school.**
- **All subject areas and teachers can play a part in tackling inequality and discrimination.**

Inclusion

Like equality and equal opportunities, the term 'inclusion' has also become a 'catch all' phrase. The term **social inclusion** refers to participation in society. It includes involvement in politics, the economy and mainstream cultural life. Its opposite is 'social exclusion', for example, the absence of black and other minority people from key areas of social, political, recreational and economic life. Education in relation to social inclusion is concerned with equipping people with knowledge and skills, and also the paper qualifications ('educational achievement'), which they need for full participation in society. The wider political task is to combat poverty, inequality, unemployment, poor housing and poor health (Richardson and Wood, op.cit. p. 15). Social deprivation that arises out of poverty, inequality, unemployment, poor housing and poor health is measured crudely within the schooling system in terms of students' entitlement to 'free school meals'.

What is an inclusive school?

An inclusive school is one in which the teaching and learning, achievements, attitudes and well-being of every young person matter. Effective schools are educationally inclusive schools. This shows not only in their performance, but also in their ethos and their willingness to offer new opportunities to students who may have experienced previous difficulties. This does not mean treating all students in the same way. Rather it involves taking account of students' varied life experiences and needs.

In *Evaluating Educational Inclusion: Guidance for Inspectors and Schools* (Ofsted 2000), it seems that the most effective schools are ones that do not take educational inclusion for granted. Instead, they constantly monitor and evaluate the progress each student makes, identifying students who may be missing out, difficult to engage, or feeling some way apart from what the school seeks to provide. They take practical steps – in the classroom and beyond – to meet students' needs effectively and promote tolerance and understanding in a diverse society (p.4).

During the past three to four years, the term 'inclusion' has gained sufficient currency to become a central feature of the revised National Curriculum and a focus of the Ofsted inspection framework. The National Curriculum Inclusion Statement requires schools, in planning and teaching the curriculum, to take regard of the following three essential principles:

- **setting suitable learning challenges;**
- **responding to the diverse needs students bring to their learning;**
- **overcoming potential barriers to learning and assessment for individuals and groups.**

(Each of the above three principles have been expanded and exemplified in the National Curriculum handbook with additional information on inclusion in the subject booklets.)

Making your school more inclusive

- **There needs to be a strong commitment to equal opportunities and social justice underpinned by explicit support from the head teacher.**
- **The perspectives of both student and parents needs to be sought.**
- **Clear procedures for recording and acting on racist/sexist incidents must be developed.**
- **An ethos that is open and vigilant, which enables students to discuss issues of justice and equity and shared concerns, needs to be generated and sustained.**
- **Communicating high expectations accompanied by a clear view that under-performance by any group is unacceptable.**
- **Reviewing curricular and pastoral approaches to ensure their sensitivity and appropriateness.**
- **Using ethnic monitoring and other forms of data collection as a routine and rigorous part of the school's/LEA's self-evaluation and management.**

The legal framework

All teachers need to be aware of the legislation with regard to equal opportunities since this has a direct impact on the school's role as a provider and an employer. The legislation is fairly complex in relation to gender, 'race' and Special Educational Needs. It is important to note that since the passing of the 1988 Education Reform Act (ERA) governing bodies have increased responsibility for all aspects of staffing, training and grievance procedures. The specific laws that have been passed in this field are:

- **The Sex Discrimination Act 1975;**
- **The Race Relations Act 1976 (as amended by the Race Relations Amendment Act 2000);**
- **The Education Act 1981 – provision for children with Special Educational Needs;**
- **The Disability Discrimination Act, 1995 and 2005;**
- **Crime and Disorder Act 1998;**
- **Special Educational Needs Code of Practice 2001;**
- **The Employment Equality (Sexual Orientation) Regulation 2003.**
- **The Children Act 2004 and the guidance on safeguarding children in education (DfES 2004a);**
- **The Equality Act 2006.**

From 1988 to 2003, the Local Government Act (1988), Section 28, made it unlawful for local education authorities to 'promote homosexuality as a pretended family relationship'. You may have heard about Section 28 – but it was repealed in September 2003. Ellis (2004) has shown that young people who identify as lesbian, gay or bisexual still experience problems related to their sexual identity in school, even though sexuality is talked about more in lessons. The Employment Equality (Sexual Orientation) Regulations that became law in December 2003 protect lesbian, gay and bisexual people (including teachers) at work – direct discrimination, indirect discrimination and harassment are all included in the legislation.

The Race Relations Act 1976 (as amended by the Race Relations [Amendment] Act 2000) places a new general (statutory) duty on public authorities (including schools) to promote race equality. The general duty has three parts:

- **eliminating unlawful race discrimination;**
- **promoting equality of opportunity;**
- **promoting good relations between people from different racial groups.**

Specific duties (also statutory) are laid down in the Act to assist schools in meeting the general duty and include:

- **a proactive approach, which builds race equality into the mainstream of schools and their existing mechanisms;**
- **a requirement for schools to prepare and maintain a written Race Equality Policy;**
- **this policy must deal with race equality explicitly and transparently;**
- **promote race equality and tackle discrimination.**

This policy must also link with other policies and its impact on staff, students and parents from different racial groups must be monitored and evaluated, with particular attention being paid to student attainment.

In practice this means:

- **collecting, comparing and evaluating data to measure performance and effectiveness;**
- **monitoring attainment and progress, exclusions, support and guidance, parental involvement, governing body membership, punishments and rewards;**
- **evaluating data, establishing what more should be done, revising and setting targets in strategic plans.**

Further guidance on the Race Relations Act 1976 (as amended by the Race Relations [Amendment] Act 2000) can be obtained from the Commission for Racial Equality at **www.cre.gov.uk**

There are two further pieces of legislation which will have an impact on the school's role as both an employer and provider of services: The Children Act (2004) and the Equality Act (2006).

The Children Act 2004 provides the legal underpinning for *Every Child Matters: Change for Children* – the programme aimed at transforming children's services. *Every Child Matters* aims to improve opportunities and outcomes for children, young people and families. The legislation is central to the promotion of inclusion in schools. It outlines five key outcomes for children:

- be healthy;
- stay safe;
- enjoy and achieve;
- make a positive contribution;
- achieve economic well-being.

These five outcomes now form the basis for the structures for supporting children in local authorities as well as Ofsted inspections. The Act places a duty on local authorities to promote co-operation and sharing of information between health and social services agencies and education, alongside partners from the private, voluntary and community sectors in order to maximise achievement of the five key outcomes. Multi-agency working is a key element of the Children Act and therefore the inclusion agenda. A series of documents have been published which provide guidance under the Act, to support local authorities and their partners in implementing new statutory duties. These can be found at **www.everychildmatters.gov.uk**

The Equality Act (2006) has three functions:

1. To create a single commission that will replace the Equal Opportunities Commission (EOC), the Commission for Racial Equality (CRE) and the Disability Rights Commission (DRC). This single commission will be called the Commission for Equality and Human Rights (CEHR).
2. To make unlawful (apart from certain exemptions) discrimination on the grounds of religion or belief or sexual orientation in the provision of goods, facilities and services, the management of premises, education and the exercise of public functions.
3. To create a duty on public authorities to promote equality of opportunity between men and women and to prohibit sex discrimination in the workplace.

Assessing and monitoring the impact of policies

Questions for assessing the impact of a school's policies, including its race equality policy, could include the following:

- **Does the school help all its students to achieve as much as they can, and get the most from what is on offer, based on their individual needs?**
- **Which groups of students are not achieving as much as they could? Why not?**
- **Is the school making sure that its policies, including its race equality policy, are not having an adverse impact on students, parents or staff from racial groups?**
- **How does the school explain any differences? Are the explanations justified? Can they be justified on non-racial grounds, such as English language difficulties?**
- **Does each relevant policy include aims to deal with differences in students' attainments (or possible differences) between racial groups? Do the policy's aims lead to action to deal with differences that have been identified (for example extra coaching for students or steps to prevent racist bullying)?**
- **What is the school doing to raise standards and promote equality of opportunity for students who seem to be underachieving and who may need extra support?**
- **What is the school doing to:**
  - **prepare students for living in a multi-ethnic society?**
  - **promote race equality and harmony?**
  - **prevent or deal with racism?**

Dealing with racial and sexual harassment

While harassment may be difficult to define, it encompasses unwelcome physical, verbal or non-verbal conduct, which may be degrading, abusive and/or offensive. A resolution carried by the European Commission's Council of Ministers (May 1990) suggests that the aim of employer policies should be 'to create a climate at work in which men and women respect one another's human integrity'. We have to acknowledge that harassment is frequently a function of power where power is exercised indiscriminately to the detriment of human rights. Research has indicated that harassment in schools of both a sexual and racial nature or of a more general form is a common part of a student's everyday experience. Often sexual or racial harassment in schools is not regarded as a problem because there have been few complaints. The reason for this may be that recipients:

- believe no action will be taken;
- are too embarrassed to make a complaint;
- fear reprisals for making a complaint.

To whom this may concern.

The girls in this class have put together their feelings towards the boys also in this class. Eversince we went into this class there has been nothing but harrisment. By now we are pretty sick of it all. if nothing is done about it we shall be forced to play truant. The facts are when we are sitting in the class we are violently assaulted, if we do not agree with them they threaten us and hit us if we answer them back. Sometimes when we want to show our feelings to them, they give us agravation. There is also a problem with them calling us insulting names, such as slags, bitch tramps, smelly cows fish, Ugly Wretch, and lots of other discusting names. Followed by a punch. They don't always hit us, unless we have sweet's or something that they want. We all must state that it is not all off the boys in this class but a fast magority of them. if one of the boys start then normally the rest follow. We must confess that it is also effecting our worck and giving is great stress and worry. There are so many problems that we can't take any more
          i hope there is something you can do to
              help us in the future. Thankyou.

Figure 14.1: Letter from a group of girls

Read the letter 'To whom it may concern'. What action do you think should be taken in the light of this letter, which the headteacher has just received? What should be in place to prevent a situation like this occurring?

(Schools are required to have a behaviour policy under Circular 10/99 that may include provision on dealing with bullying and harassment or a separate policy on harassment that is cross-referenced to the behaviour policy. The policy or policies should include clear procedures on dealing with such incidents.)

Including everyone in educational success

Closing the gap in educational attainment between various groups in society has been widely acknowledged as a pressing concern of national importance. However, it needs to be acknowledged that each of the main ethnic groups now achieves higher attainments than ever before. However, since the introduction of the GCSE there has been increasing concern among politicians, policy-makers, parents, etc., that has focused upon the differences in achievement between boys and girls.

Gender is also only one factor that affects schooling and achievement. Other factors such as class and ethnicity are strong determinants of educational achievement and thus it is danger-ous and inaccurate to imply that all boys underperform and all girls do well. The gender gap is widest in comprehensive schools and least pronounced in independent and grammar schools.

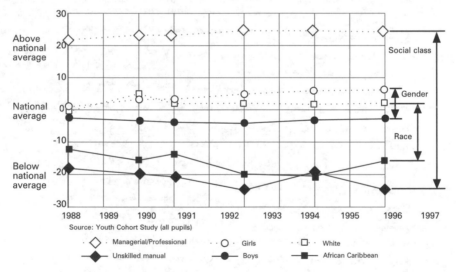

Figure 14.2: Attainment inequalities by 'race', class and gender, England and Wales, 1988–1997 (five or more higher grade GCSEs relative to the national average).

Figure 14.2 illustrates how the gender gap is significantly smaller than the gap associated with class and 'race'. In relation to the national average, African-Caribbean pupils and their peers from unskilled manual homes experience the greatest disadvantage. The trends high-lighted by this graph concur with the research by Gillborn and Mirza (2000), that:

> of the three best-known dimensions of inequality ('race', class and gender) the latter, gender, and in particular boys' underperformance, represents the narrowest

disparity. In contrast to the disproportionate media attention, [our] data shows gender to be a less problematic issue than the significant disadvantage of 'race', and the even greater inequality of class.

(Gillborn and Mirza 2000, p. 23)

Furthermore, information from the Youth Cohort Study 1999, as cited by Gillborn and Mirza (op. cit.), found that although African-Caribbean, Pakistani and Bangladeshi boys are less likely to attain five higher grade GCSEs than their white or Indian peers, all 'main ethnic groups' now achieve higher attainments than ever before. This study also confirms a previous Ofsted review of research, which showed that Indian pupils as a group were the highest performing of the main South Asian categories and stated that 'they are all achieving consistently in excess of their white counterparts'.

A summary of Gillborn and Mirza's research with specific reference to the three aspects of inequality – ethnicity, social class and gender – is outlined below.

Ethnicity and attainment

- African-Caribbean, Pakistani and Bangladeshi pupils are markedly less likely to attain five higher grade GCSEs than their white and Indian peers nationally.
- White and Indian pupils are the only groups to have improving rates of attainment in each successive survey.
- Indian pupils have made the greatest gains in the last decade: enough to overtake their white peers as a group.
- Bangladeshi pupils have improved significantly but the gap between themselves and white youngsters is much the same.
- African-Caribbean and Pakistani pupils have drawn least benefit from the rising levels of attainment: the gap between them and their white peers is bigger now than a decade ago.
- Available evidence suggests that the inequalities of attainment for African-Caribbean pupils become progressively greater as they move through the school system; such differences become more pronounced between the end of primary school and the end of secondary education.

Social class and attainment

- Since the late 1980s the attainment gap between the highest and lowest social classes has widened.
- Difficulty with definitions, and the cost of analysing suitable material, mean that little research gathers adequate data on social class background.
- The ways in which social class affects educational opportunities are multiple and complex: some factors lie outside the school, others operate through institutional processes that disadvantage particular groups of students.
- The familiar association between class and attainment can be seen to operate within each of the main ethnic groups.
- The majority of boys and girls from socially advantaged backgrounds do better in all subjects at GCSE than the majority of girls from disadvantaged families.
- Comparing like with like in terms of their class background, clear inequalities of attainment are evident for Pakistanis/Bangladeshi and African-Caribbean students.
- Inequalities of attainment are now evident for black students regardless of their class backgrounds.
- African-Caribbean students from manual backgrounds fell behind other working-class peers in levels of attainment during the late 1980s and 1990s.

- African-Caribbean students from non-manual homes are the lowest attaining of the middle-class groups. In some cases they are barely matching the attainments of working-class students in other ethnic groups.

Gender and attainment

- The gender gap is considerably smaller than the inequalities of attainment associated with ethnic origin and social class background.
- In each of the principal ethnic groups nationally, girls are more likely to achieve five higher grade GCSEs than boys of the same ethnic origin.
- Ethnic inequalities persist when comparing groups of pupils of the same sex but with different ethnic origins.
- The inequalities of attainment of Bangladeshi/Pakistani and African-Caribbean girls not only mean that they do less well than white and Indian girls, they are also less likely to attain five higher grade GCSEs than white and Indian boys.
- No group has been completely excluded from the improvement in GCSE attainments during the late 1980s and 1990s.

PRACTICAL TASK PRACTICAL TASK PRACTICAL TASK PRACTICAL TASK PRACTICAL TASK

The following scenarios are based on actual events that have taken place. With one or more trainee teacher colleagues, discuss the issues that arise and consider what their implications are for practice.

- A grandparent complained to the LEA that the primary school where his granddaughter attended had used a black doll to represent the baby Jesus. He had complained directly to the headteacher the previous year and felt that his concerns had been ignored. He found it unacceptable for Jesus Christ to be portrayed as black. 'I could understand it if the doll was slightly brown because we know that the Holy Land is in the Middle East and hot – so people could be a bit tanned.'

- Overheard in a staff room – 'I'm a white middle-aged and middle-class woman; what can I possibly do to help underachieving black boys? It's just so far removed from my world.'

- A parent makes a complaint that two other children are bullying his 15-year-old daughter in and out of the classroom. He also reported that his daughter was having nightmares and showed extreme reluctance about going to school. He then went on to say that the daughter had recently started praying to become white.

Strategies for addressing differences in attainment

IN THE CLASSROOM

The Northwards Comprehensive School database shows that the achievement of Pakistani boys is significantly lower than the average school achievement, whereas the achievement of Pakistani girls is higher than average. In July 2001, at the end of the Key Stage 3 National Literacy Strategy pilot, concern was expressed that although all pupils progressed over Year 7, the progression of Pakistani boys was not as great as any other group. The attainment gap therefore is an issue at this early stage in a pupil's secondary education. Northwards instigated an observational study of students in English groups in Year 7 and Year 8. The observations indicated, as would be expected, a wide range of ability, achievement and motivation within the group of Pakistani boys in these two year groups.

As a result of the school's observations the following actions can be initiated to possibly bring about change in outcomes for this target group.

A whole school's response may include:

- **an examination of the curriculum content to reflect the interests and prior experiences of all its students;**
- **evaluation of its teaching and learning strategies;**
- **development of whole school policies, which cover all aspects of work and behaviour.**

(The school's formally taught curriculum and the informal hidden curriculum should take into account and reflect the linguistic and cultural diversity of the school and the community it serves. The teaching and learning in school should reflect this range of diversity.)

The whole-school response is aimed at creating an ethos whereby Pakistani boys can achieve without fear of ridicule. The impact of the whole school's response can then be monitored to ascertain:

- **levels of attainment and progress;**
- **levels of engagement with school life – participation in activities both in the classroom and beyond.**

For detailed guidance refer to *Learning for All: Standards for Racial Equality in Schools*, Commission for Racial Equality at **www.cre.gov.uk**

The research into achievement has mainly focused on the extent of the differences as measured through testing and examination results and the likely reasons for the differences. It has viewed achievement in narrow terms that conflate attainment with the broader concept of achievement which could be argued as attainment plus representation, participation, etc. – in short, social inclusion. The strategies for addressing differences in attainment have focused very much on the role of the school, whereas indicators of achievement would require greater acknowledgement of the wider societal changes in the labour market that have taken place over the past ten years or more and the impact this has had on boys' attitudes to schooling as can be gleaned from the following quotation:

> The collapse of the manufacturing industry and the introduction of new technologies in the workplace have conspired to make working class boys feel useless and unwanted. The disaffection has spread to the classroom.
>
> (Martin Bright, *The Observer* March 1998)

A SUMMARY OF **KEY POINTS**

> **The terms *equal opportunities* and *equality of opportunity* have to be informed by an understanding of the concept of *equality*.**

> **The concept of *inclusion*, as used in the context of education and schooling in the present political climate, refers to the role of education and its contribution to reducing disaffection and promoting participation in the political, social and economic life of wider society.**

> **While girls generally may be doing well in schooling up to GCSE, they fail in later life to capitalise upon this seeming success and still end up occupying the low ranks in most areas of work, especially in the business sector.**

> Since the late 1980s the attainment gap between the highest and lowest social classes has widened. The ways in which social class affects educational opportunities are multiple and complex: some factors lie outside the school, others operate through institutional processes that disadvantage particular groups of students.

> Social class and gender differences are closely associated with differences in attainment but neither can account for persistent underlying ethnic inequalities: comparing like with like, African-Caribbean, Pakistani and Bangladeshi students do not enjoy equal opportunities.

The intention of this chapter was to make complex ideas accessible to trainee and beginner teachers unfamiliar with issues relating to equality and inclusion. It is vital that these understandings are put into practice so that they become central to your teaching and learning strategies. Promoting equality and inclusion is a cornerstone of being a member of one of the most influential professions in society.

Moving on

Trainees committed to furthering their understanding of inclusion relating to 'race', ethnicity and multicultural education should contact the Lead Advisor/Inspector for Ethnic Minority Achievement in their local authority. There are also CPD opportunities for NQTs organised by local authorities, professional associations and teacher unions (e.g. the NUT) that consider wider issues of addressing inequality arising through 'race', gender, sexuality, religion and socio-economic disadvantage.

FURTHER READING FURTHER READING FURTHER READING FURTHER READING

Epstein, D., Elwood, J., Hey, V. and Maw, J. (1998) *Failing Boys? Issues in Gender and Achievement*. Buckingham. Open University Press. This is a useful and accessible text which explores the complex issues relating to masculinity, schooling and achievement.

Francis, B. and Skelton, C. (2004) *Reassessing Gender and Achievement*. London. Taylor and Francis. This book draws together findings from the vast array of material on this subject.

Gaine, C. and George, R. (1999) *Gender, 'Race' and Class in Schooling: A New Introduction*. London. Falmer Press. This book provides an overview of research and key problems in the field of education and three social inequalities – gender, 'race' and class.

Gillborn, D. and Mirza, H. S. (2002) *Educational Inequality: Mapping 'Race', Class and Gender: A Synthesis of Research*. London. Ofsted.

Griffiths, M. (2003) *Action for Social Justice in Education: Fairly Different*. Buckingham. Open University.

Searle, C. (2001) *An Exclusive Education: 'Race', Class and Exclusion in British Schools*. London. Lawrence and Wishart. This text analyses the exclusionary practices of many secondary schools and puts forward policies to reverse this situation. It places educational exclusion within the wider context of social and political exclusion.

For further information on equality and inclusion, visit **www.learning matters. co.uk/education/ learnteach/chapt14.html**

Chapter glossary

Black is sometimes used as a general term for people of African, Caribbean, South Asian and other Asian origin. Black is also one of the ethnic monitoring categories used in the census. It includes Caribbeans, Africans and others who wish to describe themselves as black.

Ethnicity and ethnic group. Ethnicity is an unambiguous term, which refers to culture. An ethnic group is simply a group which shares certain cultural features such as language, religion, various customs, perhaps food and clothing preferences (Gaine and George 1999).

Gender refers to those characteristics of being female or male which are socially constructed.

Institutional racism. *The Stephen Lawrence Inquiry Report* defines institutional racism as:

> The collective failure of an organisation to provide an appropriate and professional service to people because of their colour, culture or ethnic origin. It can be seen or detected in processes, attitudes and behaviour which amount to discrimination through unwitting prejudice, ignorance, thoughtlessness and racist stereotyping which disadvantage minority ethnic people.

'Race' is a crude and superficial classification, which began in the last century; it has no biological significance to scientists today. Perhaps a useful working definition is 'a group of people who may share some physical characteristic to which social importance is attached'. Thus, the important facet of 'race' is not the skin colour, facial features or type of hair people have but the social significance which is placed upon these (Gaine and George op.cit.).

Racism. *The Stephen Lawrence Inquiry Report* defines racism as:

> ... conduct or words which advantage or disadvantage people because of their colour, culture or ethnic origin. In its more subtle form it is as damaging as in its overt form.

Using this definition, black, white or Asian people may be victims of racism. This definition of racism is consistent with the Race Relations Act. Some groups of people (for example black people, Asians, Gypsies and asylum seekers) are much more likely to suffer racism. Racism is sometimes used to refer to the power relationship between white people and black people. The basis for this viewpoint is that white people make most of the social, economic and political decisions and that these decisions may systematically disadvantage black people. 'Black' is used politically in this context to unite people who are not white or who are likely to be subjected to racism (for example Jewish people).

Racist incident is any incident that is perceived to be racist by the victim, or any other person.

Sexism is discrimination against women or men on the basis of their sex.

Social inclusion refers to participation in society. It includes involvement in politics and in the economy and mainstream cultural life.

References

Allen, J., Loveless, A., Potter, J. and Sharp, J. (2007) *Primary ICT: Knowledge, Understanding and Practice*. Exeter. Learning Matters.

Arnold, R. (2006) *Schools in Collaboration: Federations, Collegiates, and Partnerships*. EMIE at NFER Report No. 86.

Aspect (2006) *Personalised Learning: From Blueprint to Practice*. Wakefield. Aspect.

Assessment Reform Group (1999) *Assessment for Learning: Beyond the Black Box*. Cambridge. University of Cambridge School of Education.

Barbe, W. B. and Malone, M.N. (1981) What we know about modelling strategies. *Educational Leadership*, 38, 378-80.

Barratt, R. and Barratt Hacking, E. (2000) Changing my locality: conceptions of the future. *Teaching Geography*, 25(1), 17–21.

Barrs, M. (1990) *Words Not Numbers: Assessment in English*. Exeter. Short Run Press.

Basic Skills Agency (1997) *Does Numeracy Matter? Evidence from the National Child Development Study on the Impact of Poor Numerary on Adult Life*.

Bassey, M. (1989) *Teaching Practice in the Primary School*. East Grinstead. Ward Lock Educational.

Beard, R. (1993) *Teaching Literacy Balancing Perspectives*. London. Routledge.

Beard, R. (2000) *Developing Writing 3–13*. London. Hodder and Stoughton.

Bearne, E. (1999) *Use of Language Across the Secondary Curriculum*. London. Routledge.

Becta (2001) The secondary school of the future. A preliminary report to DfEE by Becta **www.becta.org.uk/news/reports/secondaryfuture/**

Becta (2002) Impa CT2. Norwich. HMSO.

Behets, D. (1990) Concerns of pre-service physical education teachers. *Journal of Teaching in Physical Education*, 10, 66-75.

Bereiter, C. and Scardamalia, M. (1987) The psychology of written composition, in Beard, R. (1993) *Teaching Literacy Balancing Perspectives.* London. Routledge.

Black, P. and Wiliam, D. (1998) *Inside the Black Box: Raising Standards Through Classroom Assessment*. London. King's College.

Black, P. *et al.* (2003) *Assessment for Learning: Putting it into Practice*. Maidenhead. Open University Press.

Bleach, K. (2000) *The Newly Qualified Secondary Teacher's Handbook.* London. David Fulton.

Booth, T., Nes, K. and Stromstad, M. (2003) *Developing Inclusive Teacher Education*. NY. Routledge.

Bruer, J. T. (1997) Education and the brain: A bridge too far. *Educational Researcher*, 26 (8), 4–16.

Bruner, J. S. (1966) *The Process of Education*. New York. Vintage.

Bruner, J. S. (1966) *Toward a Theory of Instruction*. Cambridge, MA. Harvard University Press.

Bullock Report (1975) *A Language for Life*. London. DES.

Cairney, T. H. (1995) *Pathways to Literacy*. London. Cassell.

Calderhead, J. (1987) *Exploring Teachers' Thinking*. London. Cassell.

Cano-Garcia, F. and Hughes, E.H. (2000) Learning and thinking styles: an analysis of their interrelationship and influences on academic achievement. *Educational Psychology*, 20(4), 413–430.

Capel, S., Leask, M. and Turner, T. (1995) *Learning to Teach in the Secondary School*. London. Routledge.

Carr, W. and Kemmis, S. (1986) *Becoming Critical*. London. Falmer Press.

Chasty, H. (1990) cited in P. D. Pumfrey and C. D. Elliott (eds.) (1990) *Children's Difficulties in Reading, Spelling and Writing*. London. Falmer Press.

Cheminais, R. (2000) *Special Educational Needs for Newly Qualified and Student Teachers*. London. David Fulton.

Child, D. (1986) *Psychology and the Teacher* (4th ed.). London. Cassell.

Coffield, D., Mosely, D., Hall, K. and Ecclestone, E. (2004) *Should We be Using Learning Styles: What Research Has to Say on Practice.* London. Learning and Skills Research Centre.

Cohen, E. (1994) *Designing Groupwork: Strategies for the Heterogeneous Classroom.* New York. Teachers College Press.

Cole, M. (ed.) (1999) *Professional Issues for Teachers and Student Teachers.* London. David Fulton.

Collier, V. (1987) Age and rate of acquisition of second language for academic purposes. *TESOL Quarterly*, 21, 617–641.

Cotton, J. (1995) *The Theory of Learners: An Introduction.* London. Kogan Page.

Counsell, C. (2001) Challenges facing the literacy co-ordinator. *Literacy Today*, 24.

Cowley, S. (2001) *Getting the Buggers to Behave.* London. Continuum.

Crick Report (1998) *Education for Citizenship and the Teaching of Democracy in Schools.* London. DfEE/QCA.

Cullingford, C. (2006) Children's own vision of schooling. *Education 3–13,* 34(3), 211–221.

Cummins, J. (2000) *Language, Power and Pedagogy: Bilingual Children in the Crossfire.* Clevedon. Multilingual Matters.

Dale, R. (1990) *The TVEI Story: Policy, Practice and Preparation for the Workforce.* Milton Keynes. Open University Press.

Davies, B. (2005) Youth Work: a manifesto for our times, *Youth and Society*, No. 88.

Dean, G. (2000) *Teaching Literacy in Secondary Schools.* London. David Fulton.

Demos (2005) *About Learning: Report from the Learning Working Group.* London. Demos.

DES (1978) *Special Educational Needs: Warnock Report.* London. HMSO.

DES (1981) *Education Act.* London. HMSO.

DfEE (1995) *Disability Discrimination Act.* London. HMSO.

DfEE (1996) *Education Act.* London. HMSO.

DfEE (1997) *Excellence for All Children: Meeting Special Educational Needs* (Green Paper). London. HMSO.

DfEE (1997) *Excellence in Schools.* Cm 3681. London. HMSO.

DfEE (1998) *Meeting Special Educational Needs: A Programme of Action.* London. HMSO.

DfEE (1999) *Social Inclusion: Pupil Support.* Circular 10/99. London. HMSO.

DfEE (1999) A fresh start – improving literacy and numeracy skills. *Skills and Enterprise Briefing*, Issue 5/99, London. HMSO.

DfEE (2001) *Framework for Teaching English: Years 7, 8 and 9.* DfEE.

DfEE (2001) *Key Stage 3 National Strategy Framework for Teaching Mathematics: Years 7, 8 and 9.*

DfEE (2001) *Literacy Across the Curriculum.* DfEE.

DfEE and QCA (2000) *The National Curriculum for England.* DfEE and QCA Publications.

DfES (2001) *Numeracy Across the Curriculum Notes for School-Based Training.*

DfES (2001) *Numeracy Across the Curriculum Support Materials for School-Based Training.*

DfES (2001) *Schools Achieving Success.* White Paper. HMSO.

DfES (2001) *Special Educational Needs and Disability Act.* Nottingham. DfES Publications.

DfES (2001) *Special Educational Needs: Code of Practice.* Nottingham. DfES Publications.

DfES (2002) *Qualifying to Teach*: *Professional Standards for Qualified Teacher Status and Requirements for Initial Teacher Training* (online). Available from **www.canteach.gov.uk/itt/ requirements/qualifying/standards_ printable.pdf**

DfES (2002) *Transforming the Way We Learn.* Norwich. HMSO.

DfES (2003) *Every Child Matters.* London. DfES.

DfES (2004a) *Five Year Strategy for Children and Learners.* London. DfES.

DfES (2004b) *Raising Barriers to Achievement.* London. DfES.

DfES (2005) *Higher Standards: Better Schools for All.* London. DfES.

DfES (2005) *14–19 Education and Skills White Paper.* London. DfES.

Dodds, P., Griffin, L. L. and Placek, J. H. (2001) A selected review of the literature on the development of learners' domain-specific knowledge. *Journal of Teaching in Physical Education*, 20(4), 301–313.

Doyle, W. (1979) Classroom tasks and student's abilities, in P. Peterson and H. Walberg (eds.) *Research on Teaching: Concepts, Findings and Implications*. 183–209. Berkeley, CA. McCutcheon.

Doyle, W. (1981) Research on classroom contexts. *Journal of Teacher Education*, 32(6): 3–6.

Driscoll, M.P. (1994) *Psychology for Learning*. Needham Heights, MA. Allyn and Bacon.

Ellis, V. with High, S. (2004) Something more to tell you: gay, lesbian or bisexual young people's experiences of schooling. *British Educational Research Journal*, 30(2): 213—225.

Emig, J. (1977) Writing as a mode of learning. *College Composition and Communication* 28(2): 122–128.

Epstein, D., Elwood, J., Hey, V. and Maw, J. (1998) *Failing Boys? Issues in Gender and Achievement*. Buckingham. Open University Press.

Felder, R.M. and Silverman, L.K. (1988) Learning and teaching styles in engineering education. *Engineering Education*, April, 674-680.

Fleming, N. and Baume, D. (2006) Learning styles again: VARKing up the right tree. *Educational Developments*, SEDA Ltd 7(4), 4–7

Franklin, S. (2006) VAKing out learning styles – why the notion of learning styles is unhelpful to teachers. *Education 3–13*, 34(1), 81–87.

Fuller, F. F. (1 969) Concerns of teachers: a developmental conceptualisation. *American Educational Research Journal*, 70, 263–8.

Gaine, C. and George, R. (1999) *Gender, 'Race' and Class in Schooling: A New Introduction*. London. Falmer Press.

Galili, I. and Bar, V. (1997) Children's operational knowledge about weight. *International Journal of Science Education*, 19, 317–340.

Gardner, H. (1983) *Frames of Mind: The Theory of Multiple Intelligences*. New York. Basic Books Inc.

General Medical Council Standards of Practice. Available from **www.gmc-uk.org/standards/standards_frameset.htm**

Gibbons, P. (1993) *Learning to Learn in a Second Language*. Portsmouth. Heinemann.

Gillborn, D. and Mirza, H. S. (2000) *Educational Inequality: Mapping Race, Class and Gender*. London. Ofsted.

Gipps, C. and McGilchrist, B. (1999) Primary school learners. In P. Mortimore (ed.) *Understanding Pedagogy and its Impact on Learning*. London. Paul Chapman.

Gipps. C. and Stobart, G. (1997) *Assessment: A Teacher's Guide to the Issues*. London. Hodder and Stoughton.

Glaser, R. (1976) Components of a psychology of instruction: toward a science of design. *Review of Educational Research* 46(1): 1–24.

Glaser, R. (1984) Education and thinking: the role of knowledge. *American Psychologist* 39(2): 93–104.

Goldstein, H. (1998) Response papers on **www.ioe.ac.uk/hgoldstn/**

Goleman, D. (1996) *Emotional Intelligence*. London. Bloomsbury.

Goswami, U. (2004) Neuroscience and education. *British Journal of Educational Psychology*, 74, 1–14.

Graff, H. J. (1987) *The Labyrinths of Literacy*. London. Falmer Press.

Gredler, M.E. (2001) *Learning and Instruction: Theory into Practice* (4th ed.). New York. HarperCollins.

Griffin, L. L., Dodds, P., Placek, J. H. and Tremino, F. (2001). Middle school students' conceptions of soccer: their solutions to tactical problems. *Journal of Teaching in Physical Education*, 20(4), 324–340.

Griffiths, M. (2003) *Action for Social Justice in Education: Fairly Different*. Buckingham. Open University.

Gross, J. (2002) *Special Educational Needs in the Primary School – A Practical Guide*. London. Open University Press.

GTCE Professional Code for Teachers. Available from **www.gtce.org.uk/gtcinfo/code.asp**

Guide to the Professional Conduct of Solicitors. Available from **www.guide-on-line.lawsociety.org.uk/**

Haines, S. (2006) *14–19 Education and Training and Young Disabled People*. Nuffield Review Working Paper No. 37. **www.nuffield14-19review.org.uk**

Hall, D. (2001) *Assessing the Needs of Bilingual Students: Living in Two Languages*. Abingdon. David Fulton.

Hammersley, M. (1993) On the teacher as researcher. *Educational Action Research*, 1(3).

Hargreaves, D. (1996) *Teaching as a Research Based Profession: Possibilities and Prospects*. London. Teacher Training Agency.

Hargreaves, D. (2001) The Nuttall Memorial/Carfax Lecture. BERA. 2001.

Harlen, W., Gipps, C., Broadfoot P. and Nuttall, D. (1994) Assessment and the Improvement of Education, in A. Pollard and J. Bourne, *Teaching Learning in the Primary School*. London. Routledge.

Hart, C. (1998) *Doing a Literature Review*. London. Sage.

Haydon, G. (1996) Should teachers have their own professional ethics? *Journal of Philosophy of Education*, 30(2), 301–306.

Heffler, B. (2001) Individual learning style and the learning style inventory. *Educational Studies*, 27(3), 307–316.

Hill, D. and Cole, M. (eds.) (1999) *Promoting Equality in Secondary School*. London. Cassell.

Hillage, J., Pearson, R., Anderson, A. and Tamkin, P. (1998) *Excellence in Research in Schools*. London. DfEE.

Hitchcock, G. and Hughes, D. (1995) *Research and the Teacher*. London. Routledge.

Honey, P. and Mumford, A. (1982) *The Manual of Learning Styles*. Maidenhead. Peter Honey.

Hopkins, D. (1993) *A Teacher's Guide to Classroom Research*. Buckingham. Open University Press.

Jasmine, J. (1996) *Teaching with Multiple Intelligences*. Westminster, CA. Teacher Created Materials.

Katz, L. G. (1972) Developmental stages of preschool teachers. *Elementary School Journal*, 73(1): 50–54.

Koehn, D. (1994) *The Ground of Professional Ethics*. London. Routledge.

Kohl, H. (1986) *On Becoming a Teacher*. London. Methuen.

Kolb, D. A. (1976) *Teaching Students Through Their Individual Learning Styles*. Reston, VA. Reston Publications.

Kolb, D. A. (1984) *Experiential Learning: Experience as a Source of Learning and Development*. Englewood Cliffs, NJ. Prentice-Hall.

Kolb, D.A. (1985) *Learning Styles Inventory and Technical Manual*. Boston, MA. McBer.

Kyriacou, C. (1997). *Effective Teaching in Schools: Theory and Practice (2nd ed.)*. Cheltenham. Nelson Thornes Ltd.

Kyriacou, C. (1998) *Essential Teaching Skills* (2nd ed.). Cheltenham. Stanley Thornes.

Kyriacou, C. and Stephens, P. (1999) Student teacher concerns during teaching practice. *Evaluation and Research in Education*, 13(1), 18–31.

Lave, J. (1988) *Cognition in Practice: Mind, Mathematics, and Culture in Everyday Life*. Cambridge. Cambridge University Press.

Lave, J. and Wenger, E. (1996) *Situated Learning*. Cambridge. Cambridge University Press.

Ledwick, M. (2001) *Numeracy Across the Curriculum in Secondary Schools*. Leicester. Mathematical Association.

Lewin, K. (1946) Action research and minority problems. *Journal of Social Issues*, 2, 34–6. 286, 438.

Lewis, M. and Wray, D. (2001) Implementing effective literacy strategies in the secondary school. *Educational Studies*, (27)1.

Long, M. (2000) *The Psychology of Education*. London. Routledge.

Luke, A. (1999) Education 2010 and new times: why equity and social justice matter, but differently. Paper presented at Education Queensland conference October 1999. Available from **http://education/qld.gov.au/corporate/newsbasics/docs/onlineal.doc**

Lunzer, E. and Gardner, K. (1984) *Learning from the Written Word*. Edinburgh. Oliver & Boyd.

MacBeath, J. *et al*. (2006) *The Costs of Inclusion*. A report commissioned by the National Union of Teachers concerning inclusion in schools, University of Cambridge.

Marlowe, B. A. and Page, M. L. (1998) *Creating and Sustaining a Constructivist Classroom*. Thousand Oaks, CA. Sage.

McIntyre, D. Pedder, D. and Rudduck, J. (2005) Student voice: comfortable and uncomfortable learnings for teachers. *Research Papers in Education,* 20(2):149–168.

Medwell, J. et al. (1998) *Effective Teachers of Literacy*, in M. Lewis and D. Wray (2001) Implementing effective literacy strategies In the secondary school. *Educational Studies*, (27)1.

Meek, M. (1991) *On Being Literate*. London. Bodley Head.

Meltzer, H., Gatwood, R., Goodwood, R. and Ford, T. (2000) *The Mental Health of Children and Adolescents in Great Britain*. London. TSO.

Miliband, D. (2004) Personalised learning: building a new relationship with schools. Speech made to the North of England Education Conference, 8 January, Belfast.

Monk, M. (2001) Learning in the classroom, in J. Dillon and M. Maguire (eds.) *Becoming a Teacher: Issues in Secondary Teaching*. Buckingham. Open University Press.

Montgomery, D. (1989) *Managing Behaviour Problems*. London. Hodder and Stoughton.

Morgan, C. and Morris, G. (1999) *Good Teaching and Learning*. Buckingham. Open University Press.

Mortimore, P. (2006) *Which Way Forward? An Education for the 21st Century*. London. NUT.

Moseley, D., Higgins, S. et al. (1999) *Ways forward with ICT: Effective Pedagogy Using ICT for Literacy and Numeracy in Primary Schools*. Newcastle University.

Muijs, D. and Reynolds, D. (2001) *Effective Teaching: Evidence and Practice*. London. Paul Chapman.

Myhill, D. (2000) Misconceptions and difficulties in the acquisition of metalinguistic knowledge. *Learning and Education*, 14(3), 151–163.

Myhill, D. (2001) *Better Writing*. Westley. Courseware Publications.

National Statistics (2004) *Statistics of Education: Schools in England*. London. TSO.

Nuffield Foundation (2004) *Time Trends in Adolescent Well Being*. London. Nuffield Foundation.

Nuffield Review (2004) *Curriculum for the 21st Century.* Oxford University Press.

Ofsted (1995) *Physical Education and Sport in Schools: A Survey of Good Practice*. London. HMSO.

Ofsted (2000) *Evaluating Educational Inclusion: Guidance for Inspectors and Schools*. London. Ofsted.

Ofsted (2002) *Good Teaching, Effective Departments*. London. Ofsted.

Ofsted (2004) *Standards and Quality 2002/3: The Annual Report of Her Majesty's Chief Inspector of Schools*. London. Ofsted.

Palmer, D. (2001) Students' conceptions and scientifically acceptable conceptions about gravity. *International Journal of Science Education*, 23(7), 691-706.

Papert, S. (1980) *Mindstorms: Children, Computers and Powerful Ideas*. Brighton. Harvester Press.

Pendry, A., Atha, J., Carden, S., Courtney, L., Keogh, C. and Ruston, K. (1997) Pupils' preconceptions of history. *Teaching History*, 86, 18–20.

Perks, P. and Prestage, S. (2001) *Teaching the National Numeracy Strategy at Key Stage 3*. London. David Fulton.

Phillips, D. C. and Soltis, J. (1998) *Perspectives on Learning*. New York. Columbia University.

Placek, J. H., Griffin, L. L., Dodds, P., Raymond, C., Tremino, F. and James, A. (2001) Middle school students' conceptions of fitness: A long road to a healthy lifestyle. *Journal of Teaching in Physical Education*, 20(4), 314–323.

Pope, S. and Sharma, R. (2001) Symbol sense: teachers' and students' understanding, in *Proceedings of the British Society for Research into Learning Mathematics*, 21(3), 64–69.

Porth Junior School (2000) Porth Junior School YEAR2KMAG (online). Available from **www.geoci-ties.comtyear2kmag/**

Pritchard, A. (2005) *Ways of Learning: Learning Theories and Learning Styles in the Classroom*. London. David Fulton.

QCA (1998) *ICT Across the Curriculum. An Overview*. Norwich. HMSO.

QCA (1998) *Supporting and Target Setting Process: Guidance for Effective Target Setting for Pupils with Special Educational Needs*. London. DfEE/QCA.

QCA (1999) *Information and Communication Technology. The National Curriculum for England*. Norwich. HMSO.

QCA (2000) *Language for Learning in Key Stage 3*. QCA.

QCA (2000) *A Language in Common: Assessing English as an Additional Language*. London. QCA.

QCA (2001) *Language at Work in Lessons*. QCA.

Richardson, R. and Wood, A. (1999) *Inclusive Society: Race and Identity on the Agenda*. Report produced for Race on the Agenda in partnership with Association of London Government and Save the Children. Stoke on Trent. Trentham.

Riding, R. J. and Raynor, S. G. (1998) *Cognitive Styles and Learning Strategies: Understanding Style Differences in Learning and Behaviour*. London. David Fulton.

Rink, J. E. (2001) Investigating the assumptions of pedagogy. *Journal of Teaching in Physical Education*, 20, 112–128.

Roblyer, M. D. (1996) The constructivist/objectivist debate: implications for instructional technology research. *Learning and Leading with Technology*, 24: 12–16.

Robson, R. (1993) *Real World Research*. Oxford. Blackwell.

Roelofs, E. and Terwel, J. (1999) Constructivism and authentic pedagogy: state of the art and recent developments in the Dutch national curriculum in secondary education. *Journal of Curriculum Studies*, 31(2), 201–227.

Rogers, B. (1997) *You Know the Fair Rule*. London. Prentice Hall.

Ruddock, J. (2001) The Quiet Revolution: Opening address for the DfES and TTA conference, using research and evidence to improve teaching and learning.

Rudduck, J. (2005) Pupil voice is here to stay. *QCA Futures: Meeting the Challenge*. London. QCA.

Sarason, S. B. (1993) *You Are Thinking of Teaching? Opportunities, Problems, Realities*. San Francisco. Jossey-Bass.

Sarason, S. B. and Doris, D. J. (1979) *Educational Handicap, Public Policy and Social History*. London. Macmillan.

Schön, D. (1983) *The Reflective Practitioner*. London. Temple Smith.

Schunk, D. H. (1996) *Learning Theories* (2nd ed.). Englewood Cliffs, NJ. Prentice Hall.

Searle, C. (2001) *An Exclusive Education: 'Race', Class and Exclusion in British Schools*. London. Lawrence and Wishart.

Secondary Heads Association (2001) *14 and Beyond: Proposals for the Development of a Coherent Post-14 Education Framework.* Secondary Heads Association.

Sheeran, Y. and Barnes, D. (1991) *School Writing*. Milton Keynes. Open University Press.

Shipman, M. (1983) *Assessment in Primary and Middle Schools*. Kent. Croom Helm.

Siedentrop, D. and Tannehill, D. (2000) (4th ed.) *Developing Teaching Skills in Physical Education*. Mountain View, CA. Mayfield.

Skinner, B.F. (1968) *The Technology of Teaching*. New York. Appleton-Century Crofts.

Smith, J. (2002) *The Learning Game: A Teacher's Inspirational Story*. London. Abacus.

Smith Report (2004) *Mathematics Counts: the Report of Inquiry into Post-14 Mathematics Education*. London. HMSO.

Stakes, R. and Hornby, G. (2000) (2nd ed.) *Meeting Special Needs in Mainstream Schools: A Practical Guide for Teachers*. London. David Fulton.

Stenhouse, L. (1975) *An Introduction to Curriculum Research and Development*. Oxford. Heinemann.

Sternberg, R. J. (1997) *Thinking Styles*. Cambridge. Cambridge University Press.

Stevenson, R. J. and Palmer, J. A. (1994). *Learning Principles, Processes, and Practices*. London. Cassell.

Taber, K. (2001) The mismatch between assumed prior knowledge and the learners' conceptions: a typology of learning impediments. *Educational Studies,* 27(2): 159–171.

Task Group on Assessment and Testing (TGAT) (1988) *National Curriculum, Report*. London. DES.

Terwel, J. (1999) Constructivism and its implications for curriculum theory and practice. *Journal of Curriculum Studies*, 31(2), 195–199.

Thomson, P. and Gunter, H. (2006) From consulting students to students as researchers. *British Educational Research Journal,* 32(6), 830–856.

Times Educational Supplement (2007, 5 January) Students' personal advisers, p1.

Tirosh, D. (2000) Enhancing prospective teachers' knowledge of children's conceptions: The case of divisions of fractions. *Journal of Research in Mathematics Education*, 31(1), 5–25.

TLRP (Teaching and Learning Research Programme) Personalised learning: A commentary by the teaching and learning research programme. ESRC.

Tomlinson Report (2004) *14–19 Curriculum and Qualifications Reform*. London. DfES.

Tooley, J. and Darby, D. (1998) *Educational Research – A Critique*. London. Ofsted.

Tuckey, C. (1992) Who is a scientist?: children's drawings reveal all. *Education, 3-13*, 20(2), 30-32.

Tyler, R. (1949) *Basic Principles of Curriculum and Instruction*. Chicago. University of Chicago Press.

Van Zwanenberg, N., Wilkinson, L. J. and Anderson, A. (2000) Felder and Silverman's index of learning and Mumford's learning styles questionnaire: how do they compare and do they predict academic performance? *Educational Psychologist*, 20(3), 365-380.

Verkasalo, M., Toumivaara, P. and Lindeman, M. (1996) 15-year-old pupils' and their teachers' values, and their beliefs about the values of an ideal pupil. *Educational Psychology*, 16(1), 35–47.

Walker, C. and Newman, I. (1995) What teachers believe. *Educational Research*, 37(2), 191–202.

Weber, S. and Mitchell, C. (1996) Drawing ourselves into teaching: studying the images that shape and distort teacher education. *Teaching and Teacher Education*, 12(3), 303–313.

Wetton, N. and McWhirter, J. (1988) Images and curriculum development in health education, in J. Prosser (ed.) *Image-Based Research: A Source Book for Qualitative Researchers*. Brighton: Falmer Press.

Wiliam, D., Askew, M., Rhodes, V., Brown, M. and Johnson, D. (1998) Discover, transmit or connect? Approaches to teaching numeracy in primary schools, *Equals*, Summer 1998.

Wood, D. (1998) *How Children Think and Learn* (2nd ed.). Oxford. Blackwell.

Wray, D. (1999) Teaching literacy: the foundation of good practice. *Education 3- 13*, March 1999.

Wray, D. (2001) Literacy in the Secondary School, in *Reading*.

Wray, D. and Lewis, M. (1997) *Extending Literacy: Children Reading and Writing Non-Fiction*. London. Routledge.

Young, M. and Lucas, N. (1999) Pedagogy in further education: new contexts, new theories and new possibilities, in P. Mortimore (ed.) *Understanding Pedagogy and its Impact on Learning*. London. Paul Chapman.

Index

Index for Achieving QTS Learning and Teaching in Secondary Schools

Achieving QTS

The Achieving QTS series continues to grow with nearly 50 titles in 8 separate strands. Our titles address issues of teaching and learning across both primary and secondary phases in a highly practical and accessible manner, making each title an invaluable resource for trainee teachers.

We've updated and improved 13 of our bestselling titles in line with the new Standards for QTS (September 2007). These titles are highlighted with a * in the list below.

Assessment for Learning and Teaching in Primary Schools
Mary Briggs, Angela Woodfield, Cynthia Martin and Peter Swatton
£15   176 pages   ISBN: 978 1 903300 74 9

Assessment for Learning and Teaching in Secondary Schools
Martin Fautley and Jonathan Savage
£16   160 pages   ISBN: 978 1 84445 107 4

*Learning and Teaching in Secondary Schools (third edition)
Viv Ellis
£16   192 pages   ISBN: 978 1 84445 096 1

Learning and Teaching Using ICT in Secondary Schools
John Woollard
£17.50   192 pages   ISBN: 978 1 84445 078 7

Passing the ICT Skills Test (second edition)
Clive Ferrigan
£8   80 pages   ISBN: 978 1 84445 028 2

Passing the Literacy Skills Test
Jim Johnson
£8   80 pages   ISBN: 978 1 903300 12 1

Passing the Numeracy Skills Test (third edition)
Mark Patmore,
£8   64 pages   ISBN: 978 1 903300 94 7

*Primary English: Audit and Test (third edition)
Doreen Challen
£9   64 pages   ISBN: 978 1 84445 110 4

*Primary English: Knowledge and Understanding (third edition)
Jane Medwell, George Moore, David Wray and Vivienne Griffiths
£16   240 pages   ISBN: 978 1 84445 093 0

*Primary English: Teaching Theory and Practice (third edition)
Jane Medwell, David Wray, Hilary Minns, Vivienne Griffiths and Liz Coates
£16   208 pages   ISBN: 978 1 84445 092 3

*Primary ICT: Knowledge, Understanding and Practice (third edition)
Jonathan Allen, John Potter, Jane Sharp and Keith Turvey
£16   256 pages   ISBN: 978 1 84445 094 7

*Primary Mathematics: Audit and Test (third edition)
Claire Mooney and Mike Fletcher
£9   52 pages   ISBN: 978 1 84445 111 1

*Primary Mathematics: Knowledge and Understanding (third edition)
Claire Mooney, Lindsey Ferrie, Sue Fox, Alice Hansen and Reg Wrathmell
£16   176 pages   ISBN: 978 1 84445 053 4

*Primary Mathematics: Teaching Theory and Practice (third edition)
Claire Mooney, Mary Briggs, Mike Fletcher, Alice Hansen and Judith McCullouch
£16   192 pages   ISBN: 978 1 84445 099 2

*Primary Science: Audit and Test (third edition)
John Sharp and Jenny Byrne
£9   80 pages   ISBN: 978 1 84445 109 8

*Primary Science: Knowledge and Understanding (third edition)
Graham Peacock, John Sharp, Rob Johnsey and Debbie Wright
£16   240 pages   ISBN: 978 1 84445 098 5

*Primary Science: Teaching Theory and Practice (third edition)
Rob Johnsey, John Sharp, Graham Peacock, Shirley Simon and Robin Smith
£16   144 pages   ISBN: 978 1 84445 097 8

*Professional Studies: Primary and Early Years (third edition)
Kate Jacques and Rob Hyland
£16   256 pages   ISBN: 978 1 84445 095 4

Teaching Arts in Primary Schools
Raywen Ford, Stephanie Penny, Lawry Price and Susan Young
£15   192 pages   ISBN: 978 1 903300 35 0

Teaching Design and Technology at Key Stages 1 and 2
Gill Hope
£17   224 pages   ISBN: 978 1 84445 056 5

Teaching Foundation Stage
Iris Keating
£15   200 pages   ISBN: 978 1 903300 33 6

Teaching Humanities in Primary Schools
Editor: Pat Hoodless
£15   192 pages   ISBN: 978 1 903300 36 7

Teaching Religious Education: Primary and Early Years
Elaine McCreery, Sandra Palmer and Veronica Voiels
£16   176 pages   ISBN: 978 1 84445 108 1

Achieving QTS Cross-Curricular Strand

Children's Spiritual, Moral, Social and Cultural Development
Tony Eaude
£14   128 pages   ISBN: 978 1 84445 048 0

Creativity in Primary Education
Anthony Wilson
£15   224 pages   ISBN: 978 1 84445 013 8

Creativity in Secondary Education
Jonathan Savage, Martin Fautley
£16   144 pages   ISBN: 978 1 84445 073 2

Teaching Citizenship in Primary Schools
Editor: Hilary Claire
£15   192 pages   ISBN: 978 1 84445 010 7

Teaching Literacy Across the Primary Curriculum
David Wray
£14   144 pages   ISBN: 978 1 84445 008 4

Achieving QTS Extending Knowledge in Practice

Primary English: Extending Knowledge in Practice
Jane Medwell and David Wray
£16   160 pages   ISBN: 978 1 84445 104 3

Primary ICT: Extending Knowledge in Practice
John Duffty
£16   176 pages   ISBN: 978 1 84445 055 8

Primary Mathematics: Extending Knowledge in Practice
Alice Hansen
£16   176 pages   ISBN: 978 1 84445 054 1

Primary Science: Extending Knowledge in Practice
Judith Roden, Hellen Ward and Hugh Ritchie
£16   160 pages   ISBN: 978 1 84445 106 7

Achieving QTS Practical Handbooks

Learning and Teaching with Interactive Whiteboards: Primary and Early Years
David Barber, Linda Cooper, Graham Meeson
£14   128 pages   ISBN: 978 1 84445 081 7

Learning and Teaching with Virtual Learning Environments
Helena Gillespie, Helen Boulton, Alison Hramiak and Richard Williamson
£14   144 pages   ISBN: 978 1 84445 076 3

*Successful Teaching Placement: Primary and Early Years (second edition)
Jane Medwell
£12   160 pages   ISBN: 978 1 84445 091 6

Using Resources to Support Mathematical Thinking: Primary and Early Years
Doreen Drews and Alice Hansen
£15   160 pages   ISBN: 978 1 84445 057 2

Achieving QTS Reflective Readers

Primary English Reflective Reader
Andrew Lambirth
£14   128 pages   ISBN: 978 1 84445 035 0

Primary Mathematics Reflective Reader
Louise O'Sullivan, Andrew Harris, Gina Donaldson, Gill Bottle, Margaret Sangster and Jon Wild
£14   120 pages   ISBN: 978 1 84445 036 7

Primary Professional Studies Reflective Reader
Sue Kendall-Seater
£15   192 pages   ISBN: 978 1 84445 033 6

Primary Science Reflective Reader
Judith Roden
£14   128 pages   ISBN: 978 1 84445 037 4

Primary Special Educational Needs Reflective Reader
Sue Soan
£14   136 pages   ISBN: 978 1 84445 038 1

Secondary Professional Studies Reflective Reader
Simon Hoult
£14   192 pages   ISBN: 978 1 84445 034 3

Secondary Science Reflective Reader
Gren Ireson and John Twidle
£16   128 pages   ISBN: 978 1 84445 065 7

To order please phone our order line 0845 230 9000 or send an official order or cheque to **BEBC, Albion Close, Parkstone, Poole, BH12 3LL**
Order online at www.learningmatters.co.uk